Power to the Population

STUDIES IN SECURITY AND INTERNATIONAL AFFAIRS

Power to the Population

THE POLITICAL CONSEQUENCES AND CAUSES OF DEMOGRAPHIC CHANGES

TADEUSZ KUGLER

THE UNIVERSITY OF GEORGIA PRESS
Athens

© 2023 by the University of Georgia Press
Athens, Georgia 30602
www.ugapress.org
All rights reserved
Set in 10/12.5 Minion Pro by Kaelin Chappell Broaddus

Most University of Georgia Press titles are
available from popular e-book vendors.

Printed digitally

Library of Congress Cataloging-in-Publication Data

Names: Kugler, Tadeusz, 1978– author.
Title: Power to the population : the political consequences and causes of
    demographic changes / Tadeusz Kugler.
Description: Athens : The University of Georgia Press, [2023] | Series: Studies in
    security and international affairs | Includes bibliographical references and index.
Identifiers: LCCN 2022049663 | ISBN 9780820364186 (hardback) | ISBN 9780820364155
    (paperback) | ISBN 9780820364162 (epub) | ISBN 9780820364179 (pdf)
Subjects: LCSH: Population forecasting. | Population—Political aspects. | Economic
    development. | Marginality, Social. | Social prediction.
Classification: LCC HB849.53 .K84 2023 | DDC 304.601/12—dc23/eng/20230329
LC record available at https://lccn.loc.gov/2022049663

To those who came before and those who come after.

CONTENTS

FIGURES AND TABLES

TABLES

ACKNOWLEDGMENTS

This book comes from my abiding curiosity about humanity's potential and how we seem to ignore and forget our decisions to create our modern world. The strife, struggle, limitations, and achievements of the past are forgotten seemingly within a generation. Grandchildren do not know or understand how important their grandparents' lives are to theirs as well as the generations before and then afterward. So, I dedicate this book to my parents, Jacek and Cheryl Kugler, who have always been my role models, to my grandparents who moved from farmers in the Appalachia to doctors and war refugees in Poland to statelessness in Argentina before rebuilding again in the United States. I want to thank my friends at the Transresearch Consortium (TRC) for their years of mentoring and support, particularly Johnny Thomas, Ron Tammen, and Birol Yesilada, and the universities that have been so supportive, La Sierra University, Portland State University, Claremont Graduate University, and Roger Williams University. The list gets a little long when I start to consider all the people who have influenced me, from undergraduate classes with Kenneth W. Harl to reading the works of A. F. K. Organski, Douglas Lemke, and Michael Ward. With honesty, the hope seen in fiction, the illustrations of historical maps, and what we have of human history have been as important to my curiosity as modern academic works. Always fun to remember that, at best, we only know less than a percent of human history. I appreciate all my coauthors, such as s J. Patrick Rhamey, Ali Fisunoglu, and Kyungkook Kang, for helping make this career enjoyable. Thank you Jennifer D. Sciubba, Richard Cincotta, and Eric Kaufmann for the advice and direct conversations on the wonders of demography and to all those who organize the academy and make it a place of growth. I would also like to thank Kristian Gleditsch, Patrick James, Michelle Benson-Saxton, Ismene Gizelis, Alex Braithwaite, Kathleen Gallagher Cunningham, Tom Volgy, and a substantially large amount of people who give up their time to organize ways for the rest of us to interact. Thank you for all that you do to make the academy welcoming to scholars. Lastly, to those who have been with me and near me in my personal life, EMNK, CSH, JR, SN, KM, and the whole city of Providence. You mean the world.

Power to the Population

INTRODUCTION

Why Population and Politics Matter

People are potential. The span of history represents the accumulation of human dreams, hopes, and achievements, and, ultimately, the choices of individuals shape the outcomes of societies and the futures of nations. Grandiose structures ranging from economic systems to the international community are all summations of individual choices. Choices create societies and group dynamics, and these in turn create nations. The goal of this book is to comprehensively demonstrate the links between systems, groups, nations, populations, and individuals. It aims to show how we as groups make political reality and how political reality, in turn, reshapes what we as individuals want to do or are allowed to achieve. This core concept underlies the premise of this book, written in an age of population crisis in which we find ourselves dealing with conflict, refugee waves, and plague. As global rivals circle each other hoping to not start a new world war and as the continued disparity between rich and poor becomes ever more apparent, demographic concerns are moving from a focus on population growth to anxieties about aging and the decline of human civilization itself.

This book investigates the dynamic relationship between political choices and changing populations. It explores how government policies seemingly focused on localized power and economic development can profoundly shape the demographic makeup of populations on local and global scales. The demographic future of a population—in terms of not only numbers but also diversity—is not merely the study of one place, time, or people. Demography has the potential to change the economic and political future of the world. This book acts as a comprehensive guide to predicting and evaluating different possible futures for humanity, scenarios of particular importance to decision makers. The book focuses on the optimism of what can be created by and for the population.

I look at the current choices of modern nations and societies while discussing how those choices may shape the future. One area of particular focus is how restrictions on population growth undermine our shared human prosperity. The impulse of nations to isolate from the global arena threatens not only to undermine their own economic futures but also to restrict the potential of humanity overall. Worse is the concept that all domestic problems are caused by excessive numbers of people, which has led to harsh restrictions. The worst examples have escalated to the horror of genocide and inspired the forced use of sterilization—a means of changing the future by choosing who exists in the next generation. We see all these policies in force today: nations sealing their borders to refugees, reeducation camps and forced population control, intentional attacks on civilian populations, ethnic cleansing, and, yes even at the writing of this in 2022, genocide. All of these exist in the modern world. Until recently, all were thought of as historical mistakes, horrors, and the outcomes of disreputable regimes.

The rhetoric behind policy does not matter nearly as much as what it creates. How does it change what a group can do and achieve? Hoes does it affect individuals' decisions to have children, to be employed, or to live in particular locations? Policies alter demography, but they have not been traditionally studied from this perspective, obfuscating the critically important, lasting effects of policy on the foundation of nations and the people themselves. Who we are, where we can live, what we can do, how many of us there are, and whether we are growing, aging, or dying are all the outcomes of politics. Politics and demography must be studied as a comprehensive whole.

Book Structure and Chapter Guide

The first two chapters present the proposition that politics creates population changes. They introduce the story of humanity as a means of understanding national and global history. Governments shape the future wealth and health of individuals by implementing policy without consideration of its long-term demographic effects. These effects ultimately determine whether these policies are limited or fruitful. Chapter 1 describes historical connections between population policies that induce change and the creation of developed and modern society. The analysis includes a broad range of eras but focuses on the creation of the modern world, moving beyond bare statistics.

Chapter 2's objective is to explain how politics influences what is called the "demographic transition,"—the process by which a population's demography shifts from large numbers of youth to roughly equal numbers in each generation to a larger proportion of elderly or from population growth to stagnation to decline—with a focus on economic opportunity. It connects seemingly unrelated policy choices to their long-term demographic outcomes, providing a framework for the book's later discussions of a wide range of policy issues, such as women's rights, recovery from war, immigration, and the prospects of conflict and rapid expansion, and how they link to demography.

This foundational discussion outlines how politics can first reduce mortality, which in turn increases labor availability and opens a window of opportunity that promises vast economic expansion but also carries the risk of civil war. Internal population movements and urbanization are critical components at this stage. At a later phase of the demographic transition, sharp fertility declines and expanded longevity drive increased aging, declines in population, and retirement burdens.[1] Classic economic growth theory, demographic trends, and policy choices are connected to assess the long-term demographic implications with respect to economic development. Developmental policies commonly prescribed by international organizations such as the World Bank cannot be generalized, not because of the policies themselves but due to the demography, a unique addition to political science and economic literature with significant implications on foreign aid allocations.

In chapter 3, I explore the current demographic state of much of Western Europe and the "developed" world: a stable, educated, wealthy, aging, and ultimately less energetic population. Such situations can be traced back to major population events within the last few generations. A rapid rise in fertility leading to a large youthful workforce may result in a period of massive economic growth. This "baby boom" or "youth bulge" usually transitions into a drop in birth rates in subsequent generations, resulting in an affluent and long-lived population.[2] A society like this possesses more aging people, with a shrinking younger generation to support them. This reality is currently emerging as the norm of "developed" nations but will soon spread to the rest of the world. A critical concern is that some countries lack the resources to care for a growing elderly population. Using past and present examples, I look at how many of these nations missed taking advantage of their period of economic and population growth and now face the reality of economic and political decline.

Chapter 4 considers immigration and finds the acceptance of immigrants to be an incredible advantage to a nation's interest! The ability to attract immigrants, assimilate them, and then reap the rewards of higher economic growth is a massive achievement. Analysis shows how migration, whether external or internal, unlocks the potential for the creation of new technology and the advantages of specialization. I explore a crucial question of how to provide for the basic needs of feeding, sheltering, and employing these new populations. More importantly, though, is the assessment of how political choices to support, allow, or try to curb migration will affect future economic development. The many forms of immigration offer opportunities or can limit the chance for a nation to revitalize its population.

Chapter 5 discusses war—civil or international—as the only policy choice by which vast amounts of a population can be lost (with infectious diseases only recently reminding the world of its possibility of similar levels of carnage within the last few years). We currently live in a relatively peaceful time, but we retain the ability for mass slaughter. War may be increasingly rare, but it and its effects are potentially severe and lasting. The evaluations in this chapter show that large-scale international and civil devastation (e.g., World War II and Cambodia) have dramatic long-term results on the size of populations and the composition of cohorts. In the short term, war produces massive consequences, but over time, it can enhance economic and societal change or perpetuate multigeneration devastation in which each subsequent generation has less opportunity than the one before it.[3] Recovery is uneven; it begins with a postwar baby boom that can rebuild the size of populations to a degree, but cohort distortions persist for the length of the expected life in each society. The policy conclusion is that postwar recovery may not be possible in a postwar Syria or in the ongoing war in Ukraine. Syria and Ukraine has the demographical characteristics that are aged enough that it can be a good foreshadowing of what would happen whenever older developed countries attempt recovery, which in my estimation they will not. The ability to rejuvenate after wartime devastation is an advantage seen in youthful countries not ones with developed aged populations.

Chapter 6 considers the demographic effects of discrimination against marginalized populations, focusing on gender discrimination. Discrimination limits the political and economic opportunities of a society. Crucially, it alters the most fundamental choice of all: the decision to have children. Counterintuitively, when marginalized populations live in dire circumstances, they experience expansive birth rates. The unintended effects go beyond the groups that are discriminated against, altering the political dynamics of nations—particularly in democracies, as the size of the subgroup affects voting patterns and who has political influence. Enfranchisement—which goes beyond legal changes to voting, education, or citizenship access—radically changes the possibilities for marginalized groups and the nation. Women's enfranchisement can increase a country's economic performance and concurrently push fertility rates into a sharp decline. How women are incorporated into the labor force and the types of opportunities offered to them are critical to determining future population, economic capabilities, and national power. Enfranchisement must be considered as a component of international relations at the highest levels, as it creates the fundamentals of national competition and economic development.

In chapter 7, I discuss how domestic concerns create international politics. I examine the future of world politics from the demographic perspective, with a particular emphasis on global power and hierarchy. The chapter calls back to previous discussions of domestic immigration policy and forecasts different national policy outcomes in relation to each other. I show how these domestic policies have the potential to alter the trajectories of future great powers. Power is more than treaties and wealth, for it is rooted in population size.

Chapter 8 examines the specific examples of today's two major powers, China and the United States. While these countries might be rivals, they do not have the same concerns domestically or the same options available to them for the future. In the United States, immigration will be the country's primary source of future power. In China, by contrast, success will depend on pulling the elderly back into the labor market and altering the cultural pressure to have male children. The scale of China, in other areas its chief advantage, precludes it from being able to effectively implement policy to attract immigration.

This chapter's discussion of policy and the culture of population choices shows how these two national stories have global implications. Differing forecasts that estimate ultimate national power could change considering trends toward isolationism and anti-immigration in the United States and various estimations of economic growth in China. Unlike much of the current research, I suggest that, given a continued status quo in terms of immigration policy, the United States would remain near parity with China well into the second half of the twenty-first century. U.S. dominance could increase with higher immigration, but it could lose significant national power given immigration restrictions. China possesses less flexibility for additional economic growth, and this future of two nations at near parity is, unlike what balance-of-power supporters suggest, a troubling outcome of demographic and economic change as it can increase the possibilities of conflict at levels unseen since the middle of the twentieth century.[4]

Lastly chapter 9 addresses the future, as ongoing challenges to the world order from pandemics and conflict are evaluated in terms of differing impacts and potential. Special attention is given to the current, as of 2022, COVID pandemic and conflict in Ukraine, Syrian, and the future of stagnation in politics within developed societies via nonviolent protests.

To some readers, this book may seem at times like an optimistic attempt to link political and economic stability to progressive ideals, promising that we can have both an inclusive, equitable society and capitalistic too. Others will read the book's accounts of war, discrimination, and economic failure and its overt pushback against eugenics as a pessimistic history of human failure. Neither of these perspectives captures the goals of this book. This book is about hope and agency and the heavy responsibility those ideals place upon policy makers at every level of government. It is about the continuing cycles of devastating wars and wasted opportunities to rebuild and how these failures offer us a primer on how to harness demographic changes to create a better future.

Especially in Western Europe and North America, the belief that the future will inevitably be better than the past can give us a dangerous sense of complacency. To ignore how individuals, groups, and nations have agitated and sacrificed to create a better society is to ignore human history. It also ignores the nuances inherent in the perspectives of those who are often quoted as the sources of this optimism, such as Gottfried Wilhelm Leibniz, the eighteenth-century German philosopher who asserted that we lived in "the best of all possible worlds." Leibniz did not mean that the world was perfect or that we should not strive to improve. Development is not a given or a constant.

History is not innately progressive; it is only the outcome of choices at the individual, local, national, and global levels. We look to history and see that rights have declined, economic growth has been undermined, and life expectancy has fluctuated between highs and lows. We can also see that, when societies have faced inflection points, they have not always chosen a progressive path over a regressive one. The perhaps overly noted fact that "crisis" and "opportunity" are represented by the same character in Chinese Mandarin holds true. Crisis alters futures: war, conflict, and political collapse, combined with the possibility of whole regions making the same problematic mistakes, may lead to altered demographic trajectories.

CHAPTER 1

Demography, People, and Nations

On the surface, population statistics may seem to be little more than faceless masses of data points that erase the triumphs and tragedies of everyday life. Subsuming individual lives into a vast sea of context—places of birth, times of birth, parental income, national rates of infant mortality, educational opportunities, famine, disease, war—might appear to some to reject the worth of individuals and their agency. The study of politics, in general, similarly glosses over the level of individual choice in favor of large-scale phenomena—the rise and fall of nations, the terror of wars, or the expectations that follow from economic development or governmental change—with much of the nuance of why policies are created and what they actually achieve therein lost. Nevertheless, as we dive deeper into these profound shifts, a much richer reality emerges. Politics, like other related fields such as history and economics, is at its core personal; it is the result of individual choices writ large.

Demography, the study of who makes up a society, illuminates how national policy dynamics shape regional, local, and individual welfare, but it can also show how domestic, national-level choices create change at the global level.

The danger posed by this dynamic relationship is that often local actors, especially those who make decisions on behalf of national governments, do not envision how the policies they employ to affect the lives individuals will scale up to effect societal-level change, let alone international politics. Gender equality efforts, antidiscrimination measures, policies that encourage robust immigration, and access to health care are more than just platforms to be claimed by one political party or another: they are the means through which a society can embrace a stable future or not. Demography is not destiny, but the trends contained within population statistics are momentous. Once these trends are in motion, they are remarkably hard to alter.

The world has seen fantastic successes in improving the foundational aspects of human existence. Today, we live longer, with a higher degree of physical health, than people at any time in human history. This success is a direct
outcome of political choices to fund and implement scientific advancements
to better the population. Domestic motivations for these policy choices are
less important than the results; investments in clean water, some level of public health, and even the most limited of sanitation measures can have dramatic
effects on a range of fundamental human issues, including infant and mater-
nal mortality rates. Importantly, the most effective of these policies are not the
most expensive ones or even ones that historically had worked before they
were scientifically understood. You do not need to know what a virus is or that
bacteria exist to know that sanitation works.

Radical change is a fundamental aspect of humanity, but it only occurs in
brief periods of dynamism. Demographic change occurs when societies shift
in a major way, whether in the form of a baby boom, decreased fertility, or the
integration of recently arrived cultures. These are temporary phenomena, most
often lasting the life of a single generation, which is almost nothing given the
time horizons of a society. However, if a government mismanages these potentially fruitful moments in time, it can undermine the country's whole future
trajectory.

Politics and Population

The dire dream of humanity is that when we as rational humans are betrayed,
attacked, or even dismissed, we will never trust the offending group, nation, or
even family to the same extent that we would have before. This claim suggests
that, for a society to have long-term gains, it must never suffer a conflict or—
undercutting the theory—be almost amazingly altruistic in the face of conflict, with trauma being forgiven or even forgotten. This sustained altruism in
the face of conflict and betrayal could be the primary aspect of human nature
that has allowed humanity to survive. Even after horrific events in regions of
the world with troubled histories, families, religion, hierarchies, and the sem-
blance of law endure. A true state of anarchy cannot exist and allow for the successful creation of subsequent generations. We, humans, create structure even
in the most difficult and dangerous of places in all parts of the globe. At the
same time, it is often humanity itself that makes the world a difficult and dangerous place to live. We do not, unfortunately, always create social and political structures that support the flourishing of humanity. This goal is an ideal,
not a common choice.

Paradoxically, decisions that create unideal conditions seem to define the
traditional systems of the human species. For the overwhelming majority of

the time that humans have existed, they have endured high levels of political instability, high birth rates, high levels of mortality, nearly continuous conflict, short life spans, and limited long-term economic gains undermined by even the smallest of crises, be they political or environmental. A pattern of conflict and devastation followed by decades of limited technological or population growth—knowledge created and lost repeatedly with limited (at best) ability to build upon it—has characterized human history until the modern era.

The modern expansion era only started in the nineteenth century. If we were Methuselah, we could have moved through time and space for thousands of years without seeing changes to the population's essential existence. The lives of individuals would have been seemingly static for centuries, setting aside changing religions and social styles. While cities rose and fell, the amount of urban space was limited and highly susceptible to local environmental fluctuations. While history remembers the most powerful, the richest, and those with the most to leave behind for subsequent generations, it often tells us little about the average person, who likely lived a harsh life of physical, agricultural labor, whether in the medieval, classical, or even near modern eras.

It has become much easier to feed large, growing populations, as the limitations of local land usage have given way to the significant gains of large-scale transportation. Famine, a common mortal phenomenon for most of human history, resulted not just from local farming failures and the inability to transport foodstuffs on a large scale but also, and equally important, from a lack of international and domestic markets and institutions to facilitate that transfer.

In the modern world, problems of food scarcity prior to significant climate change now emerge initially due to local political complexity and no longer due solely to environmental stresses; modern famine is an issue of political choice (or failure), not of markets or luck. Groups need a level of organization and the willingness to use it for the betterment of the population, and that is the critical component of this discussion. Not just developed versus developing but organized versus organizing.

The "demographic transition," a population phenomenon that has been identified in the statistics of nearly all nations at this point, follows a familiar curve: traditional, slow population growth becomes too-rapid growth, followed by widespread aging, with population decline likely at the end. The transition itself means a move from the expected historical norms of human existence, in which life is short and the elderly are rare, and leads to a scenario in which life expectancies are high and individuals can expect to live a life after work. The likelihood of average ages increases well into the century and the horror of a lost child is felt only by the rarest families and is not the expectation of any family.

Notice in figure 1.1 the differences between population growth rates and total estimated world population. The latter seemingly rises along a slow, in-

FIG. 1.1. Total Historical Population: Year 1–1950

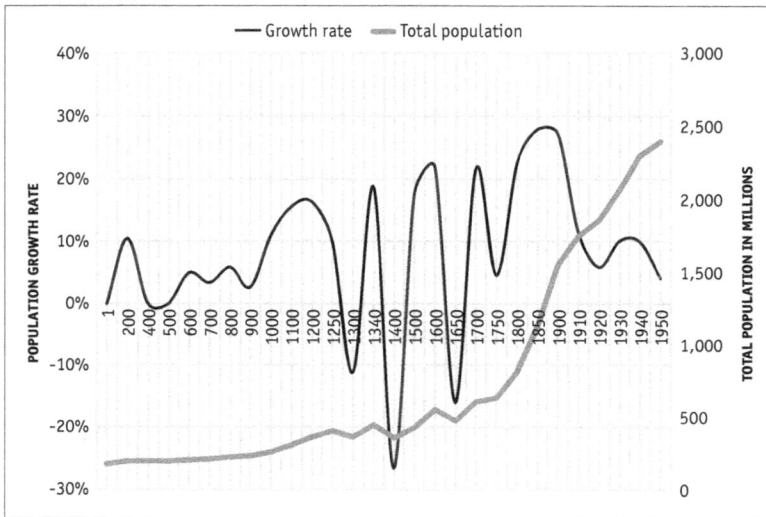

Source: U.S. Census Bureau 2016

exorable trajectory, starting in year 1 with 250 million people and ending in 1950 with 2.5 billion. While this represents a dramatic increase overall, it comes overwhelmingly from the last two hundred years. Prior growth was profoundly slow, with an increase from 250 million to only 500 million by the fourteenth century. Think about it: from year 1, it took almost a full thousand and a half years to double human population—something we did in a generation at the end of the twentieth century. Amazingly, until the tenth century, the total population of the Earth was roughly at or less than the current population of the United States. The scale of modern population potential is so vast as to undermine how we consider the past.

The growth rates themselves are fascinating; not only are there periods of rapid rise but also dramatic drops (keeping in mind that the early percentages cover centuries of growth and the later percentages cover decades). Much of this trend line corresponds with environmental trauma, such as the Black Death or plague of Justinian (and similar catastrophes). The total population data reveal stagnation, with centuries of growth wiped out due to these types of calamities. Disease itself was often a catalyst for political collapse and war in many areas, further undercutting societal and economic success. Take as an example the period between 1250 and 1640. The total population of the world remained nearly the same, at five hundred million, after all those decades. These four hundred years ultimately amounted to no population growth. The year 1640 turns out to be key, as in the years to follow are the first to show sustained substantial growth. Our current era is complex, as growth in terms of total population occurs alongside no growth in terms of growth rate.

Importantly, the story of famine, decay, reconstruction, and environmental shock is not the modern story. The possibility of a future collapse is real yet unlikely. While the chance that substantial percentages of the population could be made casualties due to nonhuman action was a concern for the majority of human history; with modern transportation, organization, and medical advancements, it is today the rarest of possibilities. Rare, however, as we all know, does not mean never.

The final editing of this book is being conducted during the worst pandemic since 1918, while hundreds of thousands of refugees continue to flee violence throughout the world. Millions have died due to the first two horsemen—plague and war—with the others of pestilence and even famine soon to come. Even with this level of carnage, a more efficient system of organization to help prevent this from happening again seems to be lost in recriminations and political choices to ignore the consequences of inaction. The COVID-19 crisis in the richer countries had, by February 2022, moved from policies of abatement to continued pressure on populations to choose to get vaccinated. The starkness of the divide between rich and poor nations is evident in these circumstances. Every single person living in the rich nations of the world, without regard to personal income, has access to life-saving vaccines at such a rate that millions of doses have been wasted and even thrown away. Doses that have been refused by millions of people within those rich nations would not have been refused, and are desperately needed, in the developing world. With the rise of the Delta then Omicron variants, which seems more virulent than the original, the timing of when medical care is administered and who receives it becomes morally apparent.

All life is equal from those in the developing world pleading for access to life-saving medications to those in the developed ignoring it and, be it by choice or ignorance, choosing to die and perpetuate the pandemic.

The COVID-19 plague is not a world war. Even though millions of people have died, either of the great wars killed more, and certainly destroyed more in terms of infrastructure, than this infection. The methods used in this book to estimate recovery are not directly applicable to our current crisis, as they have been built from analyses of massive, devastating, destructive events. The multiyear trial of COVID-19 has not yet hit that level of carnage. In turn, how countries recover from this event should be different; if anything, recovery should be quick. Houses still exist, as do factories, educational levels, and governments. Roads work, as does the internet. An economy should be easily rebuilt so long as it does not depend on travel or tourism.

Who has died matters, and it is always important to remember that numbers are people. Deaths are not statistics but personal and familial tragedies without regard to place, age, or nationality. From a strictly economic standpoint, while not ignoring the turmoil, COVID-19 has so far primarily struck people who are not heavily within the labor force or who have retired from it. We should remember of course that many of the people most affected are the ones that we as a society rely upon but do not compensate for their added risk: nurses, orderlies, sanitation workers, grocery store workers, and a host of others we have belatedly realized are now essential, a characteristic not always seen in their incomes. The stark differences in risk associated with COVID at the individual level can be blatantly seen in what jobs can be achieved at home and which need to be in person because of their physical nature. Home-based jobs tend to be much better compensated.

Even with this morality difference, COVID has not undermined industries or damaged the youth and future of nations. So far, unlike the Zika virus, it has not been shown to damage the unborn; that said, we do not yet know the costs and consequences of long COVID and chronic damage. The caveats are heavy in this section, but they are important. So far, countries have weathered the storm because their populations have.

However, this does not mean that countries will continue to weather the storm. COVID-19 is an unprecedented event. To the best of my knowledge, at no time in modern history have whole countries willingly reduced economic activity and stopped large sectors of their economy from running. Even in the depths of World War II, countries continued to produce, build, and buy while actual bombs fell on them. It is a remarkable reflection of stability that no country has yet suffered a collapsed government, rebellion, or total devastation from either COVID itself or from the actions taken to alleviate it. This is not to say that riots, demonstrations, strangeness on the internet, or publicity-hungry politicians have not all made themselves known, but these events have been folded into the usual scope of national discourse. No countries have seen uprisings, assassinations, and sustained violence, even those that have had the most sustained lockdowns or the highest number of casualties.

The Indian government, for example, remains standing, despite millions of deaths, many of which were hidden in problematic statistics caused by internal disorganization. Belgium did not collapse, though it had the highest per capita death rate in the developed world. The United States was more worried about electoral conspiracies than the deaths of nearly seven hundred thousand citizens—a higher number than everyone who has ever died in a U.S. war since the end of the Civil War in 1865. Despite the Brazilian government touting absurd, make-believe cures instead of pushing for vaccines, Iran losing actual major political actors, Japan hosting the Olympics, New Zealand going into lockdown after one case, and, of course, China censuring its data so heavily that the rest of the world has no idea how much damage it has truly sustained, governments continue to operate as well or poorly as they did prior to the pandemic.

The influence of COVID on demography is more nuanced than the direct horrors of more people dead than perished in both World Wars combined. Its lasting effects will stem from its influence on individuals' decisions related to fertility. Particularly in the developed world, COVID seems to have pushed fertility decisions later in a person's life span, whether due to job insecurity or even damage to someone's physical self. The overwhelming importance of public education has become evident now that it has been restricted. Not only does public education facilitate parents' employment, as it is where children are fed, educated, and housed during work hours, but the controversies over whether to suspend it or not also illustrate how remarkably expensive children are in terms of time, money, and political will. Can governments be trusted to sustain foundational programs in times of crisis? How consistent is this cross-nationally, and what can we expect in the future?

Are Nations Important?

A core of political science remains that nations are the primary actors on the international stage. Nations' decisions, choices, and mistakes create the world system, and political science tends to believe that this system is at a level far above the concerns of population studies. Representing policies as domestic or foreign adheres to a false binary; in today's globalized world, as rival regions and nations vie for power and larger, wealthier nations dictate the preferences of smaller, perhaps dependent, ones, any ostensibly "domestic" policy choice will inevitably affect other countries.

Countries are not equal, and part of this inequality stems from their demographic makeup. Demography limits what countries can accomplish or what policies they should consider. What, then, can countries do when faced with grievances or the possibility of international conflict? They should reconsider the basic framework of power—that of the population itself—and how it is arranged and can be expanded. International rivalries are won not by international action but by domestic choices.

Nations that choose to deploy domestic policy or to render international aid to achieve certain goals among a specific population are not acting just for the short term; these choices can reverberate through generations and may alter the basic components of the target group's existence. These policies may be directed toward economic growth and the establishment of greater (or on occasion lesser) human rights. Though they can radically change the demographic profile of a population within a generation, the evaluation of their success or failure is generally limited to a few percentage points of gross domestic product (GDP) growth or isolated declines in mortality rates. These policies are not usually evaluated in terms of their dynamic and dramatic effects on the essential quality of people's lives.

For example, policy choices of concentrated discrimination—those designed to undermine the futures of specific populations within a country—have dangerous effects. Nations often use these discriminatory practices to create unity among a group seen as more important than those who are marginalized: a country may wish to benefit a numeric majority at the expense of smaller groups, to unite people around one group identity in order to distract from other divisions (such as playing up ethnic or religious identity to draw attention away from economic divisions), or to fulfill some other motivation based on its sense of which of its subjects truly "belong" there. Worse, these discriminatory policies, combined with theories of population manipulation, often give rise to stickier discriminatory institutions.

Post–World War II cultural narratives about apocalypse focus implicitly or explicitly on the power of humanity. Disaster movies continue to be popular, and an increasing number focus on nature rebelling or punishing humankind. Keeping in mind that the most important demographic dynamic in the last century has been the movement of populations from rural to urban areas, other disaster movies show urban areas that fall prey to seemingly endless attacks by alien forces—whether monsters created from human hubris, extraterrestrials, or zombies and other forms of the undead—sometimes justified by the explanation that a faraway planet has run out of resources (or, in George Romero's zombie film series, because hell has run out of room due to overpopulation). While apocalypse is neither a practical nor critical concern, the cultural preoccupation with it seemingly has its origins in a time when substantial populations could be lost to massive, unexpected floods, famine, or disease, with the political system seemingly helpless.

Within China, the idea of apocalypse connects to the legendary origin story of the unified Chinese state. The first dynasty (somewhere between three thousand and five thousand years ago) was created after a series of floods forced a massive overhaul of the region's water management systems, and that domestic advancement allowed for the mandate of heaven to be awarded to the first government of China. In this and many other such stories, disaster demands action, which in turn creates legitimacy.

The historical record of population growth is more than just a series of numbers; it is also a question of potential. Over the course of most of human history, population losses have equated to losses of conceivable innovation and discovery. Individuals who survived were trapped in eras of isolation or illiteracy and saw most of their potential go untapped, with so much of their energy pushed into actions they needed to take to survive. In the premechanized world, food production constituted the vast majority of human endeavors, and it remains so in some parts of the developing world to this day. All that we consider to be aspects of the past—from artistic and scientific innovations to the great works of history—were accomplished in the population's limited free time.

War, Recovery, Economic Growth, and Discrimination

The importance of politics cannot be overstated. Politics facilitates the stability that nations need to create new technologies and methods of distributing wealth. The degree to which a government can maintain stability and implement policy affects its ability to extract growth, gains, and success from its population. Politics allows both subnational groups and nations to disburse resources at the scale needed to deal with the most damaging of catastrophes that humanity can endure.

Nevertheless, the gains that politics can provide in terms of long-term planning and public health, for example, must also be evaluated against the damage that politics can produce via failed policies or, worse yet, the horrors of war between nations. No known natural act is more devastating to populations than major war. The ability to decimate large-scale populations is, problematically, an achievable goal for many nations. Even countries with limited technological and military supplies can wage large-scale carnage due to the excellent ability of people to organize. War alters the presumed destiny of the populations involved. Often, casualties are concentrated in the very young and very old, and they are generally weighted toward males.

Catastrophic wars can thus disequilibrate the gender balance of a generation or more, which, combined with societal norms, can cause a great deal of demographic pressure. If more women than expected are left without male partners, it limits a society's ability to procreate. Norms and policy matter after the war, as a common postwar phenomenon is a small but expansive increase in birth rates: a baby boom. A baby boom will eventually become a youth bulge in the aging framework of a society, with all its resulting possibilities and dangers. War recovery therefore depends on the fertility choices of people in the postwar era and the legal allowances for refugees to return. After major conflicts, nations that implement restrictive fertility and immigration policies produce fewer children and see less population growth than nations that give families the freedom to choose to have children and that welcome refugees home.

Worryingly, expectations of postwar recovery may no longer be viable in the future. Conflict-ridden nations such as Syria and now Ukraine are already seeing dropping fertility rates, which in turn decreases what would be the country's expected birth rate expansion after a significant war—the bounce needed for reconstruction. Simply not enough new births are expected to facilitate the nation's recovery. Syria and other nations in similar situations will never recover. War, at least measured in terms of total population losses, will have become unrecoverable. Countries nearing the end of their demographic transition no longer have the necessary flexibility to regrow after unexpected devastation.

A youth-heavy demographic structure creates economic growth expectations without regard to what caused that structure to originate. It is important to remember, however, that a youthful composition can arise without the necessary economic system and political stability in place to turn that presumed temporary advantage into economic growth. Such growth potential has only truly come to fruition in our modern post–Industrial Revolution era. In this brief period, the vast majority of human development has been made possible thanks to technological advancements large enough to create the possibilities that a young population can unlock. A combination of people, potential, and innovation formed today's modern world.

Economic opportunity is the outcome of policy, not its driver. A market is not magic, nor is the economic system as a whole—it is merely the system by which a population is allowed to make choices given a series of potential outcomes. The willingness to invest is not a moral choice or monetary choice alone but one of opportunity and estimation, with the critical consideration being life itself: the limited number of years we all have to act, grow, and exist. We spend our scarce resources of time on chances, whether education, entrepreneurship, or even relationships, and monetary costs are only one component of decision making. Policy changes that disrupt the economic system thus cause investors to lose both money and time, the latter of which cannot be regained. Choices such as pushing off the birth of one's first child until one finishes school or finds a permanent partner are, at their core, investment—and so economic—decisions.

To study economics in isolation is to examine the leaf from the tree within the forest. A full, comprehensive evaluation must be made from population to politics, from systems of culture to those of economics. Increased wealth and the changing incentives it offers to people can reorder the societal and political systems of a population. Economic growth itself is a dynamic variable, and its effects are understudied. The classic modern example is that of women's rights as they relate to economic growth. Modern, developed nations need to engage large percentages of their populations in their economies to survive—something extraordinarily difficult to do if significant restrictions exist on the largest group within the population: women. Liberalization of restrictions causes women to reevaluate essential components of their existence, particularly procreation. Women are the key to future generations, and their choices, even in highly restrictive societies, determine the future of a country's demography.

When given a choice, women wish to work, attain income independence, and have a limited number of children. Thus, situations in which women have a say are nearly always characterized by rapid declines in fertility.

Women's choices, in turn, drive change at all levels of society. Although not all traditional societies have restricted women's choices, most do or did at one time. Radical declines in marriage and birth rates have had widespread consequences: domestic nongovernmental organizations are panicked about declines in the family, women are increasingly participating in politics, universities that were once overwhelmingly male are now majority female, largely male educated populations are increasingly composed of women, and, most importantly, subsequent generations are smaller than the ones that came before. This simple concept—that women's choices related to childbirth create society—is often overlooked when discussing the future. Population declines due to women choosing to have fewer children have been observed throughout the developed world and are directly connected to the aging of society. Societies have thus attained success in terms of both rising life expectancies and rising equity but neither without consequences.

From the Individual to the National

The most important groups in the international system are the ones we call nations. Interactions among the most powerful states continue to determine the course of international politics. At the heart of major theoretical structures—ranging from neoliberal institutionalism and power transition to realism—is a common perception that power dynamics among nations set the preconditions that guide global and regional politics.[1]

Without discounting the importance of nonstate actors or emerging institutions, such as the World Trade Organization (WTO(), United Nations (UN), all major organized religions, and the North Atlantic Treaty Organization (NATO), the relative power of nations continues to regulate the dynamics of the international system.[2] This power is directly created by the choices of and subsequently the size of each nation's population. International power is, at its core, the combination of scale and organization. Those two components form the foundations of the global political order, no matter the type of theoretical construct used to investigate it. Power is and remains that which comes from the population itself.

Power to the Populations

Power, defined as the ability of one entity to influence another to accept the first entity's policy objectives, is a complex, multidimensional concept. Consensus has emerged that power reflects a combination of demographic and economic capabilities adjusted for government efficiency and preparedness.[3] Knorr (1970) was among the early pioneers who carefully distinguished between potential power—a measure of the base capacity of a nation before mobilization—and actual power—the approximate strength of a fully mobilized country facing a direct threat.

After the December 7, 1941, Pearl Harbor attack, Admiral Isoroku Yamamoto, referring to the United States, may or may not have uttered: "I fear we have awakened a sleeping giant and filled him with a terrible resolve." This well-known phrase effectively captures the difference between active power and potential power, the latter created from the implementation of policy and reflected in population dynamics. In this book, I focus on potential power.

The changing nature of the international system, be it the rise of China or the continued reorganization of the European Union (EU), may to a degree merely reflect the new and changing opportunities that states create for themselves. Starting in the late 1970s, China's decision to liberalize, at least economically, was at its core the choice to allow its population to exercise its existing potential. The miracle rise of China's population has its roots in the repeal of government policies that spent enormous amounts of time and effort pulling the population in unsustainable and economically unrealistic directions. The small change that allowed rural villagers to sell excess produce in semi-independent markets ended what had been the largest sustained famine in the twentieth century (from the early 1950s to the late 1970s). The Chinese famine offers a dramatic example but one that must be remembered. It was caused not by environmental challenges but by fundamentally flawed, tragically unsuitable agricultural policy, which the government forced upon farmers for years even after the disaster became apparent. It is a troubling example of the incredible stability of Mao's government that even after more people had died than in all of World War II at the hands of a preventable, government-created famine, still China continued the policy year after year. As China shifted its domestic choices from catastrophic to creative, the rest of the world has needed to reconsider the interests of the largest country on Earth. Now, China has the ability to organize and project its power—an ability that it did not have for almost all of the twentieth century. The reforms in the late 1970s have thus altered the course of history in the twenty-first century.

The ability to organize politically allows for the implementation of policy, often without regard for what the policies can achieve. Flawed economic and agricultural systems are implementable, as are flawed space programs. Countries with totalitarian or authoritarian regimes can be highly effective, even if they mobilize their efficient systems to create policies that undermine the long-term stability and potential of their populations. We have seen this happen time and again throughout history, and it remains an ever-present possibility. Stable, efficient political systems do not guarantee success, however "success" is defined, but they are more capable of implementing policy once policy choices are made. By the same token, it is assumed that more efficient political systems are the richest. This is, of course, not necessarily true; they may have simply been the ones to pick more economically viable policies.

If politics is the key, potential is the driver. For instance, smaller countries, such as the European nations, remain influential due primarily to their high levels of labor efficiency and technological prowess. Neither is a fixed aspect of humanity, but both can be gained. Education systems can be built, and technology is creatable and transferable in the long run.

Scale matters for politics as much as for anything else. Larger countries have more potential, yet the range of countries' sizes is remarkable. Nations the size of small towns interact with countries that take up whole continents. Countries of thousands must deal with those with larger than a billion people. Consider the difficulties that arise when a small country deals with another country, or set of counties, close to four times larger than itself. To be equal in terms of total nominal GDP, that smaller country must be four times more productive per person than the larger country, as that is what a total GDP is at its core, the summation of all economic output of the people themselves. So if one is near four times larger in population they only have to be a quarter as productive to equal a total GDP. China has started to surpass this productivity point, and, with a higher degree of domestic stability, it may be in India's future. This is the story of the ratio between the United States and China with the United States at one quarter the size of total population than China.

To use China again as an example of how decisions made decades ago can alter a nation's future, figure 1.2 shows the age distribution of the Chinese population in the year 2000. The turn of the millennium was a historical inflection point from the optimism of the 1990s to conflict of various levels of intensity seen later in most regions of the world. China's population follows a traditional pyramid distribution, with relatively few elderly compared to the larger, younger age cohorts. Yet China's population boom ends with the thirty to thirty-four age group, which corresponds to those born in 1966–1970—before the country's tremendous economic reforms and, interestingly, before the country's one-child-per-family policy went into effect. Notice that after this cohort, most generations have not been nearly as large. The Chinese entered their population-boom phase after World War II, though it was limited in scope by the great famines that started in the 1950s. Even without undergoing large-scale economic reform, China moved toward the expected demographic structure

FIG. 1.2. China's Population Distribution in 2000 (in thousands)

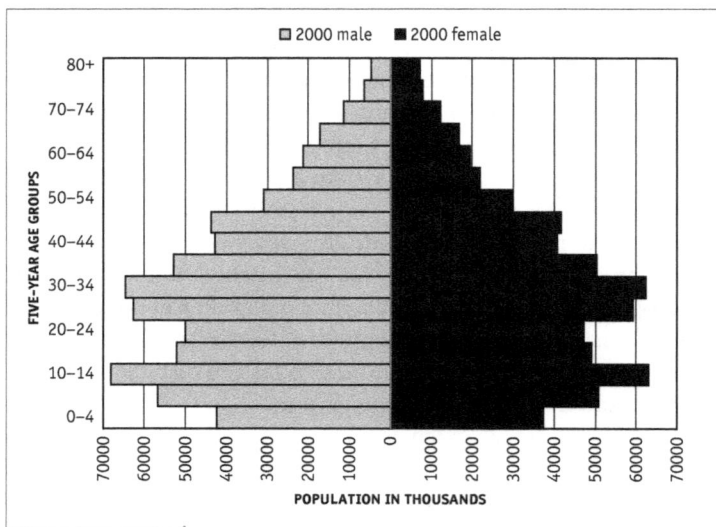

Source: United Nations, Department of Economic and Social Affairs, Population Division 2015b

of a developed society in which subsequent generations were smaller than the ones before.

Notice that the exception to this is the group between ages ten and four-teen. Critically, this generation provides a preview of China's future, with significance for international relations. The aging of China will be vast as that group moves from youth to the labor force and finally into elderhood. That generation will be stressed as it is forced to provide for China's largest elderly population in history.

The need for an increasingly efficient labor force is rooted not only in global economic competition but also in the stark reality that fewer people will be available to support an unprecedented number of elderly dependent individuals. Some Chinese scholars call this the "middle-income" trap: the idea, which I agree with, that an aging society is incapable of the sort of dramatic economic success that we have seen in China over the past forty years. This level of growth will necessarily slow when the labor force declines and the population becomes increasingly elderly (and therefore increasingly expensive). If this decline in growth happens too quickly, China will not become a wealthy country but one that is in the middle— think eastern Europe as opposed to western Europe, or Mexico as opposed to the United States. This middle group is certainly still prosperous! But a middle-income country with the demographic pattern of a wealthy country is a nation that has must meet the needs of an aging population with a comparatively low level of resources. Even worse, its era of significant economic growth is now over. The worry of stagnation caused by demography is real.

A relatively prosperous middle-income country might not have the resources it needs to fulfill the demands of its expanding elderly population. Remember, inducing mortality rates to decline, at least with relatively low-hanging methods like sanitation improvement, is inexpensive. Add some limited universal medical care based upon access to vaccines, and Chinese life expectancy is soon to become eighty years on average. That is very close to what can be enjoyed in the richest states in the world. Importantly, an eighty-year-old Chinese citizen will not have the same access to medical care as an eighty-year-old in a wealthier country, but they will have the same demands. The demands matter when we are talking about hundreds of millions of people—more elderly people in one country than the total population of the United States. The scale is vast! What kind of policy could deal with this situation? Increased immigration or some form of EU-style coalition would not have the size needed to offset domestic aging and losses in China, unlike in much of the Western world. China must hope that their labor force will be remarkably productive to compensate.

The EU-27 is a cross-national organization with high levels of economic and political integration. All the while, it attempts to define what exactly that integration, in fact, looks like. Is the EU a commonwealth, a failed alliance, or the creation of the United States of Europe? The coalition's dire combination of nationalism and disagreement on the demographic stability of the union raise questions of both free ridership and want. What do member countries gain from being part of such a union: strictly economic efficiency, with labor mobility, as a principal aspect, or something more dramatic? Small, highly efficient nations merge with neighbors under the umbrella of the EU agreement, possibly even creating an original entity that can harness what should be the largest GDP of any group in the world. This dream depends on the unity to unlock the potential power of a unified Europe. Consolidation not from conquest but by negotiation is in stark opposition to most European history. It is likely that the EU offers European countries their last chance for relevance in the international system: individually, the member states are increasingly less relevant, but combined, they are critical actors.

Here, a question of the potential energy of population arises again. The questions before a country such as Germany are simple. Is it better to be a small, wealthy nation of 80 million people with ever declining influence, or to be the largest country in a coalition of 450 million people? Does the German population vote for and care about global power? Is it better to be small, wealthy, and organized or large and influential? Would Germans have the ability to assimilate new migrants and continue to be the center of the union? The EU's costs are borne by its largest members, but so too go the benefits of influence. This type of normative decision matters. These choices can be made for a multitude of social reasons, such as domestic preferences for isolationism or idealism, but their outcomes on the international system are clear. Scale is a critical component, and without it, only organizations such as the UN) or NATO will be able to pull less-influential nations into processes that they can no longer affect due to their lack of relevant resources.

National Policies of Population

International politics matters, as does the power of nations. Policy creates prosperity. It allows for sustained peace, and it gives hope that the future will be materially and even morally better than the past. Prosperity, peace, and hope are critical to the development and creation of what humanity wants but does not yet know exists. As I mention at the beginning of this chapter, history is not innately progressive: it is a series of trends for or against liberalism, for or against free trade or institutionalism, toward or away from the creation of peace or the horrors of war. Trends move in relation to interests or ignorance, not according to some inevitable evolution toward a future by which we are measurably better.

Demography and the policies that affect it are often ignored in terms of their direct causal effects. The plans themselves are sold, marketed, and even implemented for reasons as wide as the sun, but all policies that link and create the future of nations themselves are linked to power and economic potential: two key areas of concern.

Examples of how these choices and changes affect the international system are vast. Politically, discrimination has the tendency to, over time, upend democracies. Those groups with less economic access and opportunity tend to have higher birth rates. Those with more economic opportunity have fewer children. Not always, but often, smaller, discriminated-against minorities may thus grow larger in proportion to the majority group. Add the possibility of being in a democratic system, and generational effects become evident: first in terms of voting, then political change.

For example, in South Africa, the apartheid regime became untenable as the percent of the white population became an ever declining minority, which resulted in making repression unsustainable. Smaller demographic groups may follow the same trajectory in countries such as Lebanon, Syria, India, Singapore, and Israel, even if all are much less dramatic examples than South Africa. All have groups within that have sustained rivalries. In Lebanon, with a rapidly declining Christian population, both Sunni and Shia groups see political power changing because of their population growth and growth from Syrian refugees. Syria has a similar situation with large outflows of heavily urban educated elites, again Christian or Druze populations, and increased importance of Shia from Iranian support, with the Assad regime still holding its powerbase from the Alawite minority. India continues its crisis between Hindi and Muslims, and in Singapore, ethnic rivalry from a wealthier Chinese minority to Malay and Indian immigrants continues to cause concerns. Each nation has a combination of wealthy, powerful groups with different birth rates creating distinctions between rival ethnic or religious factions. Moreover, politically distinct demographic groups are a crucial domestic concern in Israel. The divisions between these groups are not the result of actual policies of discrimination but instead arise due to disparities in access to economic opportunity and even isolation from changing gender norms. Those with what are considered traditional religious practices, for instance, have higher birth rates because they enjoy less female equality—an important consideration when asking what they want or whom they would vote for in a competitive election.

Israel is one of many countries that must consider the ramifications of how their society would change should, for example, those of Jewish faith no longer be the majority of the country. Fertility statistics show that when both Israel and the Palestinian Territories are forecast as one total population, the Muslim and Jewish communities are projected to become roughly equal in size by 2030, thanks to higher birth rates among the former. Massive differences in education, wealth, the ability to mobilize, and fertility separate these two populations. Currently, we see similar demographic dynamics playing out politically, as the ultra-orthodox subgroup in Israel has a much higher birth rate than the expected mainstream. Israel thus faces a combination of interesting demographic factors, including the questions of what to do with the significant and increasing Palestinian population and how to handle the political influence of the religious population. The country itself seems to have understood this issue from its beginning, with the "right to return," a cornerstone of Israeli immigration law first signed in 1950, intended to encourage Jewish immigration. This policy, which allowed anyone who can show even limited Jewish heritage to move to the country, no longer has the same level of influence as it once did, as traditional sources of Jewish immigration (Europe, the Middle East, and North Africa) have already moved and the remaining Jewish populations (within the United States and parts of Latin America) seem no longer to want to make that type of journey.

The famed Israel-Palestinian peace process made large an increasingly important factor as these underlying demographic foundations become a greater part of the overall whole of the country. Israel thus represents an exciting combination of domestic choice, ethnic identity, and demography as a process that is changing the political reality within a nation.

Israel is not unique. Japan also actively recruits those of Japanese descent to return to the motherland. Japan has seen a small increase in immigration from Brazil as a result. Many European nations choose to allow their diasporas, even three generations deep, to return to claim citizenship, with Ireland, Italy, and Spain all having well-worn policies to attract those they think will be the easiest to integrate (those who are, in part, their relations). Spain has also used this process as a way of publicly apologizing for past actions; they have created a process by which descendants of the Jewish population expelled during the most brutal parts of the Spanish Inquisition would be able to claim Spanish citizenship.

While Spain's immigration policy—one that memorializes historical acts that the modern population of Spain considers to be immoral—is attractive in theory, from a population standpoint, it is almost impossible to implement directly. The Inquisition itself lasted nearly four hundred years and ended nearly two hundred years ago. True, a decent number of people may have direct connections to family who suffered during this era, but how would one prove it after such an amount of time? Would Spain only allow current practicing Jews or also those who converted at some later date? How would the children of affected people, often many generations later, remember the act of fleeing? During the early sixteenth century, it was a common refrain for Jews fleeing to the Caribbean from the Spanish Inquisition to claim to be Portuguese, as they often fled through Portugal and to its overseas holdings (before it, too, started its own organized program of discrimination). That lasted for generations, even as religious affiliation waxed and waned, and it may to this day have a residual effect on culture in the region.

Will the focus be only on the Sephardic community itself, many of whom are the direct descendants of exiled Spanish Jews? The specific implementation of this type of policy (if it even can be implemented) could have a dramatic effect. A broad policy that grants visas to those with limited or no documentation includes one group of people. But if the policy were to become even broader to include all members of groups that likely had some connection to discrimination during the Inquisition, that would dramatically change the flow. Or, of course, discussion of these policies could just be rhetoric, backed by no real attempt to discover these lost refugee Jewish Spaniards. Similar situations have also arisen in Poland, with comparable processes organized for those who lost citizenship (and their children) due to the acts of the Communist government.

These small, but interesting, policies of immigration pale in comparison to the changes to the world order that are currently being wrought by the larger flows of the world. The movement of African and Asian migrants to Europe, for example, presents a fantastic opportunity. It could cause the seat of dominant power in the region to move from Germany to either France or Britain. The recent Brexit vote could, instead of undermining the union, reinforce it or even allow the union's members to reassess who should pay the necessary costs to create unity. If the remaining EU members sustained their unity, this could change the union from one that is maybe a few steps too large to one with a higher degree of consolidation and hence relevance on the international stage. The rising cases of populism within France and other countries are noteworthy countermovements, but they do not change the possibility that power dynamics may be radically transformed, and maybe even rejuvenated, given this period of crisis. The world may meet with a unified, efficient, organized EU, one with a central government that has actual coercive power, maybe even a military, and most importantly, a reason to exist. If the European population itself chooses to buy into EU institutions, sustained peace and economic growth may follow. The alternative is, of course, disintegration, with all the difficulty it would entail.

The United States matters as well. As the world's dominant power, it has served as the coercive and diplomatic force behind the institutions that have facilitated widespread prosperity. Its size, scale, and efficiency have allowed for a degree of power never before seen at the international level. While the United States has moved to exert its influence in ways that many deem problematic, it has still maintained broad support around the globe for its ideas that integration, free trade, and institutionalism matter for the international system and for humanity as a whole. The force and degree of power that the country built from its demographic core propelled the entire world to a higher degree of integration than what would have been possible without it.

The great question now is whether decline is upon the Western world. To a lesser degree, one wonders whether the United States will be able to, as I suggest in chapter 8, create and harness a successful immigration policy that allows the country to maintain the scale of power necessary to remain dominant—or at least close in power to its rising challenger, China. I would suggest that yes, this is a possibility, should the United States wish to pursue it. The United States's choice to accept immigration is so unique that it is a competitive advantage, one that must be acknowledged in discussions of how power is created, sustained, and used. The future is not inevitable; it is built from domestic choices. Even so, many decades of consistent immigration policy can be changed with just one election.

Demography as a Foundation for Future Choice

The politics of power rests on questions of choice framed by the demographic structures of a given time. Demography can facilitate amazing periods of economic growth as a youth dividend is channeled for the betterment of society. Processes of mass migration, urbanization, and maybe even democratization all come from that structure of youth before age and poverty before riches.

Aging is the inevitable outcome, but it is one that can be checked or exacerbated by choices to discriminate or not, to allow for increased gender equality or not. When societies liberalize a tradition that has historically concentrated power, money, and potential in men and decide to open these opportunities up to women, the tradeoffs are amazing. Economic growth increases to a degree that would not have been possible given older forms of social structure. Structures that limit development may have undermined human potential for generations. Successful development, in turn, relies on the capacity of the government, its stability, and the unity of the nation and its people.

Demography is the framework of the future. Trends of isolationism have reinforced the fact that the future can only be created via the expectations of the current population. While that structure can be modified to some extent by expanding the labor force and reconsidering past cultural biases, it cannot be altered dramatically via domestic policies that attempt to increase fertility.

This argument is built from a consensus that the liberal world has meaning. To create international peace, institutions must matter. To allow for expanded growth, rules governing everything from finance to physical trade, population movement, and the arguments of the nations themselves must work to maintain the stability of the world. That stability then creates additional incentives to invest, grow, and build a future for us all. To isolate is to limit potential, whether technological, cultural, or from a population standpoint. The latter is often ignored in politics because it does not influence votes, but it is this book's greatest worry.

On the contrary, trends do matter in politics. What we do next—how we deal with a society transitioning from a norm of youth and an expectation of growth to one of age, decline, or stagnation—is not a question for futurists but for us all. These demographic changes will influence all aspects of our society, from politics to film. The expectation that new cities will be built, new buildings will be larger, and the population will grow is so intrinsic to humanity that to decline is more than a statistical change—it is a paradigm shift. Yes, large areas have seen significant population losses; sparse rural regions and old mining towns sitting abandoned are common sights throughout the developed world. Nevertheless, they are not great Western cities or nations.

This discussion has the smell of fiction but is the modern reality. Population growth continues, but it is not universal. Dealing with demographic trends is the great question of politics because demography creates the system we live in and the institutions we rely upon. It will be our financial obligation and curse. With it, the "how" and the "why" of construction will also change. In no area will this be more obvious than in the global arena, as demographics influence the wax and wane of countries. The rise and fall of politics, and the importance of power, will remain.

CHAPTER 2

Feast or Famine

INVESTIGATING HOW POLITICS CREATES
DEMOGRAPHY AND THE FUTURE OF HUMANITY

The stories a society tells itself about its origins and expectations for the future reveal much about its belief structures and fears for what is to come. From expectations of home ownership to when (or if) they expect to build a family, the stories people tell frame personal choices and demographic reality. As the twentieth century gave way to the twenty-first, a demographic shift occurred within many nations from the youngest generations representing the most substantial portions of society to a new reality of aging populations and future population decline. This trend will shape the story of the new millennium, first in the developed world and then for the rest of humanity. Implicit in this modern shift is the likelihood of extraordinary economic growth, significant societal change, and the increasing importance of immigration to the maintenance of economic growth. Mapping the trajectory of this demographic transition requires an understanding of the role of politics in shaping economic trajectories and potential for progress or disaster in growing, developing nations. Politics leads to policies that can facilitate human development or undermine human potential itself. The study of how politics creates demography thus allows us to understand and frame the future of humanity.

The "Malthusian specter," as I call it, refers to the theories put forth by Anglican curate Thomas Robert Malthus in his 1798 work *An Essay on the Principle of Population*. Malthus viewed population growth as an inevitable evil. Economic prosperity and peace, he believed, would lead to higher standards of living, longer lives, and lower infant mortality, which, in turn, would drive population growth. The population would then grow and grow until standards of living inevitably decreased, resulting in famine, disease, and unrest. Malthus believed that population growth was untenable and would ultimately prevent society from progressing. He warned, "I say that the power of population is indefinitely greater than the power in the earth to produce subsistence for man."[1]

Indeed, Malthus presented this cycle of overpopulation undoing economic and other forms of progress as a divine check on humanity, forcing governments to turn away from projects that only sought to increase wealth or alleviate poverty. Instead, Malthus advocated for taxation and other disincentives to keep nations focused on securing primary resources and preventing population growth. Of course, Malthus left the inevitable question of who should then be allowed to produce children up to future generations.

The Malthusian thesis inhabits political spaces like a specter. Its ghostly shadow is largely uncredited but continues to shape governmental policies, political activism across a broad spectrum of views, and popular culture.

Pop Culture, Environmentalism, and Malthus

Let us pause for a moment to consider how fears of overpopulation, along with a frighteningly frequent call for eugenicist remedies, subtly appear without much outcry in mainstream, arguably escapist, entertainment. Focusing on North American and British popular films and television, for instance, science fiction, fantasy, horror, and disaster movies offer near unquestioning acceptance of population control policies.

Kingsman: The Secret Service, one of the top-grossing films worldwide in 2014, is a highly stylized comedy-action tale that follows working-class hero Eggsy Unwin as he embarks on a journey to join a secret elite British spy organization—the Kingsman—and defeat an evil tech billionaire named Richmond Valentine.[2] Valentine threatens to eradicate the majority of the human population in order to save the rest of the planet, all the while ensuring his own survival and that of his wealthy friends. —In the film, the lower-class protagonist Eggsy battles his rich bourgeois nemesis in his training academy, and the antagonist decides to preserve only the wealthy elite, as opposed to scientists, artists, or other figures a different fictional eugenicist may have gravitated toward. Although the film criticizes the elitism of Valentine's plot, it does little to question Valentine's initial logic that the size of the human population is an existential threat to its own survival.[3]

Instead, the narrative boils down to Eggsy rising to his proper place in the Kingsman by becoming a member of the historical aristocrats and saving his family from his mother's also lower-class criminal boyfriend, all the while pursuing the promise of sex with a princess. Unwin does "save the world," too, in that he foils Valentine's plan for the proletarians of the world to violently turn on one another while the wealthy watch from well-appointed bunkers. Valentine's central argument that overpopulation is destroying the planet, however, remains unchallenged. The hero "wins" by preventing mass murder, but within the world of the film, the planet and humanity are still doomed to be destroyed by overuse and overpopulation. The film hinges on the argument that there is a surplus of people in the world—largely from marginalized groups and whose subordination the film unquestionably accepts—from which exceptional individuals can distinguish themselves and be "rewarded" with higher socioeconomic status, privilege, and, should they reach high enough, life itself.

The public appetite for this narrative is evident in other examples, such as the 2019 blockbuster film *Avengers: Endgame* based on classic Marvel comics.[4] Again, a villain seeks to cull the population; in this case, the godlike Thanos aims to channel the power of a set of "infinity stones" to instantly halve all life in the universe, once again, to prevent the overuse of resources. Within the film itself, his logic remains unchallenged: no one offers solutions to avoid food scarcity, nor do they ask Thanos to simply use the stones' power to double the universe's resources. The latter is perplexing. Here, we have a force that could destroy half of all life in the universe but that is incapable of increasing access to resources or at least facilitating their more efficient use. Was it a lack of imagination that necessitated destroying half of life instead of ending resource scarcity, or was it an attempt to appeal to a public that finds plots featuring devastation as a solution to overpopulation more compelling than plots promoting advancement?

Thanos's worldview is bolstered by the film's dramatization of his own planet's ruin due to overcrowding. He seeks to be "fair" by making the population reduction random, and the only clear ideological counterpoint by a protagonist comes from Steve Rogers, or Captain America, who insists repeatedly and without elaboration: "We don't sacrifice people." The narrative thus presents a central tension between morality, on the one hand, and extinction, on the other. The Avengers win by allowing life itself to end at some indeterminate time in the future. Morality in this case means allowing subsequent generations to die in degradation. Meanwhile, the problem of resource scarcity remains unsolved.

The film's focus on the supposed perils of overpopulation departs from its 1992 comic book source material, in which Thanos seeks to destroy life to prove himself worthy of being the lover of Death, who is a character in the book. While the decision to change the plot can be partly attributed to a trend in mainstream films to portray more nuanced antagonists, it is nonetheless extraordinary. Romantic (albeit toxic) desire, it seems, was considered less appealing to an international audience than forced coercive population control and genocide.[5]

We can argue that even though the villains' evil plots in these films are eventually foiled, a disturbing binary emerges when the protagonists cannot offer more than a desire to protect individual relationships or vague personal codes to justify fighting back against human genocide. On the one hand, these films suggest that we must protect populations because it is "morally right," although the films do not dispute whether pursuing the villains' "logical" population-control or technological advancement policies would ultimately benefit the world. All involved seem to generally accept the premise that population control would, regardless of its moral faults, fix the world's problems. However, the films consider neither the realities of population decline nor alternative solutions such as improving efficiency, promoting creative policies, and making different personal choices.

The general acceptance of population control's viability echoes in the rhetoric of groups with a range of political stances, often united in the belief that the world's resources are scarce and must be protected by reducing the population. From the Sierra Club to the founder of Planned Parenthood, problems of scarcity focus on protecting an in-group at the expense of an out-group. As this book later discusses, these out-groups are made up of already-marginalized individuals: migrants, people in poverty, and those disempowered due to race, gender, sexuality, religion, or another minority status. The rallying call to fight overpopulation too often falls in line with nationalistic chauvinism, white supremacy, and another persistent specter haunting the world: eugenics.[6] This faulty logic appears nakedly in anti-immigration platforms and, insidiously, in subsets of more progressive movements, such as environmentalism and reproductive rights.[7]

Dear reader, please note the use of the term "subsets" in the previous sentence. This book in no way seeks to counter progressive policies. Indeed, in many cases, what the book argues to be the most humane or empathetic choices, those that increase the enfranchisement of all members of a society, are also shown to be necessary for building strong political and economic systems. What must be noted is how the threat of overpopulation—and the eugenicist policies offered as a false solution—insidiously infects groups across the political spectrum. Above and beyond the schisms in any given nation created by opposing economic philosophies, progressive versus conservative politics, or dominant religious culture, the greatest threats to a society's future are a scarcity mindset and, crucially, the belief that some of the society's members are undesirable and expendable.[8]

The popular fear of overpopulation clashes with the current expectations for declining populations in the developed world. Nearly 30 percent of the total population will disappear, leaving behind empty schools, hospitals, and even whole abandoned cities in countries such as Japan and Italy by 2050.[9] Navigating these differing outlooks for the future, as the number of children dwindle and the elderly become the largest component of society, will be the crucial issue of our time throughout the world. The new dystopian future is one of population decline—not population growth.

Considering the Demographic Transition

The demographic transition, a phenomenon seen in the population statistics of nearly all nations from the nineteenth century to today, follows a familiar curve: slow population growth transforms into a rapid population increase, resulting in a youth bulge, which becomes a broadly aging population, followed finally by a decline in total population. Demographic transition represents a shift from the cultural norms and expectations of a youthful, growing population to a new reality characterized by just the opposite.[10] This monumental change alters the very nature of human experience within a society. Consider the fall in infant mortality and the rise of life expectancy that presage the rapid growth phase of the demographic transition, which occurred in most developed countries in the twentieth century. People who came of age during this era of growth expect to live well into old age, to enjoy decades of retirement, and to never experience the horror of a lost child. Before the developed world began its demographic transition, all families expected the possibility of loss, as even the wealthiest remained powerless against the scourge of childhood diseases. These demographic shifts were first observed in the developed world, but they are now emerging in developing nations as well.

The demographic transition is best illustrated by depicting a population's age distribution as a pyramid.[11] Traditionally, the young constitute the largest proportion of a population, making up the base of the pyramid, while the elderly make up the smallest proportion at the capstone. In nations at the most extreme stage of the demographic transition, the elderly become the largest proportion of the total population, and the youngest generation is the smallest. The pyramid inverts itself, as seen in the post-transition phase illustrated in figure 2.1. Every society that has existed from the dawn of time has rested on a foundational assumption that young people would continue to be plentiful while the elderly would remain rare. This concept has shaped the politics of humanity, forcing societies to concern itself with educating, mobilizing, and imagining the future of their youth, as they were expected to eventually represent a majority.

The shift from an economically productive and youthful population to a growing elderly population in need of care is now nearly universal. Figure 2.1 illustrates the ways in which this demographic change plays out. Notice that the transition begins in traditional societies characterized by a large youth population and high mortality. Growth is limited, and yet with small technological advancements, the population expands. The society moves toward a conflux of declining mortality, reduced fertility, and increased life expectancies. The population then ages overall as the components of growth peter out, moving to the expected last stage of gradual, although slow, decline.[12]

This trend was first observed in the world's richest, most-developed coun-

FIG. 2.1. Demographic Transition

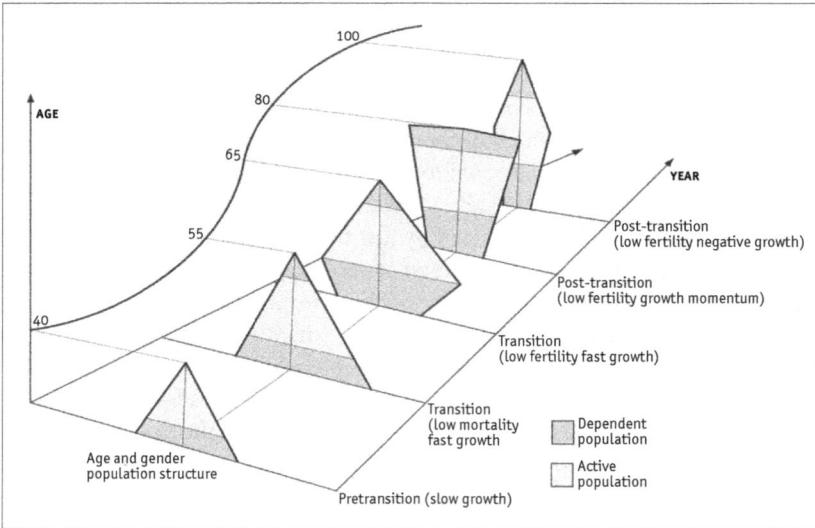

tries, but now less-developed nations are undergoing the same transformation. When exactly the demographic transition begins is surprisingly not determined by the amount of wealth a country has accumulated. Instead, even in countries with limited economic growth, it seems that external factors, such as medical advancements ameliorating mortality rates and even small investments in sanitation, create the massive changes in life expectancy that catalyze the demographic shift. This means that societies with even the most limited resources can undergo this demographic shift more easily than they can transition from poverty to wealth. This must prompt us to reconsider the future of the human population on a global scale. The major difference between these countries in transition, however, is in the scale of resources that each country has available to care for its aging majority.

Scholars studying aging populations tend to focus on this phenomenon exclusively in high-income nations or in the most successful of the developing countries, such as China. In doing so, they have overlooked that the case for a positive causal relationship between economic growth and an aging population is not as well supported as they may think. The traditional assumption is that wealth creates the context within which it is possible to have an aging society—that wealth itself is a requirement for the demographic transition. The assumption that aging is an issue only in the richest nations is wrong.

The incentives that create aging societies are not a matter of unknown market forces or the result of the accumulation of wealth but are determined, rather, by the complex interactions of individual-level choices given the available opportunities and alternatives. Opportunities for employment, education, or even entertainment are all factors that impact a person's decision to have or not to have children. The breadth of these options does not need to rise to the scale seen in western Europe or North America to have demographic effects like what we see in those regions. Nations we so often call "developing" now have levels of college education, women's labor force participation, access to the internet, and love of computer games that are nearly equal to those in developed nations. Despite continued wealth disparities, the differences between these countries are being radically reduced as technology and societal expectations become increasingly ubiquitous, all the while contributing to rapid declines in birth rates.

Dramatically, it now appears that the world is on a trajectory to consist of aging societies and that large-scale human population growth was a temporary phenomenon. The issue of aging impacts almost all nations, whether they are rich, poor, or somewhere in the middle. This trend has direct implications for economic development, as it challenges traditional expectations in transitional economies that the future will be brighter than the past. Given the need to allocate resources toward an aging population, these nations will not benefit from the opportunity to invest and grow their wealth.

In nations with a higher proportion of young people, economic growth expectations are higher, regardless of what caused the youth-heavy population structure to originate. The premise that developing societies' economies will grow faster than those of developed nations relies on the condition that poorer countries have larger, younger labor forces that they can mobilize to unlock growth. This is often an exciting and transformative point in history, when a disproportionate amount of the population waits to be allowed to create, build, and expand. However, a labor force that ages without seeing the fruits of its labor or any accumulation of wealth and success will become an aging middle-income or even poor society that will only continue to stagnate economically as their demographic structures continue to grow older. This is the key: the youthful structure of a large labor force can naturally increase without the necessary economic system and political stability in place to turn that presumed temporary advantage into actual development.

Individual choices are the critical determinants of the future of humanity, and politics and policy are their most direct systemic outcomes. People and groups can choose to embrace disorganization and violence or nurture the creation of future potential. An economy is not a mystical concept but the culmination of all the decisions made by individuals within a society. Notably, the politics of that society determine the decisions that individuals are allowed to make, whether to consume, invest, govern, or export. An economy is the outcome of a population's ability to make and create, but only in the context of the limitations imposed by that same population. Politics do not merely allow for economic opportunity to exist, nor is politics the sole outcome of economic opportunity; politics are at the root of economic growth.

Crises alter futures. War, conflict, or political collapse, as well as their potential to destabilize entire regions, can alter demographic trajectories. Demographic shifts due to tremendous loss of life during violent conflicts can trap nations within demographic profiles characterized by aging societies without the workforce or ability to achieve any significant economic growth, effectively condemning them to generations of poverty.

The demographic transition is not an unavoidable destiny. Large, youthful populations are bastions of unlocked potential, and these fleeting few decades in a nation's history are crucial, should their citizens capitalize on them and decide to propel themselves to new levels of human advancement. These delicate periods are characterized by increasing fertility and dramatic decreases in mortality. The resulting massive baby boom can serve as the fuel of the future, but it is also a potentially dangerous phenomenon. If a population is pushed into growth while its economy is left to stagnate, the worst-case result is a society that has effectively grown itself into increasing poverty and has missed what could have been the pivotal moment of its existence. The successful mobilization of a youthful population is by no means inevitable. Similarly, the eventual gradual decline that characterizes the demographic transition is not inescapable. Instead, through policies that promote education, strengthen government institutions, embrace previously marginalized groups, and welcome new migrants, governments can, whether after years of gradual change or in the wake of a sudden and traumatic event, lay the foundation for a safer, healthier, and stabler future.

What Futures Can We Expect?

Three different trajectories for future demographic change present themselves. The first follows the expectations seen in the traditional demographic transition: rich, aging populations with high levels of gender parity will continue to have limited population growth, or as I view it, limited economic potential. These societies accumulated wealth when their populations were still disproportionately youthful after a baby boom, and those riches will allow the societies to maintain themselves as their labor forces decrease and the dependency of the elderly on the young increases. The United States, Japan, South Korea, and most of the countries in Western Europe fit this profile.

The second possibility concerns nations that have improved their mortality rates and human rights records but have not experienced significant economic growth. These countries experienced a baby boom but did not wrest economic growth from their youthful workforce while they had it, and now they face the same declines in population that confront the wealthier nations. As examples, consider much of Latin America or the formerly communist nations in central Europe, such as Poland, Hungary, and the Czech Republic. These countries enjoyed public health programs, education, and, in some cases, improved gender equality, but they did not see economic growth on the scale of the countries in the first group. They chose a route that limited their development from a wealth standpoint by focusing on domestic political concerns, whether to promote an ideology or even stability. Now they have the relatively aged demography of rich nations without rich nations' finances. Political policy or international investment cannot alter this situation. Latin America offers another example of such lost demographic potential. The region's missing decades of economic growth, centered on the 1980s, undermined the economic potential of a generation but counterintuitively did not change its demographic trend; the aging continued. These countries pose a critical question: How can an older, poorer society manage?

The last and least attractive trajectory involves countries that lose the opportunity to improve their population's quality of life through access to health care, education, enfranchisement, or economic growth. For countries continually experiencing civil war, destruction, and political instability, population growth is a curse. It outstrips any possible economic growth, and each generation becomes more impoverished than the one before—a poverty trap in name and function. These countries are thankfully rare now, but many of the remaining nations to see rapidly growing populations are in this category. This third group includes many, but not all, of the sub-Saharan African nations. While North American and European news coverage tends to focus on the rapidly rising populations of India and China, the faster population growth in countries such as Pakistan, Bangladesh, and Nigeria are rarely discussed. Optimistically, if we consider all of humanity to constitute potential, these are the nations in which innovation could still originate under conditions of domestic stability.

While the demographic transition follows a well-worn path, politics can intervene at nearly every stage. Decisions that range from avoiding civil wars to investing in public health and civic infrastructure translate directly into remarkable decreases in mortality rates, particularly in child and infant mortality.

These radical declines characterize what I call stage 1 of the demographic transition. As a result of political decisions that improve child mortality rates, youth come to compose a greater percentage of the broader population, radically changing the society's *dependency ratio*,[13] that is, the ratio of those in the *labor force*[14] to those who depend on others for economic support, including both the retired and the very young. When the percentage of young people in a society increases, the full amount of *labor* increases remarkably. Political choices are thus what bring about the first phase of the demographic transition, during which the traditional pyramid-shaped age distribution of the population sees a substantial increase in its youthful base.

I discuss these youth surges, or baby booms, in chapter 3, but at this point, consider the advantages of a nation in which much of the population can be productively used in some form of developmental or economic activity. This moment in demographic history has extraordinary potential for double-digit economic growth; during this time, countries can harness their population and transition from developing to developed nations. This is a fundamental process by which economic development can occur, but it does not last forever nor is it inevitable. Most notably, it is the direct result of political choices.

Political influences also contextualize stage 2 of the demographic transition. At this stage, increased *longevity* occurs.[15] As mortality decreases and much of human misery—such as that caused by the loss of loved ones, whose labor or potential labor helped support families, communities, and nations; illness; and hunger—is abated, individuals have a greater potential for many more years of health. As mentioned in chapter 1, political decisions that lead to periods of peace eliminate or at least mitigate most forces that can destroy or upend life. These are not grand, dramatic innovations that drive large-scale declines in mortality but rather the simplest and cheapest choices of the political system, as I explain in chapter 3.

We would expect a population that has undergone rapid growth to begin reckoning with that growth's aftereffects, leading to stage 3 of the demographic transition. This phase is characterized by increased *density* or the amount of population per unit of land. This is primarily considered to be overall *density*, or the total population divided by the total landmass, but, in discussions of development, urban density becomes more important and is city specific. At roughly this point, *fertility* also begins to decline.[16] Decisions to produce children and how many to have are deeply connected to potential parents' expectations for their offspring's lives, such as what they can accomplish and, most importantly, whether they will live past infancy and into adulthood. In situations where mortality rates are high, particularly among the very young, a greater number of births and hence higher fertility rates are needed to ensure a next generation. However, when mortality declines (stage 1) and longevity increases (stage 2), fewer children are required to ensure that families live on, and thus, fertility slowly decreases (stage 3). Each phenomenon influences the next, all following indirectly from the policies that set the initial stage of the demographic transition into motion.[17]

During this stage, the average number of children born to each woman falls from almost double digits to fewer than two. Fertility rates that decline below two are especially significant; a woman who produces two children effectively replaces the two people needed to produce them, thus maintaining the size of the population. Stage 3 is also accompanied by *aging*, which is defined as an increase in the elderly proportion of the total population or the average age of the nation itself. It is the natural outcome of declines in fertility that result from individuals' choices to no longer have large families.

As the momentum brought about by the increased size of earlier population cohorts reaches its natural conclusion, the most challenging aspects of the demographic transition become evident and demarcate stage 4 of our model. Here, we have arguably the most unique and interesting of periods. Nations throughout the world are experiencing declining labor forces, and with this trend comes the potential for retired individuals to comprise the largest share of the population. Issues of medical care and pensions become critical, as do questions of how successfully the nation created wealth during its growth period. Following this stage, and because of the increased economic burden imposed by an aging population on smaller subsequent generations, our model and story concludes with stage 5, which is characterized by *population decline*.

The Choices We Make Shape Our Futures

It is vital to remember that these stages, with some degree of malleability, are only the ripples of that first political step: the initial policies that led to decreased mortality and set the stage for the traditional demographic transition. The chain of events that then follows, from increased density to declining fertility and aging, even the shift from a rural to an urban society, are in themselves not policies or decisions of any political system.

While these stages follow an expected progression of demographic transition, it is crucial to note that, at each stage, horrific actions can undermine destiny. Conflict, war, and the horrors of mass population loss can alter the economic growth that should or could have been. Politics are thus not only the key to a potentially transformative acceleration in economic development and human progress but also a potential catalyst for intense and lasting damage as a country ages.

Even in the most authoritarian regimes, politics cannot increase fertility. Politics also cannot halt, in the long run, the increased population density in cities. Nevertheless, it can modulate the intensity of these trends specifically by choosing whether to effect *enfranchisement* at any stage in our model but the last. Without political enfranchisement, the demographic transition can lead to polarization within a population. Whereas some groups may see the advantages of boom-based growth, other classes of the population may have lower mortality rates via spillover health effects but not otherwise benefit from the society's economic gains. Once entrenched, this polarization is particularly problematic; it becomes intractable when the growth era ends, leading to demands for welfare, affirmative action, and other methods of income redistribution rather than acceptance of disparities in wealth and security.

Enfranchisement does not only mean the legal granting of rights or removing of explicit discrimination. More broadly, it involves creating circumstances in which members of previously marginalized groups can exercise their rights and be allowed to attain the economic, social, and political benefits available to the already enfranchised groups. Enfranchisement is an economic necessity for a nation interested in wealth creation. It enables a state to mobilize an additional labor force, but it also pushes down fertility rates concurrently. While enfranchisement results in declines in discrimination across all marginalized groups of people, most importantly, it leads to gender mobilization. This is a critical concept and one that I investigate thoroughly in later chapters.

The economic role and future of women are vital because women make up the majority of the population. The scale of this statement is important. So much of the human progress gained in the modern developed world is attributable to the enfranchisement of women. Furthermore, no other group continues to have more untapped potential to unlock the possibilities of the future.

However, expanding women's rights can increase or exacerbate fertility declines. It can lead to earlier-than-expected population aging, as I discuss in terms of Japan later in this book. When it comes to the enfranchisement of women, the complex interactions of policy and beliefs, including access to income, work, discrimination, and societal norms can alter the trajectory of an aging population, although this effect is mitigated in countries nearing the end of the demographic transition, such as those in the developed world. The enfranchisement of women is thus one of those rare policies that can transform nations, and how society contends with population decline is complicated by how it deals with women's rights.

Immigration, like enfranchisement, is not an inevitability but a phenomenon influenced heavily by political choice. Immigration policy—the simple process of allowing new people into a country—becomes the last and only reliable method to sustain a society after it has progressed through stages 4 and 5 of the demographic transition. Movement can radically alter central aspects of an individual's life, whether it be their life expectancy, income, or even their immediate safety. Migration also refreshes the population that receives immigrants. While immmigration policy may be driven by the economic necessity of an influx into the labor force, this logic is certainly not the only type of policy that affects immigration. Isolationism and xenophobia may disrupt a country's attempts to arrive at domestic agreement on the implementation of a coherent immigration policy, but nevertheless, these perspectives do not diminish human migration's potential and its importance for economic growth.

Now that I have laid out the expected trajectory of a demographic transition, consider how familiar this narrative is and how similar it seems to the trajectories of so many countries in the Western developed world. However, remember that stages 1 through 5 are the phases that would be expected without any large-scale disruptions, such as war, famine, or other kinds of political turbulence. These are the stories of western, central, and eastern Europe; of North and South America; of most of East Asia and increasingly the rest of the continent itself.

Challenges of Demographic Change While Developing

This more challenging story is seen throughout much of sub-Saharan Africa and South Asia. Conflict and crisis have continuously disrupted these states, though they also have accrued many of the benefits of global changes in public health standards and the resulting declines in mortality. They persist, and within them, there is extraordinary potential. Currently, in most places on Earth, mortality still decreases even during periods of significant conflict. Nations such as Nigeria, Pakistan, and the Central African Republic all show these trends. While massive labor and youth increases are observed in these nations, they are not accompanied by the expected or hoped-for economic gains. Nevertheless, even those nations historically riven by war still posess the potential for dramatic change.[18]

Further, in nations beset by conflict, emigration becomes a necessity rather than an individual choice. These nations become sources of immigration, potentially creating an exasperating situation of aging due to the loss of emigrating youth. These nations also often enforce traditional norms that further the disenfranchisement of women, thus preventing these societies from making otherwise expected gains. For these countries, the last stage—so unlike the trend seen throughout most of the world—is continued population increase even with lower fertility rates. These events are the outcomes of choices linking politics of stability with cultural choices to discriminate, changing life expectancies, job opportunities, and immigration possibilities.

Change Can Happen

Even in situations that appear to be dire, the destiny of a nation can be revitalized by political choices. Governments can capitalize on high levels of political rights, the density afforded by cities, increased life expectancy, and hopefully the economic gains harvested during critical periods of youthful ambition. Nations can change, and with them, the potential of an untapped population can arise. Even nations racked by dire conflict and chaos can be revitalized with the help of stable politics and peace. Worryingly—as worry must be acknowledged—great heights of economic success may not be attained in societies with more aged populations. Potential can be lost, but it never reaches zero. A population can once again achieve success. Optimism is the abiding goal of this book, as no country has reached a stage of stagnant poverty and an aged population.

CHAPTER 3

The Outcomes of Youthful and Aging Populations

A society's potential comes from its young—a statement that might pain the souls of the elderly, but a reality. Among a youthful population, choices abound, only limited by the scope of opportunity that geography and society can provide. The inevitability of aging comes now not only to individuals but also to nations themselves. With it comes a reduction in potential itself.

Potential of a Youthful Population: Conflict, Change, and Growth

Youth has the potential to drive innovation, reshape political systems, and create economic growth.[1] Most societies do not need to innovate from zero; they can apply and implement already-existing technology and policy choices to unlock future success. Taking advantage of opportunity is thus a matter of stability and will, not of creation from scratch. When opportunity and a youthful population combine, a great amount of change, growth, and achievement can be accomplished. [2]

Although the world on the whole is young, youth is not distributed equally across nations. Figure 3.1 shows the United Nations' (UN) estimates of youth by economic development characterization, providing a crude yet useful illustration of the scale of difference between young and old countries. The ranges are remarkable—from below 30 percent of the population under age twenty-five in the most-developed nations, such as the United States and the countries of Western Europe, to two times that number in the least-developed countries, including most of sub-Saharan Africa and central Asia.

The most interesting category is the one in the middle. The less-developed countries are those in the process of moving from the least-developed category to the most-developed category. A quick point to make: in the modern era, all

FIG. 3.1. A World of the Young

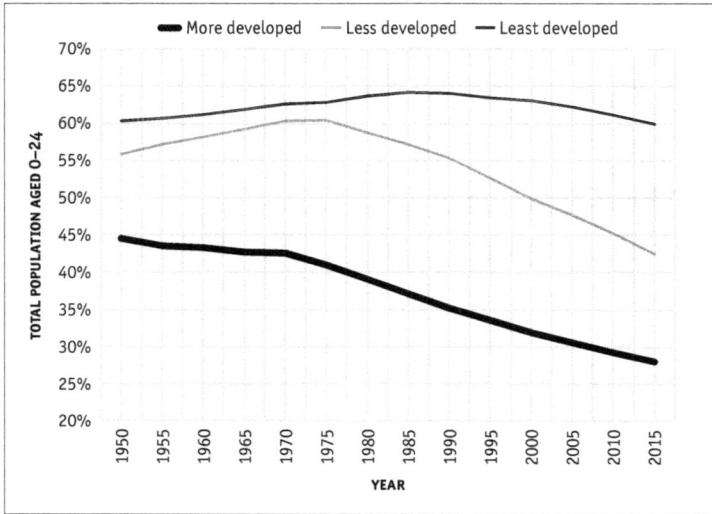

Source: United Nations, Department of Economic and Social Affairs, Population Division 2015b

nations, even those with the most limited economic growth or stability, will age. It is only in dire situations, be they caused by conflict or sustained poverty, that countries will maintain a stable traditional demographic profile with a robust young population and fewer older people.

The data for less-developed countries illustrates that by 2016, these countries had reached a demographic profile very similar to that of the more-developed world sixty years before—well along the transition from young to old, with about 43 percent of the population under age twenty-five. The less-developed countries, though, have a crucial advantage: they are undergoing one of the most profound, dynamic, and fundamental changes of humanity with the benefit of having watched other countries go through the same transition. Knowing what to expect—and seeing the results of the older world's policies—can hopefully guide these countries to make better decisions in all manner of policy realms, from social services to education systems to retirement policies and a wide range of financial and legal frameworks. Notice that the least-developed countries today have a percentage of youth that matches the youth levels in the less-developed countries in 1975.

This observation is optimistic, but with it should come a warning. Again, dear readers, remember that aging is inevitable almost everywhere in the world. If the success of a development strategy is dependent on the total amount of youth in a society, and the least-developed countries are becoming increasingly old, then they, therefore, have less time than those who developed earlier to gain the same levels of outcome from the same policies. The potential is now that developing countries will have the demographic patterns of the rich but remain the very poorest in the world. These countries may then find themselves stuck in an aging, stagnant demographic structure, never able to achieve the success seen in so much of the world around them.

Youth Is Change, and Change Can Be the Unknown

The story so far has been one of optimism with a focus on generalizable policies that efficient stable governments can take and implement. The universality of education, effective government, and sanitation is clear. This story cannot be fully considered without the alternative, which is that youth create, youth riot, youth believe, and youth destroy. While, if harnessed correctly, youth can reshape the future of the world, young people can also incite crisis and violence, damning themselves and their descendants to lost potential. The very same youthful population structure that can lead to high levels of economic growth in some cases can under different circumstances lead to conflict and undermine society. Youthful nations are fragile. In them, we see the greatest chances for civil war and regime changes. Violence is a possibility, and change does not have to be for the better.

Perspectives that herald the economic potential of youth, therefore, should not ignore the complex nature of economic development. Stable financial systems, the rule of law, allowance for entrepreneurship, the maintenance of land rights, and even the stability of a trustworthy currency are all needed for a functioning economy. The basic concepts of ownership and investment, in addition, allow for the creation of economic opportunity. These are not secrets—they are policies that can be copied and implemented.

Large sections of the world are well run, peaceful, and have high levels of infrastructure development and education. They have taken that list of successful policies to create growth and implemented them all. All other things being equal, with every policy conducive to economic development in place, how does age affect a country's capacity for economic growth? What can nations do once they fulfill the list of requirements for growth, from the rule of law to women's rights? And when does age undermine the expected outcomes of these policies?

Figure 3.2 uses an amalgamation of both high- and middle-income countries and compares average age to gross domestic product (GDP) growth to investigate the possibility that a nation's age might determine its capacity for economic growth.[3] The data suggests, as shown by the downward-sloping re-

FIG. 3.2. Average Age of the Country Related to Economic Growth

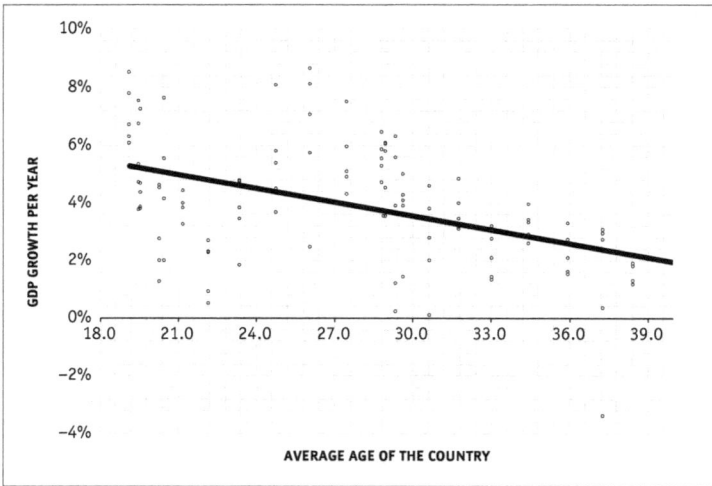

Source: World Bank (2016)

gression line, that there is a negative correlation between average GDP growth per year and average age—that is, the older a country is, the less likely it is to show sustained economic growth.

Aging and decline is not a certainty—given policy changes that can mitigate these trends, such as immigration—but it is nonetheless a common characteristic across nations, as illustrated by what we have observed in these two largest subsections of the international community, middle and high income countries, over the past fifty years. This suggests that for most of the world, because of aging populations, nations must become accustomed with a new economic expectation of close to or below 2 percent GDP growth per year. Compared to the traditional expectations of nearly 5 percent GDP growth, this is a dramatically smaller number with huge ramifications for everything from individual incomes to national defense budgets. The world has not seen 2 percent growth since two hundred years before the Industrial Revolution.

In 1980, there was an inflection point where the median age in the high-income countries began to increase steadily as GDP growth trended downward. The three lines in figure 3.3 illustrate this narrative. The dotted line tracks the median age of the population (corresponding to the secondary axis), the black line shows the percentage of the population under age twenty-five (on the primary axis), and the grey line is a trend line of GDP growth for the group of high-income countries considered here. This line is not connected to an axis but used in a general sense to illustrate the countries' economic position in

FIG. 3.3. The Amount of Youth and Age of the Population Linked to Economic Growth

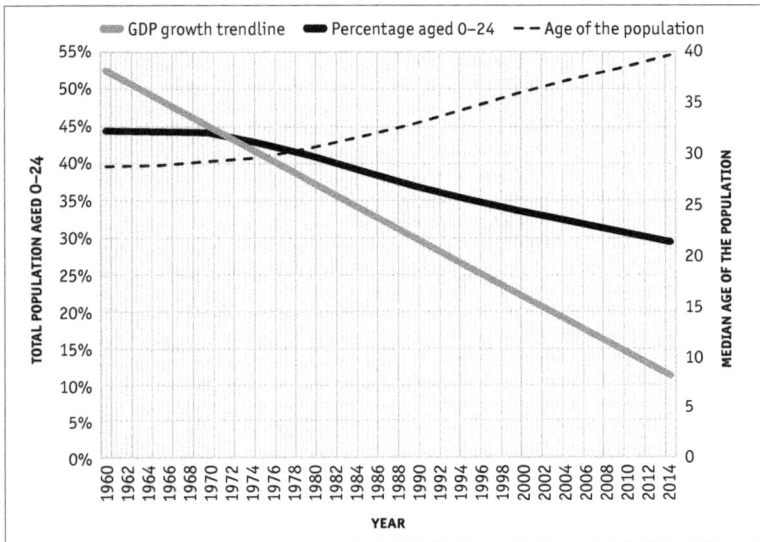

Source: United Nations, Department of Economic and Social Affairs, Population Division 2015b; World Bank 2016

those years. The trend down in economic growth is, again, a component of the modern world created by aging.

In 1980, the developed world arrived at a both figurative and literal crossroads of data points. The median age of the group hit thirty years of age, and the countries collectively saw a decrease in youth, defined here as the percentage of the total population under age twenty-five, to only 40 percent. This point is worth remembering and could be a descriptive statistical congruence. That is, when society hits a median age of thirty, with 40 percent of its total population under age twenty-five, its economic growth starts to decline at a faster rate. I call this intersection the 30/40 point. To be clear, this is a term meant to facilitate descriptive discussion and is not designed to indicate a complex causal relationship.

The economic decline observed after the 30/40 point is most likely due to governments investing more in their elderly populations than in their young ones, or perhaps the point is simply the nexus at which subsequent decreased growth is a sign of already-achieved economic success.

I would suggest that countries with this 30/40 demographic likely no longer expect to see high levels of population growth, but how this is concretely affected by and affects the demographic transition is yet to be determined. This point is useful because it can help us identify which nations have started the

FIG. 3.4. GDP Growth and Average Age in High-Income Countries

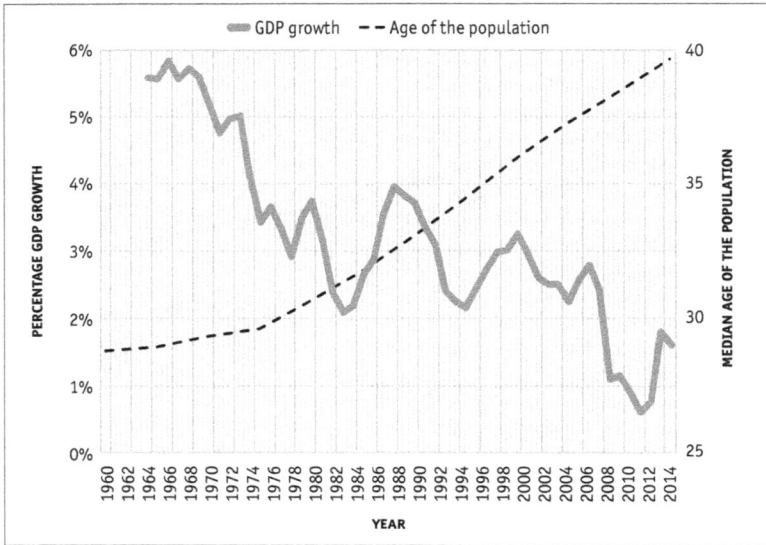

Source: United Nations, Department of Economic and Social Affairs, Population Division 2015b;
World Bank 2016

trajectory downward in total youth. If we assume that aging is the outcome of economic success, then this event has been misclassified as a crisis and should be considered a part of the composition of an organized successful society. However, suppose the transition starts via external processes such as international health aid and spillover effects such as access to new medications, technologies, and other factors that might not have anything to do with the domestic organization and are entirely due to global innovation. These influences could possibly create demographic patterns similar to those seen in nations where only domestic choices have influenced the transition to aging and the slowing of economic development. We have an interesting problematic convex in which countries must put their population to good use before starting a steep decline in potential—decline that may be caused not by their own choices but those of the world around them.

Outliers to this pattern do exist. China, for instance, had GDP growth far higher than expected—near double digits—when it hit its 30/40 point. I discuss China in detail later in this book.

Figure 3.4 examines the relationship between GDP growth and average age in high-income countries.[4] A few noteworthy components jump from the graphic; the first being that GDP growth rates above 4 percent are rare in the developed world. In only a brief period in the early 1980s did high-income countries see growth at or above that number. Between 2000 and 2015, those same countries, the richest in the world, had reached a point that 3 percent is an ideal year. Growth is and will likely be slow in the developed world unless some massive technological change occurs. Economic growth should have the possibility of additional decline as these rich developing countries age; stagnation is a possibility.

Figure 3.4 again illustrates the connection between age and GDP growth in high-income countries. Dear reader, it is important to remember that an economy is not Pavlovian: it is a complex network of competing interests, with the international system's problems or successes helping to propel it high or low. We can see this in the relatively volatile range of GDP growth percentages. In the 1960s, GDP growth neared 6 percent before inching down, slowly and with some spikes, to our contemporary economic reality of between 0 and 3 percent growth. The economic and population growth trends are both evident. As a society ages, it slows in growth and innovation; nations accrue the most significant gains when they are young.

From Population Boom to Population Poverty

What is the future of the world? Should we expect to see states with high growth rates, population booms, and continued instability in politics; a future in which the fastest-growing nations are also the most violent; a cycle of population growth, violence, and yet more population growth; a cycle of doom and destruction out of the most apocalyptic works of the followers of Malthus?[5] Will we become a species in perpetual decline? It is dangerous to assume, however, that a wide range of countries will inevitably undergo a similar move from young to old. This trend is not inevitable nor should it be taken as such.

The poverty trap is one worst-case possibility. Poverty traps occur when population growth outpaces economic growth, causing each generation to be larger and poorer per capita than the one before it. The dire prediction that accompanies this trap is that nations will see massive increases in population with only limited political stability or small improvements in public health. Nations may be able to implement policies to decrease mortality quickly, but these same nations might not be able to translate their growing populations into economic growth. The poverty trap could thus create a near-apocalyptic scenario, with a mass of youth looking for hope in politics or industry but finding nothing but disorganization and chaos. This situation could even come about because of well-intentioned global health aid that provides just enough assistance to decrease mortality but not enough to create economic opportunities for the people saved. This combination has the potential to create the foundation for future mass migration and continued political unrest.

Discussions about the demographic trajectories of the sub-Saharan region, Pakistan, Afghanistan, and parts of the Middle East, such as Yemen or Sudan, are ongoing.[6] Many worries about food shortages caused by the domestic governments' inability to invest, initiating a feedback loop in which these governments' increased reliance on international nongovernment organizations (NGOs) may in turn create a free-rider problem and undermine the governments' reliability. Others worry that economic growth, no matter how fast, will not keep up with the rising demand for employment in these nations.

Oil-export-oriented countries, be they central Asian or Middle Eastern, represent a unique mismatch of population growth and economic growth: a dangerous combination of high GDP growth, increased entitlement programs, improvements in public health, and limited employment demand from a highly automated industry. The economies in these nations do not dependent on the skill sets—or even the existence—of their populations. Their wealth does not come from their people but from the happenstance of geology. This set of factors threatens to undermine the wealth of these states and the stability of their political systems.[7]

The bane of an oil-exporting country with vast resources and income is its population. The country's people are generally superfluous to its economy, as massed, industrialized, and automated oil extraction needs very few employees to facilitate a great deal of gains. These oil-rich countries thus have broad, youthful populations that are not relevant to the prevailing economy—a worst-case scenario of population underutilization.

When we stop to consider what these youthful populations might want, we should be careful about making assumptions. These populations live in highly restricted countries. They may seek economic growth, possibility, and a greater degree of prosperity, or, in some cases, they might like a higher degree of religious control or even the imposition of a harsher system of restriction. These restrictions often undermine women's rights, which, in turn, would change the next generation's demographic characteristics. In these vibrant, youthful periods, the outcomes of government and individual choices can shift or undermine the expected trajectory of the demographic transition.

Youth Bulge versus Demographic Dividend: The Example of China

The sense of doom so common in many discussions of demographic studies is evident in the code phrase "youth bulge": a term increasingly, and wrongly, synonymous with devastation. "Demographic dividend" is the alternative: a buzzword designed to give credence to the concept that a large untapped labor force is a national benefit. Both describe the same phenomenon: the surprise of a baby boom and the subsequent dramatically high levels of youth, which

FIG. 3.5. Century of Change: China's Population (in Thousands), 1950–2050

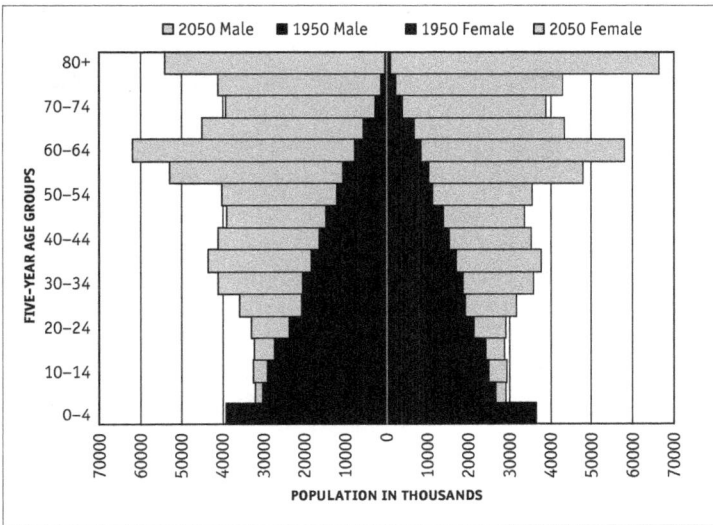

Source: United Nations, Department of Economic and Social Affairs, Population Division 2015b

come to constitute the majority of the population. The outcomes of this unique ratio of old to young are fascinating to the future of the world. While youth bulge suggests that this situation will turn into conflict, demographic dividend suggests that the outcome will be economic success.

Baby booms can have a variety of causes. The most common cause is increased access to basic-level health care, while the more complicated cause is the aftereffects of war. Think of the "baby boomer" generation in the United States, that large cohort of people born in the period of postwar euphoria right after the end of World War II. These massive baby booms are opportunity untapped; they are the physical embodiment of youth bulges and demographic dividends.

No country better represents the positive outcomes of the potential of youth then the rise of China. Figure 3.5 illustrates the scale of demographic change in China. The black bars of the graphic shows the demographic pyramid of China as it stood in 1950—which is a beautiful example of a "traditional society" made up of a majority of young people and very few elderly people. It is in the grey bars of the figure, representing the 2050 projections, that first the youth bulge and then the demographic transition itself can be investigated. The projected age sixty to sixty-four cohort is larger than any other subset of the population of China or at any time in the expected future. This cohort is larger than any seen in 1950, and it was followed by a significantly smaller generation.

A traditional society, such as that of China in 1950 starts with a pyramid structure, with few elderly people and lots of children. In this kind of society, the labor force is disunited or so fixated on the work that is necessary for life that investments are limited. When a boom happens, it begins in that cohort from age zero to four. In China in 1950, notice how much larger this group was than the preceding generations. This group represented the first births after (or near the end of) the Chinese civil war—a brutal, bloody era, but a classic situation that would cause a significant postwar baby boom, in which increased political stability, food safety, public health, and economic growth result in increased fertility. This population boom swelled the number of young people far beyond history's expectations.

Again, dear reader, notice that this population projection suggests that the youngest Chinese population cohorts will become even smaller than the equivalent cohort in 1950.[8] In this hundred-year period, China will have gone from a classic demographic pattern to a massive baby boom, to smaller generations, and in the future to population aging and total population decline. This story has changed the economics of the world and, with it, the global political structure. The economic growth that can arise from a youth bulge is vast. Countries such as Pakistan, Bangladesh, and Indonesia could all see double-digit GDP growth, unlocking the resources necessary for the bloom of potential within their populations.

In this way, crisis created an opportunity! After China withstood massive conflict and civil war, it then had the potential to harness a larger-than-expected youthful population. Let us now consider this story and what an alternative world would have been should the rise of China not have started in the 1980s but in the future by 2050. Could a aged, poor society have seen the same outcomes of liberalization policies given different labor forces? My suggestion is no. The rise of China is not only because of its total population but more importantly the age specifics of that population.

Let us be just a little more complex and consider that a baby boom is not just a onetime occurrence and that they cause little subsequent booms, or "boomlets," due to the effects of births, marriages, and timing. That is, people born in the 1950s were married in the 1970s and having children by the 1980s. In turn, the generation born in the 1980s was larger than would have otherwise been expected without that original 1950s boom. This same phenomenon is seen in the United States with a very large baby boomer population, people born from 1946–64, smaller subsequent generation X 1965–80, then much larger millennial 1981–96 and now generation Z 1997–now before probable decline. The baby boom from the 1990s will have aged to such a degree by 2050 that the largest cohort in China will be near retirement. This group was first born in the decade of the Clinton administration's heady days, the fall of the USSR, and the creation of the World Trade Organization.

This story of rapid radical change is remarkable having seen that early 1950s boom pushed into a nearly liberalized labor market with the new higher educated promarket 1990s generation reinforcing reforms of the 1980s. The country's sheer potential capability was unlocked, potential so vast it over-whelmed the expectations seen in the historical record—an outlier in place and practice but an important one. It was the right policy with the right popu-lation at the right time, which is amazing to see, more difficult to copy.

What, then, will come for the Chinese millennials born after the great re-forms, who have never seen conflict and who have never known anything but continued economic success? Most assume that they will see the same pros-perity that their parents have enjoyed for fifty years. However, this prosper-ity is slowing dramatically, exacerbated by domestic policies such as China's one-child-per-family policy, other forced family-planning programs, migra-tion controls, and trade wars, all of which have had the effect of undercutting the country's future economic success.

Again, that 30/40 point, with a median population age of thirty years and 40 percent of the population under the age of twenty-five, is a sign of change. The Chinese hit this demographic crossroads in the year 2000 and still saw double-digit GDP growth in 2007 (11 percent), but by 2015, GDP growth had fallen a full four points lower (to just above 7 percent). Setting aside for the mo-ment the reliability of China's economic statistics, we could be seeing the nexus point of change.

By 2050, the fuel of Chinese development, that postwar baby boom and its boomlets, will become part of the country's largest demographic group—the retired. With this transition, the gains that could have been made by the demographic dividend will have been lost. The change is already upon China, with 2016 (or close to it) marking the year their labor force shrunk. From this point on, expectations of Chinese prosperity must be reconsidered, changing the calculus of global power, domestic tranquility of the Chinese people, and the worries of a ruling class. The Chinese have not seen the possibility of eco-nomic stagnation in generations, but now, stagnation is a near-future domestic political concern.[9]

The process from boom to economic growth is similar throughout much of the world. It combines financial policies and policies conducive to entrepre-neurship with large-scale industrialization and employment opportunities—complicated policies for the Communist state that created modern China. Pol-icy choices are linked with the potential to create a new world.

From Traditional Societies to a Modern World

Countries with relatively young populations have a wide range of economic and political possibilities. Figure 3.6 highlights similarities across a select list of countries. Starting with China, notice that its population aged to such a degree

FIG. 3.6. Young but Not Forever

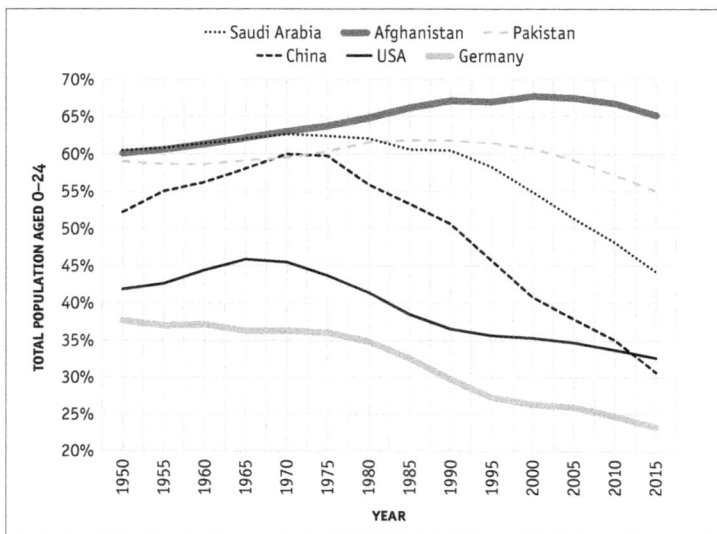

Source: United Nations, Department of Economic and Social Affairs, Population Division 2015b

that, in 2016, it had fewer youth under age twenty-five than the United States. In Chapter 8, I examine how the demographic trends and futures of these two countries will affect the international system. This change is so extreme that China's youth population will be like that of 1990 Germany—a country with limited immigration and well into its demographic transition by that point. No longer is China a traditional society by this point; it is starting to show age characteristics like those of modern Western European nations.

The comparison between China and Germany reveals a disconnect between age and development, as those young Chinese workers will not have the same levels of productivity or education as their equivalents in 1990s Germany. While 2015 China and 1990 Germany share a similar demographic structure, their economies are quite different, as Germany at that point was a truly developed society with high levels of education, wealth, urbanization, and all the advantages a few centuries of accrued wealth can attain.

To take another example, Saudi Arabia's youth population has changed along sharp trajectories. In a society with such a stratified family concept and in which extreme amounts of pressure are placed on child production, we would expect the percentage of young people to remain relatively stable over time or even increase continuously. We could go so far as to say that Saudi Arabia, more than any other country, should have the highest expected level of continuous population growth. It is among the most restrictive countries in the world in terms of women's rights. The size of the family in Saudi Arabia increases social prestige, and the country has enough wealth to pay for health and social services, all of which would seem to lead to a population boom unprecedented in human history. The data, however, reveal that this country is not only starting its demographic transition but also entering the stage at which youth sharply decline. The traditional argument that declining birth rates are caused by a combination of women's rights and economic growth flies into the reality of Saudi Arabia and hence to a remarkable question of the weight of those possibilities. It could be that even the smallest amount of increasing disposable income undermines birth rates so quickly that the effect of development outweighs the effects of human rights on demographic transition: what an example! A supposedly traditional society reinforced by political and religious edicts—disregarding for the moment its isolationism—begins its transition. Even so, a large percentage of the population, 45 percent, remains under the age of twenty-five. Saudi Arabia still has the structure for vast amounts of economic growth if that population can be harnessed.

In the cases of Pakistan and Afghanistan, both countries' youth populations are relatively stable. This makes sense given each country's relatively high degree of domestic political and economic difficulty, as this instability tends to cause continuous population growth. This can in the worse cases create a cycle of instability creating the foundation for yet more instability. Should a different path be found, and it has in so many other countries, then optimism should be real for these countries to also enjoy the possibilities created from sustained peace.

This optimistic outlook can be applied to most nations. Youth are vital and should be a prized, relevant asset. However, it is important to remember that this asset is not fixed. Youth represent change, but it can also be lost or wasted. This concept is a radical one: it differs from the common belief that potential change is dangerous and instead moves toward a new idea of gain.

Traditionally in development literature, rising populations are viewed with concern. International political efforts commonly focus on incentives to increase contraception usage and other more direct methods of decreasing the birth rate. Family-planning policies are often considered key to economic growth, the idea being that slower population growth would allow for GDP to grow at a faster rate, which in turn would make the generation to follow richer. Even assuming near-zero economic growth, if population growth could be limited, stagnated, or even decreased, then, on a per capita basis, a country would gain. Combine this with increased access to education systems or additional investments among that new, smaller generation, and you have a theoretical example of a prosperous state.

In practice, organizations as varied as the Sierra Club and the UN recommended forcibly manipulating national demographic structures as a way of creating economic growth. These policies have only been implemented on a large scale, however, in China and India. Forced sterilization campaigns and the undermining of the human right to choose to have children are difficult to consider legitimate, but the basic mathematics of these policies resonates. All things being equal, if a birth rate falls while economic growth remains stable, the next generation will be richer. This per person gain is complex. Should a government decide to stimulate GDP per capita growth through generational manipulation, it must carefully weigh its expected short-term outcomes against the likely losses associated with having fewer-than-expected youth and hence a smaller-than-expected labor force in the future. What happens to retirement or to childcare, education systems, or labor itself? If population change is forced on a system that is already entering a demographic transition, such as China, should leaders then exacerbate not only the positive economic effects seen in those next fifty years but also the problems associated with aging itself? These effects, at least in the case of China, are already becoming evident.

Success! The Outcomes of Aging Populations

An aging world is a fantastic achievement. With life expectancies now well into the eighties and likely to pass the century mark in the not-too-distant future, millions of people have enjoyed more decades of life.[10] Old age is a relatively new phenomenon in human history. Societal norms that hinge on age, from when we expect to lose our parents and loved ones to how we arrange our own priorities in anticipation of an extraordinarily extended life, reorder all our hopes and expectations. Imagine how strange it would be to jump centuries into the past only to see cities filled with children and teenagers acting as adults and for the elderly to be almost unknown. Now, make that jump into the future, where children will be rare, and the elderly will be the core of society.

Within Jonathan Swift's famous 1727 travelogue *Gulliver's Travels*, the titular hero visits a series of fantastic and magical nations. Within many are the outcomes of failed projects and politics, and Gulliver is confronted in realms such as Balnibarbi and Glubbdubdrib with a host of expansive empiricist, scientific babble used to control populations and undergird policy. Each nation suffers from its own combination of social dysfunction and income inequality. Swift's criticisms are, I think, as cutting now as they likely were in the 1800s. The most relevant of these realms to our discussion and one of my favorite concepts in fiction is that of Luggnagg, a land in which a small percentage of the population is randomly immortal.[11]

Gulliver at first embraces the overwhelming possibilities unlocked by immortality, even more so from an era in the eighteenth century in which death was of constant concern. What could he do with unlimited time: education, wealth accruement, holding of marriage, children, even the responsibilities of adulthood? He quickly learns that the reality of immortality is ennui and depression. To the population of this small land, the immortals are a stark reminder to enjoy life. The Strulburghs are prone to depression from about age thirty to eighty years old, at which point they became "opinionative, peevish, covetous, morose, vain, talkative; but incapable of Friendship, and dead to all-natural Affection, which never descended below their grandchildren."[12]

At age eighty, the state declares the Strulburghs dead, redistributes their estates, gives them a small pension on which to live, and renders them legally ineligible for employment or property ownership. They live forever in relative poverty and in poor mental and physical health, as well as on the pittance of the society. A short life of health and economic stability is held up as worth more than immortality in an inevitably decaying body. Swift may have conceived of this fictional nation assuming that the future could not be made up of nations populated by the old, dependent on a much smaller youthful labor force.

Swift's admittedly dramatic vision, however, is now widely imagined to be the future of the developed world—a fictional world, to be sure, but one that some of our more argumentative millennial activists do discuss, likely in jest. The change from a society that expects expenditures for dependents to go primarily toward the youngest members of society to one in which expenditures for pensions and elderly care constitute the largest proportion of entitlement programs is a profound shift.

Policies to ameliorate this shift have been attempted widely throughout the world from direct cash payments for children, marketing techniques focusing on ethnic nationalism, discussion of limiting access to contraception, or some combination of the whole, with only limited success.[13] Still, the search for new labor markets to support larger dependent elderly populations is becoming increasingly critical.[14] Within the United States, the general aging of the population has forced recent attempts to widen the workforce; these attempts, rather than being viewed merely as a social benefit, are now considered economically crucial. Pulling a more significant proportion of the disabled population and women into the workforce, as well as pushing off retirement for the elderly, are all components of, if not requirements for, the future. The stress of successfully extending life expectancy is the great political question of our age: not how to merely survive but to thrive with nations aging to a degree never seen before in human history.

The possibility of achieving something never seen before in human society is fantastic. So often, domestic political arguments boil down to rehashes of old ideas: restrict or not, give rights or not, invest or not. Regimes come to look so similar that they are lost within the crowd of history. Nations seems to face identical choices between different policies, as do the problems of nations and groups in general. The issue of aging, however, is unique in the scope of human history. Apart from some small, isolated groups losing their young to new economic opportunities outside the community, no group the size of modern nations has ever had to deal with this level of age. It changes every aspect of society, and the effect is so large as to be nearly incomprehensible when taken into historical context. This is a new world.

As with so much that involves demography, some scholars suggest that this change is apocalyptic. With titles such as Jonathan V. Last's *What to Expect When No One's Expecting* and front-page articles in the *New York Times* and the *Economist*, they paint a dire future of a world in decline or stagnation, no longer able to sustain the essential components of a society.[15] Last also ties demographic change to large-scale secularization movements and considers falling birth rates to be an immediate moral outrage. These demographers thus agree with many of the more conservative and religious groups around the world that women's choices not to have children represent some form of societal failure.

The idea that the traditional world is one in which lots of children are the norm ignores the societal pressure and economic reality tied to the birth rate itself. In most human societies, when women are given a choice, they choose to have fewer children. It is only in societies that actively decrease women's ability to choose—not only in terms of births but also in terms of employment, religion, political influence, and basic equality—that birth rates retain levels seen in earlier, more restrictive generations. The rise of women's rights in part creates an aging society, so the backlash against declining family size largely focuses on women as cause and concern.

Highly religious groups do maintain higher birth rates on average, but even the most religious countries in the world are undergoing declines in fertility. Saudi Arabia presents a good example of this phenomenon. Religious institutions are not immune to societal change, even if they are often slower to reorganize. The economic costs of decreasing women's rights increase proportionally as economic development increases. Where originally a family relies on one job with a multitude of dependent children, as economic development and labor competition increase, laborers choose fewer dependents both in terms of children and with additional income of the wife. The dramatic difference in total income between these two families expands generation to generation, and the direct costs of large family sizes and limited employment of women increase dramatically.

Development remains possible for most of the world, and that development should provide the fuel necessary to compensate for an aging population.[16] Change, even a change so unique as widespread aging, does not foretell a destiny of devastation; it instead underscores the reality that new issues need new government actions. The research on the topic is new, and frankly, due to the necessity of forecasting, opinions vary widely as to kinds of policy interventions that are required.[17] We are in an exciting time, but with an important caveat: because of the unique nature of these aging trends from a historical standpoint, policy failure is likely. A great advantage to the developing world will be the chance to evaluate the developed world's missed opportunities, and no greater issues remain than that of age.[18]

Scholars have even suggested that worldwide aging trends could create a new *geriatric peace* in the international system.[19] Children could become too rare, and hence too valuable, for families to allow them to serve in militaries. Alternatively, because of the reduced labor force, military enrollment would be comparatively too expensive to sustain. Combine that with many nations no longer able politically to support even low casualty rates and you have a combination of factors that could very well deter countries from using force as liberally as many did in the twentieth century.

We could even discuss a temporary advantage given to less-developed countries that are not yet faced with aging populations. Presuming a combination of semicapable military technology, increased size, willingness to suffer casualties, and capacity, these comparatively youthful states could eventually be a formidable military force in comparison to today's most powerful major nations, at least the ones well into the demographic transition.

Taking a bit more of a sophisticated look at aging and mortality, let us now investigate age-specific evaluations of life expectancy.[20] For example, in developed nations, individuals at age sixty-five can expect to live an additional nineteen years; should they reach the age of seventy, they will likely live another fifteen years. Compare that to the life expectancy at age zero: seventy-eight years. The advantage of living to an older age is that the elderly have avoided many of the accidents or questionable decisions of youth; they have not succumbed to an unexpected disease or some other unlikely mishap. They have survived, and that very survival helps to explain why they are expected to live even longer. Expected years are more informative than a single, blanket life expectancy when evaluating countries' demographic profiles.

Continuing our comparisons, let us now look at age-specific life expectancies in both the less- and least-developed nations. Within the least-developed world, an individual who reaches age sixty-five can hope to live an additional fourteen years, and at seventy, eleven years. Those in the world's less-developed countries can expect to live another fifteen and twelve years at sixty-five and seventy, respectively.[21]

As humans reach extreme ages, medical technology loses its ability to effect large gains in life expectancy for a simple reason: money does not create immortality.[22] It can radically reduce infant mortality and especially child mortality, but moving life expectancy from seventy to seventy-five or into the nineties is much harder to achieve. At each step, technology becomes both more expensive and less effective. Continuing our use of dates to help us measure development, the same expectations of life seen in the less-developed regions at those age categories would have been the expectations within the developed world during the 1980s. The 1980s were a period of loud music, the Cold War, and remarkably awful cars, but they are not that far back in the historical record. Age-specific life expectancies in the least-developed countries were roughly at the level seen in developed countries in the early 1960s. A time of better looking, if less safe, cars, wide ranges in music, and again the Cold War.

The least- and less-developed states can catch up to the developed world! Life can be expanded on, education created, and all the horrors of infant mortality minimized. These feats can be and have been accomplished.

Expectations of age at the highest levels are increasing, with life expectancies in the most-developed and less-developed countries expected to converge by 2050.[23] It will be the end of the century before life expectancies in the least-developed countries catch up. This brings us to a problem with these types of estimations: the technological and policy platforms that can facilitate extensions of life already exist. It is thus not a question of estimated innovation but the implementation of existing technology. Calculations that it would take over eighty years for the least-developed countries to converge with the 2015 version of the developed world ignore this fact; eighty years would seem to be more than enough time for four generations of people to create and implement technology that already exists. Estimations are important and provide the foundation for policy creation, but they should not be considered as from the light of Nostradamus; they are highly technical and skilled forecasts with error terms, and they are certainly not written in stone.

Dong, Milholland, and Vijg (2016) estimate that humans' maximum life expectancy is 115 years (barring a yet-unknown technological advancement), 115 years! Over a whole century of development, education, production, and human endeavor, would we arrive at the issue seen in Swift's Luggnagg? That is, would humans become less productive as they age to such an extreme degree? Importantly, as the answer to this question may very well be built into genetics itself, we should not forget that using less sophisticated methods of forecasting estimations have been wrong with Malthus in only one example. We cannot just assume that life expectancy will increase by some certain percentage based upon past successes. Biology does have limits![24] For 160 years, we have increased our life expectancy by close to a quarter of a year each year. This trend represents a tremendous change to human capacity and our ability to expand intellectually and personally.

We may run into the issue that, given the organizational ability and technological innovation needed to create such expectations of long life, we need some new form of expanded productivity to support this organization and innovation. Those we consider now to be of extreme age may need to shift from dependency to once again being part of the labor force. These considerations seemingly move into the realm of fiction or philosophical conceptions of the future, but they are rather close to current issues of policy. We ignore just how massively our frame of reference has shifted regarding life expectancy— from life ending at roughly one's early sixties (or when careers ended) to one's "golden years" lasting decades.[25]

Depending on the Workforce for Society

The concept and complexity of the dependency ratio need explanation. The first type of dependency ratio is based on the number of elderly people in a society in comparison to that society's labor force or its total working-age population, which is most often thought to include all people between the ages of sixteen and sixty-five. Other versions can deal with the ratios of women to men, labor to children, or some summation of them all.

The assumptions used to define the parameters of the groups compared in the dependency ratio are critical. The considerations of how long people generally work, different kinds of labor, and cultural norms all affect the age at which to assume an individual, or group, moves from the "labor" category to the "dependent" category. Who is young, old, and middle-aged, as well as who should be employed or retired, are remarkably important distinctions within a society. Consider how cultural assumptions come into play.

Let us take the case of a modern developed nation well into its demographic transition, such as the United States or a country in Western Europe. These countries are aging—depending on rates of immigration maybe quickly—and they will without question see pressure on their pension plans and entitlement programs as their populations grow older. Ignoring that complexity for a moment, let us look at assumptions.

Exciting questions can help us pin down a key assumption: What does, or should, the labor market look like in the developed world? What should we expect future generations to consider the norm in terms of educational attainment before entering the workforce: college, higher education in general? The number of years individuals spend in education is rising globally, and those years push back one's full entry into the labor market. When does retirement, or what should be retirement, become a possibility? Figure 3.7 shows some of the complexity inherent in these questions. Using UN medium population projections, I compare two different versions of the dependency ratio.[26] The first assumes that, in the future, people will spend more years in education and will not fully emerge into the labor market until the age of twenty-five. Afterward, because of increased pressures or simply increased life expectancy, the new expected retirement age will be seventy. The second version uses the more tradi-

FIG. 3.7. Differing Dependency Ratios in the Modern World

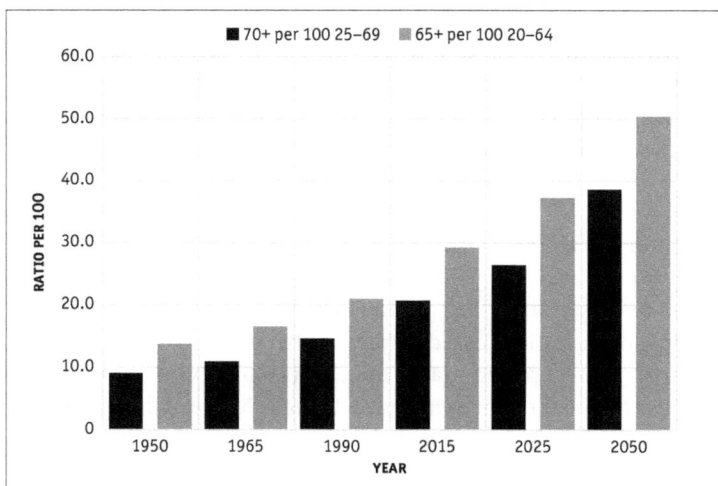

Source: United Nations, Department of Economic and Social Affairs, Population Division 2015b

tional assumptions of the developed world, with expectations of entering the labor market at age twenty and retiring at sixty-five. As we are working with averages, those expectations are closer to the modern experience (if a little more accurate twenty years ago).

Small changes in expectations have great effects on the outcomes of the data. The ranges are remarkable, and this difference of ratio to assumptions is a critical part of policy evaluation. Starting in 1950, the differences are minor: seven people per one hundred in the retirement-at-seventy scenario versus thirteen per one hundred in the retirement-at-sixty-five scenario. It is only as the decades move along that the differences in our assumptions about labor force entry and retirement become important. By 1990, the two versions show a difference of seven per one hundred, and in 2015, a difference of nine per one hundred. These numbers show both the overall aging of society and the differences in the assumptions between what scholars could proclaim are how the labor force operates in this society. The estimation of retirement, physical degeneration, could be just that, an estimation that the existence of a successful aged workforce would disprove or at least change the mathematics of dependency.

The 2050 projections are the most striking, with the dependency ratio in the retirement-at-sixty-five case increasing to an incredible fifty per one hundred. In terms of policy, that ratio is overwhelming: it is near ten times more than what a traditional society or one from earlier in the twentieth century would have expected and imagined the total population in terms of that ratio. The alternative projection, with a retirement age of seventy, reaches the still high but not as dramatic ratio of thirty-eight per one hundred, which is close to what the retirement-at-sixty-five world would see in 2025.

Efforts to organize for the future are thus created and shaped by expectations of what that future entails. The differences in these two dependency ratio models can be traced back to a series of choices: choices about retirement age or forced retirement, an expectation of younger (rather than older) workers in entry level jobs, expectations concerning advanced higher education, and questions of discrimination. The economic makeup of the nation in question is also a factor.

A wide range of professions, such as the referees in Italian professional soccer, most major police forces, and airline pilots, enforce retirement ages. Each of these careers makes the argument that the jobs themselves cause a degree of physical damage, or risk, that requires a younger workforce and a higher degree of payment in retirement as compensation. Required retirement ages in these professions are often relatively low, starting in the low sixties (or even fifties) or after a set number of years of service (typically twenty), meaning that retirement both comes early and is sticky.[27] The stickiness stems from the often highly restrictive, heavily unionized labor markets for these professions, with policies negotiated over many, typically contentious, years.

These forced retirement policies consider health and physical safety to be standard, relatively inflexible metrics, with no real consideration given to advancements in medical technology or individuals' actual physical health. The policies often ignore changing levels of substantial work-related risk as well as differences in individual workers themselves.

The potential future burden of a high dependency ratio is a legitimate concern for aging populations, but it is one that can be addressed with policy. Societies may enact a variety of policies to move a greater degree of the population into the labor force, up to and including investment in different types of industries. The capacity of a nation to enact liberalization policies or renegotiate with workforces is often a violent domestic issue, but one that is necessary. There is a need for dramatic change in how we organize the labor market, as it is not clear that the developed world's current systems of medical and entitlement programs will be able to handle the demands of fifty per one hundred dependency ratios. While this surprising number may inspire many to worry about the impending collapse of economic systems across the developed world, this fear assumes that countries will not course correct their actions and even beliefs to account for their aging populations.

The Example of Japan

Age affects all aspects of politics. Japan is a classic and, frankly, an extreme example. Current projections show Japan moving from an average age of forty-six in 2015 to over fifty-three in 2050: a seemingly small change, but one that would make Japan the oldest society on earth. Consider an average age of fifty-three! The typical Japanese person would be just over ten years from retirement, well into middle age, with grown children.

Japan's total population is expected to decrease by over twenty million people between 2015 and 2050. Imagine the radical changes this will necessitate in civic planning at all levels of domestic politics: common worries of where or when to build new schools, libraries, roads, or systems of public transportation will be reconsidered as demand declines radically and rapidly. The extent of rail networks will need to be reevaluated, as their financial stability depends on certain levels of ridership. Japan's cities will have been built for a population that no longer exists. The size of this projected decline is extraordinary, roughly equivalent to Canada's total population—the great cities of Toronto, Montreal, Vancouver, and all in between from Edmonton to Calgary—no longer existing in Japan. It is difficult not to be overly dramatic, but the specter of a few hundred thousand buildings sitting empty is a remarkable image.

Japan thus faces the policy question of how to build down its infrastructure, with the core of the issue being what to do with millions of elderly people living in great cities with a fraction of their original population. How will this projected population affect the sustainability of rail networks or hospitals? What will it mean for the necessary finances of building maintenance or maintenance of electrical grids? Much civil construction is founded on assumptions of usage without significant decline. The associated fixed infrastructural costs are a critical problem with modern civic planning, at least in Japan, which now needs to worry about how to deal with such decline.

The politics of implementing infrastructure changes are also problematic. Could Japan buy out its population and forcibly move them to new locations? Would this mean consolidating the suburbs and villages by moving most communities to the existing, still-dense cities? The country must also worry about a potentially large number of highly isolated individuals with a limited ability to care for themselves or to have someone care for them. Notice that these are not just social costs but direct financial burdens—how does one pay for trains, roads, rails, power plants, and other infrastructure in regions no longer populated? How much would it cost to tear down? Can it even be removed at all? The political choices will depend on the complexity of Japan's domestic system, but, in any case, they will not be easy, as the scale of the projected decline is more extensive than any decline to this point in human history.

The cultural losses of abandoned ancestral villages and temples, lost rural dialects, and forgotten festivals and other cultural practices are all important considerations as well. A society's population is not merely the engine of economics but also the creator of all that is human. Population losses on such a grand scale will limit what can be remembered in the next generation, and they have the potential to center the new, smaller population around less widely shared cultural traits, likely those that characterize the remaining large, amalgamated cities. An important consideration—and one that has the potential to limit the effectiveness of consolidation policies—is personal sacrifice linked with regional cultures. Like all larger countries, Japan has regional beliefs, festivals, and religious practices, many of which are endemic to specific areas. Amalgamation can dilute or even destroy those deeply held beliefs, which might be worth enough to individuals that they would stay in regions in stark decline just to hold on to them.

Later in this book, I investigate policies of immigration, which are critical to maintaining population scale in periods of rapid fertility decline. This approach is nonetheless politically difficult, even in countries with the highest projected future demand for domestic labor. While Japan has slightly lessened its formidable immigration restrictions, it has also invested widely in the field of robotics as a way of decreasing the human labor it will need in the future. Japan's goal is to create a technological alternative to immigration policy. Robotic technology may eventually be used to care for the elderly or to increase the automation within Japanese industry to an even higher degree. Robotic companions are even being designed to show comfort to isolated elderly individuals.

Japan's industrial economy has traditionally been fueled not merely by innovation but also by large numbers of youthful farm workers moving to the cities, into the plants, and then into the developed world. Japan tends to downplay this part of its story of development, choosing to focus instead on the rapid technological changes and innovations that created the country's digital age. The average age of a Japanese farmer in 2015 had moved past the midsixties, showing that this rural source of labor is long gone, whether acknowledged or not.[28]

What Does It Mean for a Population to Decline in an Economically Growing World?

Economic growth in the developed world, even at near 0 percent, is nominally extraordinary. For countries with the world's largest GDPs, a percentage point or two of growth represents an incredible amount of money. A total economy is not an individual's income, though! Do individuals gain from large-scale economic growth? Do people even know how their own income ranks in comparison to incomes in the rest of the world? These are critical political questions.

It is common for individuals to compare their situation not to the historical past but to their parents' and friends' shared history. Radical changes in life
expectancy, urbanization, and industrialization are no longer frequent occurrences in the modern individual's experience. I would suggest that this change
in expectations of what life to individuals will entail causes friction within the
political system. The rise of extreme parties prescribing change or a return to
some past "golden age" ignores the demographic makeup of today's societies or
chooses to scapegoat the international system for population challenges.

We must remember that discussion of dramatic demographic change
should not be limited to the realm of academic research on population or economics. The political and cultural implications of population shifts for or-
dinary people are likewise vast and important. Marketing to the young in a
primarily elderly population is an exciting choice, as is the wonders of neo-
urbanization and the rebuilding of major cities from car dependent to public transportation and walking while moving out of the paradigm of dispersed
population to a dense one. Combine these characteristics with the creation of
massive communities for the elderly, which will hopefully be designed for all to
make personal connections between retirees and to avoid the distressing possibility of physical and cultural isolation. It will be essential to consider these
psychological, personal, and architectural factors.

Support for a basic level of income should increase as a smaller total number of children, and then even fewer grandchildren, inherit wealth from their
parents and grandparents, a trend that threatens to increasingly concentrate
wealth in the hands of a few. Declining birth rates play a role in this phenomenon, as did the income disparities of previous generations. Think of your own
grandparents. How many children did they have? Did you come from a large
or a small family? Are your family members close? Did the older generations
support everyone in the family equally, or did they finance college education
for the men but not the women? Think again about your generation. Do you
have brothers and sisters? Consider the same questions on equity. Now think
about what happens if family size shrinks. Each subsequent generation can expect to receive even larger amounts of inheritance, with families who gain the
most being those who had the most in those previous generations. As wealth
is linked to smaller families, those who earn the most tend to have the fewest
children, who in turn receive a larger inheritance, and the cycle of wealth concentration continues to increase in momentum.

This trend is projected to continue to concentrate wealth even in light of
the possibility that more wealth may be used up during extended retirement
periods. Combine that with the wonders of compound interest and the likelihood of having made real estate investments decades in the past (depending on
area, race, gender, etc.), and there is the potential for a high percentage of the
population to become wealthy, with their grandchildren the likely benefits of

that wealth accumulation. This process may also facilitate the growth of a small percentage of the population that is divorced from the labor market: those who rely upon previous generations' accrued wealth and make up a full-time, life-long leisure class. This group is not yet large enough to affect dependency ratios, but it is large enough to change some aspects of the luxury market and political support for entitlement programs, as this group has a disproportionate influence on most domestic political systems. Disposable income means campaign contributions and policy influence. This policy influence is likely to translate into reduced tax rates, particularly for inheritance taxes or those on investments and rather than programs that effect most of the population.

Seemingly intractable domestic policy issues often boil down to nothing more than the realization that how long we will live has far outpaced previous generations' expectations! The clearest example is the problem of pensions. Whether pensions are called "Social Security" or simply "retirement," all have the same basic core concept: that the pensioner is allocated a set amount of money until death. Whether a company or a country bears this cost, it is still based on forecasts of age. Should those forecasts be off by even a little bit, the pension system will fail, undermined by the simple fact that people live longer than expected and there is no longer enough money to pay them.

Consider Social Security in the United States. This program was developed based on the idea that individuals would retire within seven years of their forecasted life expectancy. At the time, the argument was that most people will work until they are no longer physically able to do so, and for their last few years, they need just enough money to survive. That is, just enough for food and shelter in a wealthy, modern country, not for a "golden years" standard of retirement. The problem became the political inability to increase the retirement age enough, as the program moved from paying for seven years of retirement to ten, and now almost to twenty—a full generation's equivalent of time. (This is even considering the small increases in the retirement age from fifty-five to sixty-five, and now to sixty-seven.) One might assume that there is a simple solution to this problem that would restore financial stability: just increase the retirement age in relation to the average life expectancy so that the gap between the onset of benefits and death is always seven years.

The political naiveté of that statement, however, is stunning, and it ignores the power of the elderly within the U.S. political system. It also ignores the biological truth that, at some point, people lose their physical and mental ability to operate. While the timing of this inevitable decline can be estimated, it cannot be predicted precisely. At this point in one's life, retirement becomes not a reward for work but a consequence of the inability to work. The future of welfare in all its many forms must be based on a system that both allows for individual flexibility and incentivizes further employment.

The attitudes and opinions of the elderly matter more now than they have in previous generations, simply because more elderly people are still alive.[29] The elderly, with all their interests, attitudes, and beliefs, influence our current society to a higher degree than they have at any previous time in human history. As generations have become more differentiated, the outsize influence of the oldest generations has hampered the ability of the youngest generations to effect change. This pattern becomes particularly acute when we consider the different voting patterns of different age cohorts. Voters are polarized by more than just gender, race, or region: they are also significantly polarized by age, young versus old.

Age-related political issues may be increasingly pushing the overt partisanship of modern politics into the camps of young versus old or generations battling over even the most minute of problems. Regional differences abound between rural and urban communities and from state to state, yet the age disagreements—parents versus children and grandparents—are a real concern. Politics can undermine family relationships, and the question of how to pay for entitlement programs is so often divorced from how we vote for those programs.

A country's style of government, in turn, matters for its ability to anticipate and incorporate the concerns of its population into policy. The differing interests of young and old thus interlock with the political system. The ability for minor political parties to be represented in parliament for example differs initially with the amount of votes needed to change the political strategy of age specific campaigns. In democracies, too, prominent politicians connect with constituencies and rely on the support of those groups to keep their hold on power. From the Cuban expatriate community in Florida to the continued anticommunist Vietnam protests in California, generations hold to the crises of their time, in those two cases primarily the concerns are of the 1960s, to the exclusion of the problems of today. Although these are historical concerns, both remain important in domestic politics if the older people for whom they are relevant have a say.

CHAPTER 4

Movement

FORCED AND VOLUNTARY IMMIGRATION

Questions of individual agency regularly boil down to debates over nature versus nurture. In the case of demographic and development studies, the relevant question is often, to what degree can individual agency prevail over environmental circumstances? Where one is born drastically affects their access to education, health care, professional and career success. The disparities between different geographic regions are direct outcomes of governmental policy. Nations choose which geographical areas will have less opportunity, less life, and fewer opportunities for individual attainment. These influences on personal life are exasperated when taken to a global level with the outcomes of geography not only by chance of the physical world but by the outcome of other people's interests.

Questions of how much of an effect our choices as individuals can have on our own lives—as opposed to the choices that have been made for us by our location—are important considerations for the structure of government itself. The rationale for many systems of governance seems to be that the individual matters more than the group. A great deal of European (and, consequently, North American) political philosophy emphasizes individual choice, an idea that has attained a global reach via colonization and continued economic and political pressure. Focusing on this tradition (as opposed to the many others found in the histories of South and East Asian or African nations), consider this argument from Thomas Hobbes's 1651 *Leviathan*: government, however authoritarian, exists through the consent of individuals who come together and choose a "sovereign," which can be an individual or a stand-in for the state. Without government, Hobbes holds, there is nothing:

> There is no place for industry because the fruit thereof is uncertain: and consequently no culture of the earth; no navigation, nor use of the commodities that may be imported by sea; no commodious building; no instruments of moving

and removing such things as require much force; no knowledge of the face of the earth; no account of time; no arts; no letters; no society; and which is worst of all, continual fear, and danger of violent death; and the life of man, solitary, poor, nasty, brutish, and short.[1]

Government, according to Hobbes, permits individuals to reap the benefits of communal life and, at the same time, discourages the strongest in the group from preying upon the weakest. Even though people naturally love liberty—and dominion over others—they voluntarily choose to place "restraint upon themselves . . . to tie them by fear of punishment to the performance of their covenants."[2] Nevertheless, if the state does not fulfill the expected benefits of individual submission, those who had consented to be ruled by the state are not bound to their previous agreement. This concept is commonly referred to as the social contract: the agreement between individuals and the state that allows the state to exist.

A similar fable of why government exists lies at the heart of other key philosophies. John Locke's 1689 *Two Treatises of Government* offers a variation on Hobbes's perspective, arguing that societies form to protect individual property and life with liberty; that government should be representative rather than absolute; and that if the state represses freedom (which Locke conflates with property), the contract is broken and revolution must occur.[3] Genevan philosopher Jean-Jacques Rousseau's work helped form the ideological foundation of the French Revolution. His 1754 *A Discourse on Inequality* disputes the wisdom of society's basis in property: "The first man who, having enclosed a piece of ground, be thought himself of saying This is mine and found people simple enough to believe him, was the real founder of civil society."[4] In that and his later work, *The Social Contract; or, Principles of Political Right* (1762), however, Rousseau emphasizes that, for a government to be legitimate, it must represent the will of the people it governs. The sovereign he envisions must accept the positions of a popular majority--positions to which both individuals and the state must conform.

In Hobbes, Locke, and Rousseau, there is an assumption that people born into social contracts consent to be bound to them. However, no official ceremony brings citizens into the covenant; their agreement to the contract rests mostly on the fact that they remain in the geographic location governed by their state. The very act of existence within a border is the basis of legitimacy itself! What an amazing concept: that governments are both created by the people and for the people but that the people themselves are the outcome of random chance. Most of them never made the choice to become a part of a country; it was made for them by birth.

Do We Have a Choice to Leave?

While these philosophers do not explicitly acknowledge the centrality of demographic circumstances to their work or the importance of random chance to an individual's national identity, these factors are, nonetheless, critical to their arguments—perhaps as much as or even more so than individual choice. How much choice do individuals, especially those from marginalized groups, realistically have over where they live or which state governs them? Although it is possible to create and shape our life trajectories through many kinds of significant choices, we remain limited by structure, economic opportunity, and, more importantly, our abilities to make life-altering decisions, such as education or investment.

Amid the many works on social contracts in the long eighteenth century (1660–1830), Scottish philosopher David Hume points out many of these limitations. When, he asks, did people ever agree to some original contract? How much of the population actually "consented," apart from those in what would become the ruling class? Writing before the American War for Independence, the French Revolution, or the founding of Haiti, Hume looked to Western Europe, where much of the social contract discourse had originated and circulated.

Hume did not find much evidence that most people actively entered any sort of contract with the state, and he found just as little evidence that individuals, if they were so inclined, had the power to leave it: "Can we seriously say, that a poor peasant or artisan has a free choice to leave his country, when he knows no foreign language or manners, and lives from day to day, by the small wages which he acquires?"[5] The majority of those born in one place face significant obstacles if they want to change their circumstances. Instead, it can only be said that a few privileged migrants truly consent to any social contract: "The truest tacit consent of this kind, that is ever observed, is when a foreigner settles in any country and is beforehand acquainted with the prince, and government, and laws, to which he must submit."[6] Even this, Hume held, comes with caveats: Does the new state welcome the migrant? Does the old fully let them go?

Immigration flow can tell us much about both the recipient country and the originator. In most cases, a country with large amounts of immigration population has allowed foreign-born people across its boarders for years. Places that allow their population to leave can in most cases be so limited in governance that they cannot control their territory or its population has a decent degree of liberty. A prime characteristic of traditional dictatorships, such as North Korea or Eritrea, is the profound difficulty their citizens have in leaving. We should not gloss over the specifics of individual countries, but these rough guides as to the domestic choices of countries are useful to consider.

While politics is all important, so too is this limited discussion of philosophy. Most major democracies declare the importance of citizenship, but they seemingly prefer those who have not made the choice to become citizens—that is, native-born individuals—over those who do—immigrants. Where flows of people go has more to do with where they can go than what they hope to gain. Where immigrants believe they can move tells us a great deal about where they come from and why they move.

The Future of the Developed World Is Based on Immigration

As I discuss in chapter 2, immigration is critical to the success of most advanced societies. Developed societies that have already completed the demographic transition, mobilized their female workforce, and educated their population face minimal or frequently negative growth rates. These nations have already implemented policies of investment in education or infrastructure that have unlocked the potential of their population, and they are now at a stage at which continued growth increasingly depends on the fruit of technological investment. Or, perhaps, they have accepted a hopefully happy future of wealthy stagnation, in which future generations have nearly the same levels of income as past generations and major innovations are seen in imports. In these nations, the typical policy recommendations for economic development have already been successful.

The wonders of success must be proclaimed: roads, rail, universal literacy, education, electricity, health care, and stable democratic governments with effective court systems. A stagnant economy does not need to mean that museums cannot be amazing, summer fests cannot be filled with wonders, or change cannot happen, from investment in green energy to momentum toward universal internet access. Success and stagnation as a wealthy, successful country does not equal doom and decline but instead prompts a reevaluation of the levels and kinds of change a population needs or wants. A declining population is part of this world of success, and some schools may be shut down due to a lack of young students. Some towns may no longer have residents besides some elderly holdovers, and some industries may be abandoned due to a declining work force.

While these wealthy nations enjoy a high standard of living overall, these population patterns exacerbate their relative decline in power. The potential for economic growth in these countries is in part contingent on the size and characteristics of the population itself. Immigration is thus important to the developed world because it provides a partial remedy to this decline; it can help these countries maintain stable populations and even increase their population size. Immigrants become labor, become the young children in schools that otherwise would have shut down, become sources of innovation, and create a new future for a country. However way we wish to call it, be it society or economy, they are the outcome of people's decisions to buy, move, and believe. Less can create less, and an aging population has different interests than a youthful one. Where, then, does a nation want to be?

In developing societies, particularly those in which fertility rates exceed economic growth—frequently labeled "failing societies" because the next generation is likely to be weaker and poorer than the previous one—immigration is not a viable solution to economic or political troubles let alone increasing national power. Unlike the developed societies, most developing nations are unlikely to enhance their power potential by augmenting their population size. Often, states turn instead to fertility reduction measures to keep population growth in line with income growth. Indeed, China adopted its one-child policy precisely because it believed that it could not concurrently sustain economic growth and high fertility rates. This policy will prevent China from reaching its fullest potential in the middle of the twenty-first century. China has made the aggressive domestic choice to force a reduction of its population and, with it, a reduction of the country's potential.

Consider the issue of national power. Unlike fertility, international immigration is a way for nations to acquire productive populations quickly, increase human capital, and contribute both immediately and in the long term to the economy. Increasing power in this way is most useful for developed nations—Japan, the United States, or Western European countries—where the ratio of capital to labor is high. It is a far less useful option for developing countries such as China or India, where large internal rural to urban migrations provide a ready, abundant supply of human capital.[7] Immigration into the least-developed societies—Sudan, Yemen, or Bolivia, for instance—is only useful selectively, as general immigration adds to these countries' high fertility rates, reducing their economic growth and preventing these societies from escaping the poverty trap.[8]

Domestic policies of immigration can thus translate into power and long-term economic growth in developed countries. If a country with declining global influence wishes to reverse this trend on the international scene, it must reconsider its immigration policy. Immigration gives developed nations the ability to effect dynamic change in their standing in the international system by changing their most fundamental structural core—the size of their population.[9]

Migration and the Means to Move

This book investigates the outcomes of actions, with all choices involving a gamble between positive and negative outcomes. The "correct" decisions in life or economic development can be the optimal choices even if they do not result in "success." Education is an objective gain, less discrimination is an objective gain, and even increased employment, with all the dramatic upheaval it can bring to a society, is still a reasonably straightforward type of gain.

Migration is not. It is the outcome of danger, force, or limited and missed opportunities. It is among the most dramatic choices an individual can conceivably make. It alters one's current circumstances and, equally important, what one's children will become, as they transition from "us" to a new "them." The children of immigrants are not immigrants even if they are often amalgamated with the foreign born in national statistics. They are not what their parents were, but something new. This change can be unexpectedly jarring to an immigrant family and may cause difficulties, no matter which family and homeland are involved. Be they Polish, Argentine, Persian, or Japanese, all immigration populations, at least in the United States, have a dividing line between who is born in the new country and who immigrates to it. The complexity of being "first generation" is a common part of the postimmigration story.

Migration can be either international or domestic, and neither is easy, free, or without risk. Mass migratory movements, whether composed of economic migrants, refugees, or in-migrants moving to urban areas, can fundamentally alter the reality of a nation and change the potential of its population. Movement, for all its complexity, is a critical component of human demography and its overall capacity for change.

If no more important question can be answered than where one would want to live, what, then, are the implications of living in a particular place? First, some locations are simply more beneficial than others in terms of being closer to employment or other opportunities. When people migrate to a more advantageous economic situation, this is called economic migration. Many people also move toward safety—a type of forced migration. The differences between the two are too often overlooked, but they can be summarized as such: one group wants to move for opportunity, and the other must move to survive. Yes, there is overlap, as violence is often associated with economic disasters, but there is at least an intellectual difference between a refugee, who *must* move, and an economic migrant, who *wants* to move.

We can also consider location as a pure choice, ignoring for the moment legal or cultural restrictions and any costs associated with moving. Geography itself is not equal. Locations may have a temperate environment or fewer diseases; they may be significant due to their centralization of politics, capital, or art; and they may even shoulder expectations of future greatness. The pull of certain locations transcends their economy and has to do with culture. These pull factors influence individual choice, create a concept of the risk associated with moving, and mean that flows from and to certain locations are influenced by more than just a Pavlovian impulse toward economic gain. Whether the

FIG. 4.1. The Pull of the Developed World (in Thousands)

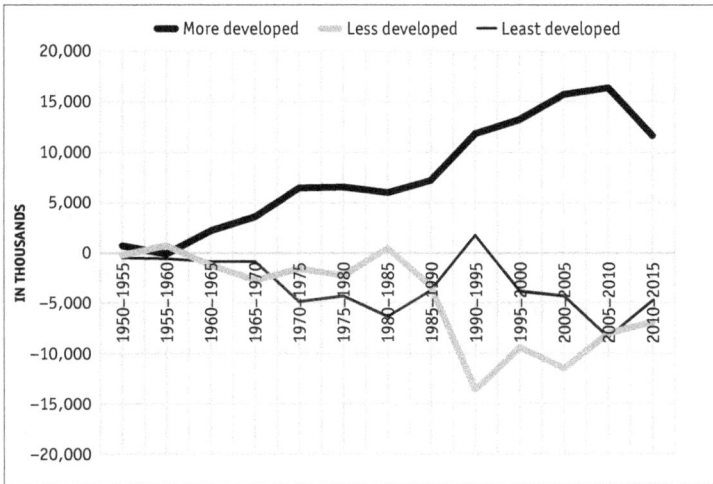

Source: United Nations, Department of Economic and Social Affairs, Population Division 2015b

outcomes of historical happenstance or policy, a location's pull factors thus become its competitive advantages.

Think of the cultural stereotypes of American cities: a Polish Chicago, Italian Newark, Irish Boston, or Cuban Miami. The histories of these cities extend far beyond these stereotypes, but because of prior immigration, the cities continue to see population streams from their associated countries, in part due to immigrants' limited information on the rest of the country. Newcomers tend to move to the major cities, ones filled with immigrants, precisely because they are major cities filled with immigrants. Hence, they are both the ones people would know and maybe even ones that immigrants have preexisting connections to, be they family or friends. The choice of where to migrate is not the outcome of a cost-benefit analysis but one that is heavily influenced by limited, common information. In countries the size of the United States or in regions like the European Union, it would be economically beneficial if immigrants had a greater degree of information and could make more informed decisions. These decisions could help restart rural economies or reverse the population loss seen in many secondary cities throughout the developed world.

Figure 4.1 illustrates the flows of population from the less- and least-developed countries of the world to the more-developed regions from 1950 to 2015. Within the popular literature on the subject, the phrase "age of migration" has become increasingly universal. This age is characterized by millions of migrants flowing from location to location; some moved north from Latin America to North America or from sub-Saharan Africa to Europe, while east–west migration occurred throughout Asia as individuals fled areas of conflict or economic degradation. Today, migration is at a level that has not been seen in a hundred years since the original age of migration in the eighteenth and nineteenth centuries. This era saw millions of people move east to west across the world, primarily from the Old to New Worlds, for a host of reasons, whether they were refugees, economic migrants, adherents of certain religions, or of course forced migrants and slaves. Mass migration is not a historical anomaly but a long-term trend that has only seen a temporary downturn. Recipient nations throughout the Western world are the outcomes of these movements, and they remember the methods and strife necessary to receive, assimilate, and grow new citizens. Many nations have made the choice to accept migrants, a choice that most nations have already made historically, and they should have no reason not to make the same choice now.

A modern concern, missing from most discussions of current migration trends, is the possibility of a reconsideration toward where flows can move and how many people would still want to move.[10] Mass migration is likely but not certain to continue, and the specter of aging demography is an important characteristic of its usefulness. For instance, figure 4.1 shows declines in migration closely associated with the Great Recession of 2008. At that time, demand for labor fell dramatically in the developed world, and equally crucial, the financial crisis also hit the countries experiencing outflow. Combined, these factors undercut both the pull and the push factors of migration. That is, potential migrants no longer had the pull of employment or the resources to invest in the trip itself. The effects of resources and growth are not yet well understood components of the decision making of migrants. Economic disasters in the developed world reduce the direct monetary reasons to move, but the effects of reduced prosperity in the developed world often spill over into the developing world. These countries, too, see declines in income and resources, and individuals thus cannot save up enough money to allow for movement. Economic stagnation in the wealthy world could undermine the argument that moving allows for future prosperity to a possible migrant.

What, then, is the most important fact during the long series of crises in the past twenty years? Refugees have come in waves from Syria, Afghanistan, Ethiopia, Sudan, Miramar, Yemen, Fiji, and others. A long list of issues in central America include both crime and natural disasters as can be seen in Haiti and Venezuela. While writing these sentences, I have been struck that I cannot think of a single region in the world that does not have reasons for individuals to be forced to become a refugee nor one that would seem to be calming.

How is the incentive to move to a new location undergoing strife balanced with the gamble of comparing what you have in your home country to what you hope to gain somewhere else? Leaving safety issues for another discussion, put yourself into the mind of a migrant. Why would you move? What do you hope to gain, and what do you risk?

Some have argued that as economic development becomes the norm internationally, the traditional push-pull factors that create much of the incentive to emigrate will become less potent. Current U.S. policy hopes to reduce emigration from Central America by increasing aid to those countries, which would hopefully create some degree of economic reason not to leave. I would suggest, however, a counterargument: because poverty is a reality that results from having a limited set of choices, small amounts of development in these countries will enable once-impoverished people to make the choice to emigrate.

Migration is not free, and as more people gain the necessary resources to move, they will. Even for those who live in growing societies, no more significant change can be made to better their own lives and their children's lives than moving to wealthier and more prosperous regions of the world. The gulf between the more-developed countries and less-developed countries, so crucial to global development strategies and the possibility of economic convergence, still exists. Thus, people in less-developed countries still have legitimate reasons to move even if the material conditions in their home country improve.

Politics is another significant factor that can help or hinder migration flows. Authoritarian governments, for instance, are particularly good at keeping people within their borders, and the dismantling of several such governments in the beginning of the 1990s, such as the Soviet Union and a host of client state dictatorships in the West, resulted in substantial increases in global movement (see figure 4.1).

This new, unrestricted ability to move created an enormous wave of immigration over the next twenty-five years, which has only possibly crested recently. With most countries having achieved some degree of economic recovery after the financial distress of 2008 by 2020, it is an interesting question whether immigration flows will again increase, especially considering the rising anti-immigration sentiment and xenophobia in many receiving countries. The demand to move is also in flux with everything from war to climate being a push factor. Competition can be an aspect of future immigration policy should it be acknowledged as a core aspect of economics and power. Where immigrants choose to go differentiate those developed countries that grow from those that stagnate.

Immigration to Education to the Future

If the number of available workers is the issue, then the solution is clear: increase the labor force. The most effective method of doing so is immigration.

Immigrants diversify the labor force and thus make it stronger. So often, however, countries attempt to limit who can migrate, generally favoring the highly educated and the rich. This creates a tension in which immigrants are allowed to enter a country so long as they fit a certain concept of gain, but the tasks and jobs that immigrants are needed to fulfill may not need the services of these highly educated or rich individuals. Wealthy, highly educated immigrants will likely not fill jobs that rely upon physical labor or a willingness to work in difficult conditions. Countries need more than scientists, accountants, and wealthy elites; they need agricultural labor and hospital orderlies. I would argue that people who can offer these services are more important than landed elites buying expensive condos.

Immigration is not a question limited to a single generation. Should a more educated workforce be needed at a high level in the future, the most effective means of creating that is to educate the first-generation children of immigrants. Consider what else an education system does for a nation. While it increases skills, it creates a shared foundation of national identity. Education systems are a significant part of the creation of shared hopes, dreams, and values.

The education system in most of the Western world has had profound effects on the labor force's aspirations. Physically demanding and well-paid jobs are not considered as prestigious or desired as seemingly lower-paid office work. Education changes what kinds of jobs people expect to do, for both newly arrived individuals and domestic groups. The norm moves away from traditional jobs as farm laborers, factory workers, and other manual-labor jobs, as these occupations become automated to a point. While automation cannot universally replace physical labor, much can be replaced or at least be augmented by it. That said, individuals are still necessary in some subsets of industry; tasks need people, and money is not sufficient to attract new workers.

Textile Industry and the Changing Labor Force

To illustrate the ramifications of a highly educated population on industrial production, we can consider how a traditionally domestic skill—sewing—and its transmission has changed over time. Four generations ago, it was typical for families in the United States to have sewing knowledge, and the household itself was tasked with providing clothing necessities. Households expected to buy small kits of unfinished clothing that could then be sewn together or even whole cloth to start from scratch. Individuals' sewing knowledge became an essential part of early textile industrialization, as large numbers of principally female workers moved from agricultural work to working in factories. The household skill of sewing was thus commodified into an industrial one.

Due to generational changes and increased automation, the prevalence of household-made clothing decreased dramatically. No longer saved for special occasions or children's wear, expendable clothing became ubiquitous, with the new expectation of multiple sets of clothes becoming the norm. Only a generation before, this would have been only seen among the privileged. Again, another generation and forced public education, and with it, the idea that maybe those individuals, newly educated, should work in jobs unrelated to factories. Jobs, again, are important not only as a source of income but also as an expression of interests, particularly those created by family, friends, and societal pressure.

Due to these generational transitions, immigration has become the core of the textile industry's labor force. No longer can it rely on the skills of primarily rural workers moving to the cities for opportunity; the industry must look to immigration to sustain itself. This trend can be seen in the stories of Los Angeles; New York; Lewiston, Maine; and Fall River, Massachusetts. Each city was a center of textiles, and central to each is a story of waves of population moving into demanding jobs in textile factories. In Maine, it was Irish and French Canadians; in Los Angeles, it was Chinese, Mexicans, and Irish again. In New York, it was Jewish, Italian, Irish, and workers of nearly every origin on Earth. Within the great textile city of Fall River, factories started with Irish and Italian workers and ended with the Portuguese, from locales as wide ranging as Cape Verde and the Azores. The textile industry was dependent not on just one period of immigration but on a sustained flow, due to differing skill sets and changing interests.

Immigration thus has the potential to change the basic story of a society. New arrivals can sustain industries that the domestic labor force no longer has any interest in. This interest is not just a question of salary but also one of expectations. What kind of worker do educated domestic workers envision to be a "successful" individual, what about immigrant workers? These expectations can influence who is more inclined to take white-collar or blue-collar jobs, factory or farm labor, retail work, or fast-food work.

What kind of employment do people want for themselves and their children? Do they focus on earning the highest possible salary without regard to safety and the physical nature of the work? Are their sights set on jobs that require college or even graduate school or jobs restricted by qualification requirements such as lawyers, accountants, and doctors? Would they follow the choices of their parents, learning from their expertise in how to do the job, what to work on, and what is needed? The children of lawyers should presumably know more about law than children of parents who hold other kinds of jobs, just as children in military families would know more about the military or families of academics about academia. Even the knowledge that a job exists can be remarkably important for setting expectations. These social considerations matter in the changing world of development and create the need to allow for new populations to fulfill jobs that the current one has no interest in pursuing, create some new form of automation, or be willing to lose industries: again, choice.

Outcomes of Migration

Consider how dramatic the choice to migrate is for the family, nation, and individual—to leave all one knows, cares about, and could be for the hope or even the expectation of a better future on a far-flung shore. The very phrase "risk acceptance" underplays the level of danger intrinsic to that choice.

Immigrants are more willing to accept these risks if the society to which they are moving holds the promise of economic success. Once they arrive in their new country, the opportunities available to them are determined by a combination of legal restrictions and, most importantly, cultural attitudes. No matter how willing a new transplant is to invest or to work hard, the attitudes of society toward immigrant populations are crucial determinants of immigrants' success. Several characteristics of the immigrant experience can be traced to this social fact. The first is that immigrant flows follow previous immigrant flows, as older generations in the new country help to create a shared framework for integration or serve as a method of entry.

Traditionally, many migrants hold their first jobs in the enterprises of their more established compatriots. These immigrant-owned businesses often form the backbone of an entire social system, sometimes reinforced by religious institutions or language programs, that offers immigrants both a new sense of self and support in more difficult times. Depending on the domestic population's attitudes toward the nonnative group, these institutions may serve as helpful steps toward acclimatization or as vehicles for isolation.

Many countries in the developed world now face the challenge of becoming an attractive destination for immigrants. As these nations age, their dependence on immigration becomes an even more critical factor in everything from long-term industrialization to the stability of their pension systems.

Currently, the single largest recipient of migrants in the world is the United States, a nation primarily made up of immigrants and their descendants. Today, most new immigrants come from Asia, with Latin America the second-most-common region of origin. Both new waves of immigrants move throughout the country, but they are still primarily centered on major urban environments with large ethnically Asian and Latino enclaves. Historically, the United States saw massive waves of immigration from Europe and, of course, forced migration from Africa in the form of the slave trade. While these older immigrant populations are now largely assimilated, new immigrant communities often settle in neighborhoods that once housed large concentrations of older foreign-born populations, with "Little Italies" or "Little Warsaws" turning into "Koreatowns," for instance. The New World stands nearly alone in the diversity of its immigrants, with the United States almost singular in the ethnic range of its population.

In Europe, the most popular destinations for immigrants are first the United Kingdom (UK), then France, and the Netherlands, Spain, and Italy following. Each of these countries is undergoing profound domestic disagreement on this topic. Most immigrants to these countries derive from the nations' former colonies, as new arrivals—be they Indonesians, Algerians, or from the Caribbean—are likely to have a continued cultural affinity with older generations in the destination country. These countries are appealing destinations for immigrants because each has an attractive developed labor market, a need for the new population, and the resulting historical and cultural ties to home country populations and cultures.

Immigration is much more complex when waves of new arrivals are composed of groups that do not have a history of acceptance in the destination country. Even in countries with large foreign-born populations and a history of immigration, new pressures can cause political friction.

Furthermore, immigration has shown a tendency to accrue to countries that have already experienced significant immigration flows and not to new locations in which immigrants might be able to achieve greater gains.[11] Compounding this problem are issues of scale, with hundreds of thousands of people in transit at any one time. The demographic transition is no longer an issue unique to developed countries; it will soon also be an issue of the developing world. China, famously, is projected to be older than the United States in 2050, and the country likely hit the peak of its labor force in 2013. In addition, over four hundred thousand people emigrate from China every year, with similar numbers seen throughout the developing world. Many people leave the world's fastest-growing economies to immigrate to countries that have already developed.

The stories of migration shown in figure 4.2 are remarkable. Again, consider the difference between the United States and Western Europe, the two wealthiest regions of the world.[12] Except for 1960–1965 (a period that correlates with refugee movement after difficulties in communist-dominated Eastern Europe), the United States has seen remarkably higher inflows, particularly after the liberalization period of the 1990s. Such influxes have not been seen in the immigration record since the beginning of the twentieth century.

Only in 2014 has Germany, the largest economy in Europe, surpassed the UK in terms of total migrants. For the first time since the end of World War II, Germany has become a central destination for immigrants. This example highlights the critical concept that a country's economic strength alone is not sufficient to attract immigration. As the largest country with significant ag-

FIG. 4.2. Flows to the Developed World (in Thousands)

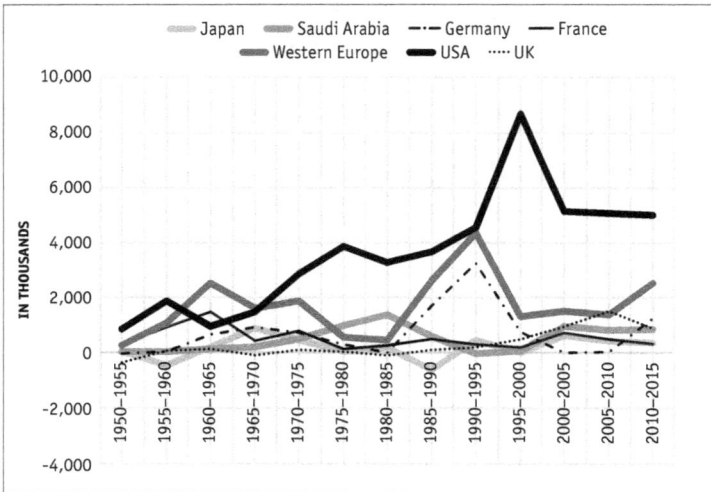

Source: United Nations, Department of Economic and Social Affairs, Population Division 2015b

ing issues, Germany has historically had very little real migration. This wave of newcomers is more associated with recent conflicts in Syria and Afghanistan than it is with any changes Germany has made to its domestic policy.

The most remarkable example of aging is Japan, a country that was until recently the second-largest economy in the world and a significant manufacturing power. While Japan has a clear need for new labor to replenish its rapidly aging workforce, it only allows one hundred thousand people a year to migrate to the country. This number is equivalent to one month's worth of new arrivals in the United States or arrivals over half a year in the UK.

Saudi Arabia is another interesting example. Nearly two times more people migrate to Saudi Arabia than to Japan, even with legal restrictions governing citizenship and the country's fixation on temporary, hence controllable, workers. Naturalization is not part of this immigration story. Saudi Arabia's current economic issues are tied to new attempts to move domestic workers into jobs currently undertaken by foreigners. The fact that many foreign workers are subjected to highly problematic work conditions makes the prospect of implementing this policy a challenge. The distinction that Saudi Arabia draws between temporary migrants and those allowed to move on a path toward citizenship has the potential to create two very different groups of immigrants. The temporary group will not have the same long-term beneficial effects on Saudi Arabian society, as members of this group are unlikely to invest or attempt to stay in a country that gives them only limited legal protection. A large temporary-worker population leaves Saudi Arabia vulnerable to rapid popu-

FIG. 4.3. Flow out of Development (in Thousands)

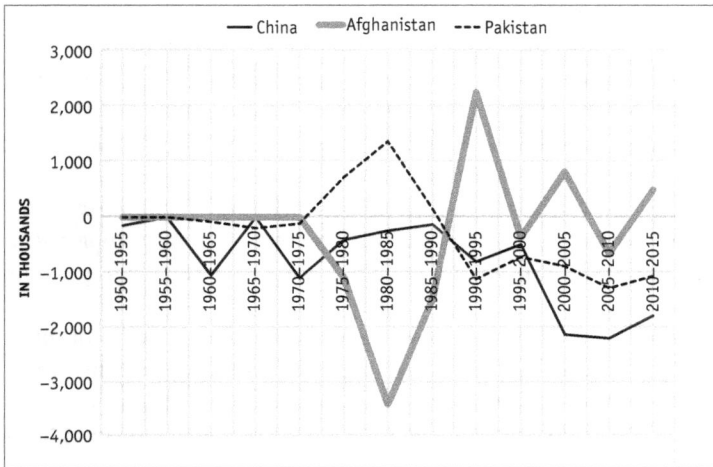

Source: United Nations, Department of Economic and Social Affairs, Population Division 2015b

lation loss during periods of economic disturbance. During such crisis periods, bankrupt companies retract workers' visas, and the government attempts to force foreign workers to leave the country to prop up unemployment rates. Migrations, as these examples show, are not equal; they are dependent on the legal and social realities within the receiving countries.

The case of Afghanistan is of particular importance, given the discussion of both forced and voluntary migration. It also allows us to move beyond discussion of the developed nations and on to a discussion of the developing world. The United Nations' UN data in figure 4.3 capture not merely the dramatic flows out of Afghanistan but also the equally dramatic returns. These waves of movement in and out of the country are connected to domestic conflict—civil strife creates movement, but the kind that is temporary not perpetual. This population moves not by choice but by force and, when given the chance to return, takes it.

Afghanistan serves as an important case against becoming too complacent in forecasting. As this book finishes its last editing in 2022, the Taliban has taken over the country. Hundreds of thousands of people are fleeing intentionally and internally. The Taliban claims that they will not direct harsh reprisals against their newly defeated foes or instigate the violent governance they had become known for during the 1990s. What they decide will create or reenforce ever larger waves from the country should violence by this newly formed government become the norm. If they do in fact create some form of repressive but stable peace those waves should be smaller, likely much smaller. For recovery of the nation, they need peace and it will be up to them to decide if that becomes the future of the Afghani people.

In the case of China, the outflow has been nearly constant for almost fifty years. Millions of Chinese people have taken opportunities outside of China, and this trend increased dramatically at the turn of the millennium. Even with some small decline in outflow after the financial crisis, this is a clear signal that development itself, in the most prosperous country over the last generation, is not the only critical factor driving population movement. The new resources that its population gains through development become the funds people use to move to perceived better opportunities abroad, not to stay, invest, or grow the local economy.

Pakistan's total migration flows can be traced to a combination of influences. The most important are those resulting from conflicts. From the Indian partition to the creation of Bangladesh and the decades of Afghan wars, waves of refugees have moved to Pakistan. The subsequent consistent level of outflow is likely explainable as a combination of economic and possibly forced migration due to domestic instability and continued conflict. Even with occasional high-level insurgency and authoritarian regimes, Pakistan has not had the same degree of outflow that is seen in China. This difference can be attributed to the importance of resources influencing one's ability to decide to migrate.

Consider again, dear reader, the mind of an immigrant. Where do they go, and what do they know about that destination? Is that knowledge from personal experience, be it education or tourism? Is it from extended family? Could it be from movies, TV, or pop culture? For much of the twentieth century, flows move through locations, such as Western Europe, which has traditionally been a source and a midway point to the United States, that could also have been ideal destination points for migrants. This could be the case because of a combination of knowledge, stereotypes, prior ethnic and family migration, and, most likely, evaluation of costs, visas, and the benefits of the move. Opportunity is not merely a case of GDP per capita but a summation of many other considerations, with the scale of migration changing countries' fundamental core.

From Immigration to Assimilation and Citizenship

Assimilation, defined here as a foreign-born population achieving similar economic and educational attainment as the native-born population within at least three generations, is not an easy process. Commonly, when immigrants first arrive in their new country, they face near-universal discrimination. They may experience segregation and ghettoization due to a combination of their own preferences and societal prejudices.

Countries that receive a significant number of immigrants thus face the question of how they can expand their integration efforts. Time is an essential component of these policies, and they are not something that can just be done and be done with. They are like infrastructure development—buildings, roads, bridges—in that they are foundations of our civic society that need continued and constant maintenance. These are not policies for today but those that last generations, and because of this multigenerational quality, assimilation is not an action but an existence.

Cultivating domestic labor is expensive. From birth to education, both a family and a society pay significant direct and indirect costs for every individual. Immigrant labor, however, provides countries with pure economic gains as migrants diversify and revitalize the labor forces of their adopted countries. Immigrants' nations of origin may experience a "brain drain" with negative long-term consequences, but these consequences do not extend to the receiving country. To gain the advantage of not only welcoming another person but also one that is educated at any level is a pure gain—depending, crucially, on costs associated with assimilation.

Policies of mandatory education are critical, as they pull children from their ethnic social communities and into the greater whole. Primary and secondary education also create the expectation, at least in most developed countries, that students will move on to higher education. Education thus decreases the ability for an individual to self-segregate within their foreign-born community, and educational success, tied to income success, decreases the importance of ethnic social support systems.

This change in support changes the immigration cost-benefit calculation. Integration is not an issue of the receiving-country culture alone but one that depends on the immigrant subgroup itself and what is lost, gained, and modified by the move toward the whole. Dilution of original cultural traits is a given and should be acknowledged. Assimilation by its very nature modifies what new generations born in a new location want from their own lives; what they think is important, influential, interesting, and funny; and therefore, what is worth their time to use, buy, and enjoy. The process of assimilation changes the attitudes between older and younger generations more dramatically than the overall society does, and this fracture can be damaging to these families.

Consider the most dramatic measurement of assimilation: out marriage, or the choice to connect not with an ethnically, religiously, or culturally similar individual but with someone from the "other." Who that "other" is usually matters less than the choice of out marriage itself. These unions may force both the domestic and immigrant groups to reconsider what it means to be one of them. Will local religious institution acknowledge those who have not grown up in the faith? Are outsiders allowed to convert or, if not, to be present in a wide range of ceremonies, such as those that proclaim adulthood, belief, marriage, or even the importance of spring?

Language knowledge declines rapidly after the first generation with the most important question being will organizations of cultural significance that have traditionally been monolingual, such the Greek or Russian Churches, continue to have sustained importance when the new generations cannot speak the language and have parents, loved ones, and friends who are not of the same ethnic backgrounds? Are they still welcome, and hence, can the organization be sustainable for the future? These questions are universal, applying to all kinds of groups, from the Japanese Buddhist Church of America to Polish, German, and Portuguese heritage societies. All make a choice, either to sustain themselves by inviting in the new changing generations or to remain based on the first generation, or isolated ethnic identity, and slowly die out with it.

Interestingly, the choice to marry someone of a different race or ethnicity is heavily correlated with education level and incomes. Is there a causal relationship here? Consider the effects of higher education. Universities bring together tens or even hundreds of thousands of young people in a centralized geographic location, often away from their parents, religious institutions, and, most crucially, social pressure. Moving, dating, and interacting outside of cultural expectations become easier and more efficient in that environment. While this experience of higher education is common, it is not universal. Education can also be isolating, composed of only one religious group, stratum of wealth, political interest, or race, as it was not all that long ago in the United States. The positive effects of forced integration are not necessarily something that students are aware they are going to enjoy when entering educational institutions.

One effect of this unawareness is linked with how relationships work, which is to say we date those we know. Lower-educated people date lower-educated people, and highly educated people date highly educated people. Of course, this is not true in all cases, but it is increasing with economic polarization. This general trend toward same-education marriages means that those immigrant groups that push higher education as an intrinsic good are also those who assimilate the most and have tended to have the highest levels of income success.

Countries that seek to discourage immigration often turn to legal restrictions on marriage, property ownership, and even the citizenship of children—all policies that undercut the willingness of migrants to move, assimilate, and become successful contributors to their adopted society.[13] Assimilation is not only an economic phenomenon but also a profoundly cultural one. Much of the controversy surrounding assimilation is based upon the level of cultural variance that immigrants bring to a society. This objection is a complex endogenous problem, as change is a constant in any culture. Attempts to restrict immigration policy as a means of reducing cultural change are unlikely to succeed.[14] The fear of change cannot be discounted, with nations creating immigration blockades due to the assumption that immigrants cannot or will not assimilate. However, in terms of migrants being able to access the tools they need for economic growth and political equality, assimilation is the key to success.

Countries have already made many of the choices needed to unlock the potential offered by migration flows—and some are still in 2022 concurrently resisted. Nations heavily made up of immigrants and their descendants then seem to have issues with immigration. Public education is a popular policy that is critical to successful immigration, but it is also one that people against immigration cite as a reason to close borders. Anti-immigrant advocates say that it is not the place of education to teach children what citizenship is or should be. Take policies regarding interracial marriage, for example. While today interracial marriage is legal in the United States, it was banned until the second half of the twentieth century and to this day is banned in major democratic countries such as Israel. How can these regressive policies still exist in modern democratic republics?

Other countries have policies grounded in religion that may make them attractive to newcomers. For instance, it is possible in some countries to convert religions, but religious conversion is also banned in much of the world, principally the Islamic world. Some countries have religious restrictions on women's and men's ability to work and be educated in the same locations.

Many of these diverse cultural mores are particularly notable for their effect on women. The reality of different marriage systems—from arranged marriages, to marriages founded on a dowry structure, to love marriages—must also be considered from this lens. The story and success of assimilation thus depends on a series of interlocked cultural and legal frameworks.

For immigrants to find success in their new countries, opportunities must exist—opportunities to grow a family unit, access employment and education, and lastly, as the enlightenment would suggest, move toward citizenship. Forever being a "foreigner," no matter how well treated, undermines one's chance to become a part of an adopted nation. The opportunities available are all based on policy choices of the recipient nation. So often, the most popular domestic policy choice is to insulate, restrict, and segregate rather than to allow for assimilation and create the necessary frameworks for success.

The Economics of Isolationism

The simplicity of this argument belies the actual complexity of these policy choices. The economics are relatively straightforward. Evidence shows that economic success follows new influxes of population. As I discuss, however, diversifying skill sets, increasing populations, and altering future demographic trends toward aging do not come without costs. Apart from the potential economic costs of pensions or social services, countries must reflect on their willingness for their future to look different, be it ethnically or even physiognomically. This consideration is not necessarily a xenophobic one, but one that gets to the heart of the national question: what is or should be the basis of citizenship in a country? Should citizenship be a historical accident or based on a myth, based on a shared language or ethnic identity? Do countries with a higher degree of historical complexity, be it postcolonial complexity or the experience of handling immigrant waves in the past, have an advantage when it comes to assimilating future waves of immigrants?

My suggested answer to this last question is yes. Policies of assimilation take decades to achieve and, more importantly, can be modified to allow for future success. A multitude of nations can use them, but the time needed to develop, incorporate, and revise them is significant, as is the time needed to deal with any conflict they may inspire. Thus, choices about assimilation are not short-term policy decisions, which election-driven politics so often focus on, but can only be achieved after decades of dedication. Even countries that have had success with assimilation policies can still see political backlashes and conflict, which may overshadow any initial achievement.

The possible rise of isolationism or even traditional nationalism throughout the Western world is a worrying example of these attitudes. Those who promote these perspectives fixate on perceived losses from accepting immigrants but ignore the potential gains. Many express concerns about a change to their country's dominant culture or even race, and they are all too willing to blame the minority for the struggles of their economy. Immigrants have been traditionally a scapegoat for unrelated problems, whether crime, job losses, or widespread societal change. Blaming the foreigner for a country's own choices is a popular propaganda technique.

While today's globalized economy can certainly create economic gains, these gains are neither simple nor constant, and they are not distributed evenly among all people. This disconnect may have, in part, motivated both the recent Brexit vote and the election of U.S. president Donald Trump. People who feel disenfranchised in today's economy discuss the past as if it could exist again from a purely economic standpoint, an unsupportable argument. The circumstances that created the world of the 1950s are no longer viable today, even with zero immigration, in the twenty-first century. The story seen in most of the Western world after World War II should be familiar. Massive successful recovery and economic booms from the devastated cities of West Germany to the ruins of Japan, and the great industrial centers of the United States. The ability for someone with limited formal education to enter massive factories, ones that are unionized; be given decent wages and benefits; and then build equity in one's life and for one's family was possible postwar. This possibility, which we should remember included very difficult working conditions, is no longer an option for much of the population, even those who would enjoy that form of labor. Innovation has automized jobs that at one time employed people who made careers of the job. These major companies that employed hundreds of thousands now employ tens of thousands but produce far more. The need for more advanced training has decreased the opportunities of those who have a work ethic but no longer have access to a career in which the willingness to work would lead to a successful financial life. The age of mass employment in manufacturing is over, and it has been lost not to globalization but to innovation.

Today's economy relies on the mechanization of industry, the need for higher education, and the move from mass physical labor to service jobs. The higher-paying union jobs of the past have become less secure and, worse yet, less culturally prestigious. While this dramatic transformation in the economic landscape is irreversible, it can still be used as an electoral convenience. Radical policy changes, in turn, can arise from elections. It is a dangerous assumption that institutionalism or even law creates stability; elections do have consequences, particularly in those nations that have concentrated power in the executive branch, such as the United States. Elections can change radically who is in power and that affects all aspects of immigration. Even if the fundamental arguments used to undermine immigration are difficult to support economically, they are not difficult to support politically.

No one was more affected by the Trump presidency than refugees who would have been allowed to gain asylum in America but were abandoned midway through the application process and left on the southern borders of Texas or in refugee camps in Syria, Iraq, and Turkey. The United States may have also deliberately increased the time needed for processing of paperwork as a method of reducing legal immigration, including of Afghani allies seeking protection. The idea was to make the process so slow it could then no longer exist even if the law had not changed. It is not only the individuals themselves who had expected protection and a better life but also those would have been born in America, Americans who now might never exist.

Refugees and asylum seekers are often the easiest for countries to reject. Here, we should distinguish between forced migration and other kinds of migration. Forced migration is motivated by conflict, often civil war or international attack. These events trigger a population flow composed of people who fear being caught up in their country's widespread violence or who fear being targeted by campaigns of ethnic cleansing or genocide. These people do not choose the horror of movement; they move as a matter of necessity, as in many cases they are running for their lives. These individuals are thus distinct from economic migrants, who are bound together by a shared belief in movement for economic opportunity.

The division between the two is essential, as economic migrants generally work, strive, and dream of movement, and forced migrants wish to return to their homelands. This means asylum could be considered temporary, and refugees may likely use their income for survival and to save money for their eventual return. It can take a generation or more before individuals realize that their homeland might now be a dream and that home is where they are now. These stories of hypothetical return—for example, after communism falls, Castro dies, the military dictator leaves, or even the country itself is re-created—become sources of friction from generation to generation, as each subsequent cohort moves to stages in which their homeland is found in stories, food at fairs, and a few pictures on the walls of Grandma's house. This is trauma given shape and form, and it is one difference between the lives of those who move because they can for the hope of a better life and those who move because they must.

"Refugee" is a legal distinction within the international system. In the United States, refugees are defined as individuals who have fled their country of origin, gained protection within a third country, and then apply from there to the United States for physical protection. If this protection is granted, they can then further apply for a permanent green card visa. The most common path for refugees wishing to enter the United States is through a refugee camp overseen by the UN. After entering the UN system, people may endure one and a half to two years of processing, background checks, and waiting to enter the United States.

This system has occasionally been overwhelmed during times of crisis, such as the end of the Vietnam War or periods of Cold War–associated violence in Cuba or Hungary. In these cases, asylum seekers must apply at the U.S. border directly. Most of these applicants are denied. Refugees admitted at the border compose only a small fraction of the total refugees and traditional immigrants permitted into the United States. For instance, compare Syrian refugees, who start the process in UN camps in Jordan, Turkey, or Lebanon, to Central American asylum seekers (many of whom are children), who are turned away or released into Texas after a quick legal process at the U.S.-Mexico border, followed by a much more complex bureaucratic process in the immigration courts.

A common criticism of refugees is the worry that they will bring terrorism into a country. The idea is that, because people are fleeing a certain location, they could then infect their new country with the trauma and damage of their homeland. Opponents fear that the charity of the refugee acceptance process will turn to violence. This refrain has been common throughout Europe during the current Syrian refugee crisis and has been trotted out during every other similar situation in modern history.

Famously, during World War II, worries of German spies hidden within groups of Jewish refugees led the United States and many other countries around the world to ignore the visa applications of thousands of Jewish refugees, leading to their deaths during the Holocaust. These deaths were caused because of the conspiracy theories that small amounts of German spies could hide among refugees and then somehow devastate the United States. However silly this seems, the popularity of that argument was used by anti-immigration movements, such as the original "America First" organization, to undermine the case for ever allowing refugees into the country, even during the worst war in human history. Antirefugee organizations are also often anti-immigration more generally.

The most well-known casualty of U.S. refugee policy was Anne Frank, who was waiting with her family for a visa to travel to the United States and became trapped in Amsterdam. Her father, Otto, had already received his visa and could have left, but he made the choice to stay with his family hoping that their visas would arrive quickly.

These antimovements, in general, are all motivated by fear—fear of the other, the unexpected, or what is perceived as strange. In nations holding on to national homogeneity myths or even in those that have had waves of migration, new populations are always the most restricted, even more so when they have arrived from a conflict zone. Let us consider the reliability of these concerns with Nowrasteh (2016) who investigates these worries in an insightful policy-based brief that presents some genuinely remarkable statistics. The work amalgamates every terrorist act committed by a foreign-born person in the United States from 1975 to 2015. It then links each terrorist to the type of visa they used to enter the country. The idea is to connect the act of terror itself to the level of security that allowed the perpetrator's entrance.

As an example, in the current U.S. political environment, those who oppose immigration are primarily concerned about undocumented immigrants and refugees. In 2016, it was estimated that around eleven million people living in the United States were undocumented—the lowest number in eight years. From 1975 to 2015, only ten undocumented individuals committed (or tried to commit) acts of terrorism within the United States, and only one of these incidents resulted in murder (six people were killed in the 1993 World Trade Center bombing, committed by Ahmed Ajaj). So, if we only worry about those undocumented immigrants successful at committing murder, the ratio would be twenty-six million undocumented immigrants for every one that commits murder—a remarkable number. Only one undocumented immigrant in modern U.S. history has become a successful terrorist.

We can make a similar claim using the broader category of refugees. Of the over 3.2 million refugees that have been admitted to the United States since 1975, only twenty have committed or attempted to commit terrorist acts. A total of three individuals died as a result. Interestingly, those deaths can be primarily attributed to inter-Cuban refugee politics, with both anticommunist and procommunist factions targeting each other in the late 1970s.

Looking at the highly developed countries that are participants in the Visa Waiver Program, all are American allies and have very similar laws and legal structures. The advantage of this system is the ability to travel to a nation with only a passport and without the need to procure a tourist visa. Of the 388 million people who have traveled to the United States using this system since 1975, none have committed a successful act of terrorist murder, and only three have been charged or arrested for possible acts. Consider the economic impact on tourism, on entertainment, on the airline industry, if travel from these countries were shut down or subjected to more checks and restrictions.

Overall, this data suggests that we live in a peaceful time. Terrorism in the United States is rare, and, in most years, zero Americans have died in terrorist incidents perpetrated by foreign-born actors. The problem is that the influence is outside the level of danger. The fear of an action drives the policy not the specifics of the danger. The importance is in more than the casualties created but the change in domestic policy it influences. The acts then become more than realistic as worries outweigh the damage. The fear of terrorism is dramatically higher than the reality of its dangers.

Do immigration's benefits to society outweigh the possibility that, at some point, a foreign-born person will a commit a crime that results in a casualty? A quick economic analysis would suggest that it is much better to have a larger, more diverse population than a smaller, more homogeneous one. I would not suggest that the anti-immigration-policy people should be ignored under an avalanche of statistics but that, as with all things, policy decisions should be supported by data.

What should receiving countries consider to be the acceptable level of risk when taking on immigrants, be they forced migrants or otherwise? Should the death of one person, for example, preclude the massive advantages that immigrants can offer to countries with the necessary systems in place to foster real assimilation? While risk cannot be ignored, it can be measured, quantified, and evaluated. Differentiating between the two flows of population, forced migrants and economic migrants, does somewhat change the calculation. Those who take advantage of the choice to move are likely to have a higher degree of interest in their new country.

Forced migration changes that dynamic. People take this action out of necessity, not by choice. The act of movement is considered the last step in a journey to escape violence, not the first step on a journey to economic success. Two divergent paths thus equal the same choice: movement.

The different psychological implications of these two immigration trajectories could help explain some of the issues associated with assimilation throughout the world. While this psychological standpoint may change over generations, with grandchildren having differing attitudes than their grandparents toward the culture of their family's destination country, it should not be ignored when estimating the economic benefit of new forced population flows in places like Western Europe—Germany and Sweden in particular.

The few hundred thousand asylum seekers entering Germany during the Syrian civil war moved due to safety issues, not because of choice. They entered a country without a high population of foreign-born individuals, or at least very few individuals born farther away than the surrounding nations. The refugees could fulfill labor shortages in eastern Germany, which is also the region that has the least interest in or willingness to work toward cross-cultural assimilation. A problematic combination of local disinterest and maybe even limited interest from the migrants themselves has thus generated an uneasy dynamic between the refugees and native-born German population.

When refugees begin to pour into a new country in large numbers, time is of the essence. Governments must work quickly to put employment and education policies in place, especially in countries that do not have preexisting networks of people from the refugees' home countries. Without this political support, refugee groups risk becoming isolated in their disinterest, which can be reinforced by the actions of the native-born groups surrounding them. This isolation is a worst-case situation, as it can quickly devolve into segregation, then limitation, and then economic disability. The resulting societal disenfranchisement of refugee groups would only work to support preexisting prejudices against them, creating a circle of disappointment and disruption. If the government misses the opportunity to reach refugees right when they arrive, a refugee crisis can turn into a multigenerational crisis. Should these individuals become isolated or, even worse, be unable to secure visas and then face forced removal from the country, more complicated or even violent acts may be expected.

The scale of forced migration can often seem insurmountable, with millions of people flowing across borders. In 2015, over 20 percent of the population of Lebanon—over a million people—and 10 percent of the population of Jordan—six hundred thousand people—were Syrian refugees. In some cases, the Syrian population looks first to achieve safety before moving further into Europe. Turkey has seen a significant number of the more urban and highly educated Syrians, who may have less interest in staying in Turkey in the long run. As the war continues, these refugees are the most likely to continue to move west into Europe. Other Syrians migrated to live with family members or familiar ethnic communities across borders. Many Syrian Kurds moved to the autonomous Kurdish region in Iraq because of the belief that fellow Kurds can be trusted more than other groups during a sectarian conflict. Syrian refugees in Lebanon, for example, are predominantly Shia Muslim, and some are supported by the charity of Hezbollah, which is a major political force in the country, has troops within Syria, and is a terrorist organization according to the United States.

The numbers of Syrian refugees in these Middle Eastern countries are high, but they are not outside the range of the total percentage of foreign-born individuals in many destination countries. The numbers themselves are also not larger than those seen directly after World War II or other conflicts in the twentieth century. The great question is, if refugees from Syria are not allowed to move beyond the first ring of neighboring countries and into nations with labor markets in need of more workers, then what is the capacity to reincorporate them productively into society?

The displaced Syrian population represents pure opportunity. The potential gains to be drawn from these people could be immense, so long as they can be tapped. The worst case would be for isolated populations sitting in UN camps to become dependent on the international charity system, waiting to be allowed to return home, maybe in vain. Giving refugees opportunities for education, investment, and the ability to build lives provides not just economic benefits for nations but also psychological benefits for individuals; these are methods by which a traumatized group can move forward from past trauma. Isolation of these forced migrants would only serve to undercut a whole generation's aspirations for a better life.

An example may be seen in Pakistan. In 2016, Afghan refugees from nearly two decades of war began to be repatriated across the border from Pakistan to Afghanistan. This refugee population had lived in Pakistan for almost a whole generation, and many of them never knew anywhere else. After being blamed for rising violence and increased cross-border issues, they were forced to return to a land fighting a civil war. The newest refugees in 2021 from that war were banned from crossing the border.

The problems of isolated, lost refugee populations can be seen throughout much of Africa. Kenya and the Central African Republic host some of the world's largest UN-organized refugee camps. Although international awareness of the Syrian civil war and Syrian refugees is high, this conflict has not spawned the largest total amount of refugees. That distinction belongs to the conflicts seen in sub-Saharan Africa.

New technologies help isolated, displaced refugees connect with the outside world, at least financially. The World Bank and World Food Programme provide direct payments to refugees via biometrically secured cash cards, which can be targeted toward single mothers with children or used to decrease losses or corruption by limiting the various middlemen between funders and fund recipients. These cards give individuals and families more flexibility; instead of lining up for daily rations, they can enter an actual market and purchase what they need, including food, clothing, childcare goods, or even medicine. The cards thus link refugees to the local economy, give the local economy a boost, and could, if linked to further liberalization, be a step toward starting the population's assimilation process. Similar programs are used as part of national food stamp programs. Importantly, the cards represent the realization that people in difficult situations can be trusted to care for themselves. The trust that these programs place in them helps them rebuild. Mental support is as vital as economic support.

Turning again to the situation in Syria, the opportunities it presents for both individual and country-level advancement are complicated but exciting. Syrian society is polarized by wealth, religion, politics, urbanization, and race. Before the war, the urban elite had access to reasonably well-established higher education institutions. Engineering, mathematics, and a well-regarded tradition of poetry are all parts of Syrian society. Some estimates suggest that these urban elites have made up the bulk of the forced migration waves—a brain drain via violence. Should the war continue to expand, further expulsions are possible, not necessarily because people face direct threats but because they face lost opportunities. Children reaching college age or even graduates looking for first jobs may look to pursue these opportunities in other countries. The economic or labor market strife associated with domestic upheaval thus causes migration for a concurrent reason: not only does civil war push away those seeking safety but it also pushes away those hoping to regain their expected opportunities.

Syria's neighbors each deal with the influx of civil war refugees in different ways. In Lebanon, at least in 2021, the Syrian population is allowed to merge with the domestic population. Refugees can start new businesses, become politically active, and maybe even create a higher degree of economic success for themselves than they would have been able to otherwise. The caveat is that the Lebanese government has shown only a limited ability to create domestic policy consensus around any major policy, refugee policy included. In Turkey, policies for handling refugees are still unclear. Some attempts to allow refugee children into state-sponsored schools are in the works, but those institutions seem to be built within refugee camps themselves. The Turkish government is also in the process of facilitating and funding access for Syrians to Turkish higher education. However, many of these policies are now in doubt due to recent political upheavals, which have resulted in the mass firings of academics and teachers throughout the country. Jordan has allowed less integration and seems more worried about conflict crossing borders than long-term population integration. Each country can benefit from substantial economic growth, or at least growth in population size, should it decide to allow full integration.

In countries with declining labor forces and increasingly dependent elderly populations, many have suggested that future national stability is only possible through increased immigration.[15] In Germany's case, even large-scale migration from Syria is not projected to be enough to compensate for expectations of future population decline. In these discussions, the demographic transition is code for a national decline, and immigration is seen as maintaining the status quo instead of offering dynamic change. Most often, policies intended to increase fertility are more popular, if less compelling, than policies intended to increase immigration.

Issues of brain drain, multiculturalism, and the actual ability to use or (for the nonimmigrant population) to accept immigrant labor are vast. Discrimination, social stigmas, and increasing xenophobia are common in countries that have attempted liberal immigration policies and even those that have limited total immigration. Many nations, such as the United Arab Emirates and Bahrain, have high restrictions on citizenship and employment, and they have made no attempt to tap into the most important aspect of immigration: multigenerational change. They think of immigration as a short-term solution to a long-term problem. This is often a politically accessible policy; temporary work visas are increasingly becoming popular, too, as an alternative to policies that facilitate permanent immigration to the United States.[16]

Most modern immigration systems involve a series of different methods for entry. Temporary visas for students or agricultural laborers are common. Permanent visas granted based on some exceptional ability (be it sport, music, or technological skill) are also nearly universal. Most countries also have some form of visa available to the rich that involves the outright purchase of entry or citizenship. These visas can often be based upon something as simple as a large domestic real estate investment. In the United States, lottery systems and family reunification visas account for the largest proportion of total immigrants. International law has created the concept of a refugee, but it has never codified what a country's obligations are to refugees directly. That is still a domestic policy choice.

Relatively recently, some countries have reformed their immigration policies to focus on limiting immigration to predominantly educated or wealthy individuals. Canada, the UK, and Australia, for instance, use point-based systems to determine who is permitted to immigrate. Most of these systems were developed after policies justified by racial segregation were struck down during the 1960s. Each program has been modified over the years, but the programs typically award points based on levels or types of education, locations of education, and common types of employment. Each policy has a different point scheme, with characteristics like type of education, level of wealth, demand for labor by particular industries, and personal connections to people already in the country worth different point values.

These systems also consider an individual's potential to invest in the nation, a factor that concentrates population flows to the rich or at least to the educated. Countries will often deliberately try to attract wealthy, well-educated potential migrants with policies that advantage them, exacerbating the brain drain of highly educated migrants who seek higher incomes than those available in their countries of origin. Countries have an easier time justifying such policies domestically; the costs versus benefits of allowing new doctors or PhDs into the country, for instance, are relatively straightforward. The human and physical capital that immigrants bring with them has become key to flows of migration. Increasingly, skills are an immigrant's ticket into a destination country.[17] Many countries have attempted to maximize these types of immigration flows. Canada and Australia, as examples, have instituted extensive financial requirements that allow for investment into the country to gain residency and a points-based visa system that gives higher score for more education attainment to attract primarily highly skilled labor or the wealthy.[18]

The concern is that this approach ignores the benefits of a diversified worker base. A fixation on higher education helps fuel a technological economy, but it does not sustain industries dependent on physical labor, such as agriculture and manufacturing. These policies also have fewer direct demographic effects in the next generation. Most migrant families have a slightly higher birth rate than what would be expected if they had not migrated, and they almost always have higher birth rates in that first generation than those of the native-born population. In countries that attract the most-educated migrants, this effect is not nearly as significant. The long-term demographic benefits of migration to a country thus decrease, as the children of first-generation migrants do not exist in the numbers necessary to offset the effects of aging societies. The increased labor force lasts for one generation at best, but it will not rejuvenate the country. As most countries with this form of immigration have harsh caps on the total number of visas that can be allocated, these policies will not likely change the trajectory of these countries' demographic transitions. Long-term demographic considerations are not a part of most major immigration policies worldwide.

Contentious domestic battles over immigration policy help explain these attempts at population manipulation. While governments ostensibly focus on attracting richer and more highly educated population flows, these selective immigration policies may have the effect of perpetuating class or racial biases. It remains to be seen if these policies will create a new version of the nineteenth-century paranoia of an upper class uninterested in or even unattached to a nation itself. Wealthy, highly educated individuals may condense into a class with various citizenships and passports, with no more connection to any country than a summer home or an investment property. The beginnings of such a class may be seen in the new rich in Vancouver who originate from Hong Kong or the oligarchs in London paying for a new life on the money they made in the Middle East or Russia. Will the children of this new landless, wealthy elite want to assimilate to their new countries or even care (or notice) that they are in one?

This is less easy to quantify but more critical for the long run as those societal ties create national group belief. Migration rates themselves are an essential data point with table 4.1 showing net migration rates per one thousand people in a wide range of countries, which differs from my earlier discussion in terms of total flows. Notice that the scale of immigration can be remarkable in smaller countries. Simply, the smaller the total population, the simpler it is for immigration to have a profound effect.

The United Arab Emirates (UAE) is a good example, having seen a net migration rate as high as 109 per 1,000 people. This degree of immigration is only possible in small countries with high pull factors and legal opportunities. This country has a vast need for physical labor and construction work, but its population is uninterested in those tasks. The UAE thus provides an excellent example of how national identity or legal issues can be hidden within migration totals. Because the UAE so heavily depends on controlled temporary labor, this inordinately high migration rate will not necessarily determine the country's future; residency in the UAE is limited to the terms of one's current employment, and migrants have only the most limited means to create a more permanent life. Called the *kafala* (roughly, "sponsorship") system, would-be migrants are linked via visas and controls to their employers. This program is like the temporary-worker visa system seen in the U.S. agricultural industry, but employers and the government retain a higher degree of enforcement and control. The UAE is not the only country within the Middle East to use this style of immigration; we can also see it in Saudi Arabia, Bahrain, Kuwait, Oman, and Qatar.

This system limits the interests of the migrants themselves to signing single contracts, earning income, and then moving home, giving a high degree of control to employers. Migrants cannot even leave the country if they want to.[19] These policies have the effect of undermining the potential that the immigration population could bring to the country, but domestic governments may choose these policies because they believe that more permanent migration would overwhelm the domestic population and fundamentally change the country's politics, ethnicity, and/or religion. All these concerns are probably valid. It is the pay that brings nonpermanent workers to the region not a belief in a long-term future. As projects end, the construction jobs end and so the workers leave. This is similar with domestic household labor or even the knowledge sector. Nearly everyone is a temporary worker and plans for their personal future assuming that they will leave. As employment demand decreases so too will population—rapidly.

Saudi Arabia has much of the same characteristics as the UAE but not nearly on the same scale, with migration rates close to those of Canada and

TABLE 4.1. Net Migration Rates of Select Countries (per One Thousand Population)

	2000–2005	2005–2010	2010–2015
USA	3.6	3.3	3.2
China	-0.3	-0.3	-0.3
UK	3.3	5.0	2.8
France	2.5	1.5	1.0
Germany	0.0	0.1	3.1
Russia	2.4	3.0	1.6
Japan	1.0	0.7	0.6
India	-0.4	-0.5	-0.4
Pakistan	-1.2	-1.6	-1.2
Nigeria	-0.3	-0.4	-0.4
Mexico	-5.3	-0.7	-0.9
Poland	0.2	0.0	-0.4
United Arab Emirates	62.7	109.1	9.3
Saudi Arabia	8.2	6.2	5.7
Canada	6.5	7.4	6.7
Sweden	3.2	5.7	5.7

Sweden. All three countries have used different methods to attract migrants, with Canada a proponent of the points-based, family ties, and human capital systems. Sweden attracts many economic migrants, but it has increasingly come to attract many forced migrants, too, as it has stepped up as a leader in Europe during the Syrian refugee crisis. Saudi Arabia has a near-zero population of refugees and asylum seekers. Temporary visa workers (such as those in the UAE) are the only migrants allowed into the kingdom. While Canada, Sweden, and Saudi Arabia have similar total migration rates, they have used radically different methods to achieve them. Each country's system—one based on economic maximization in Canada, one based on morality in Sweden, and one based on controlled task-based employment in Saudi Arabia—will have different long-term consequences.

The consistent U.S. migration rate may not be as high as the extreme rates seen in the UAE, but it is far higher than the migration rates of its closest economic competition in the Western European states and, of course, both India and China. The latter two have had small essential levels of out-migration and are expected to see that trend continue into the near future. The sustained rates in the United States, far above expectations even given its economic size, confirm it as a nation of immigration. Nevertheless, flows could still be higher as demand for labor increases during the demographic transition.

We also see, again, the paradox of Germany. Germany has the largest economy in Europe and a manufacturing base that is the largest exporter of its type in the world; it will need a vast increase in its labor force soon, but it has not seen nearly enough of a population influx—that is, until the recent humanitarian crises in Afghanistan and Syria, which explain the higher-than-average migration rates starting in 2010. Movements went from near 0 to 3.1 per 1,000. While these numbers may seem small in total, they are radical given Germany's earlier anti-immigration policy decisions.

The sources of migration are changing. It was an old cliché that Poles moved west or that Mexicans and Nigerians moved north to the United States and Europe, respectively. All three countries are no longer the most significant sources of migrant labor in their regions. Each country has populations well into the millions living in foreign lands, sometimes under duress, with new anti-immigration groups in the United States and even violence seen against Poles in the UK after Brexit. While fewer immigrants now come to the United States from Mexico, immigration flows from Central America still travel *through* Mexico. Flows come from a multitude of central African countries, with migrants leaving for both economic and conflict reasons hoping to move to Europe as their land of opportunity or at least safety.

Beyond Migration

Migration is a complicated story: one of movement, potential, acceptance, and rejection, facilitated or discouraged by a combination of law, access, hope, and worry. Over the last thirty years, new migrant populations have given birth to rising economic growth and even more diverse economic and manufacturing systems in their adopted countries, with industries such as agriculture, textiles, and technology seeing significant gains. Migration has also decreased the incomes of the lowest-educated individuals in these receiving countries, changed the countries' racial makeup, and in some cases altered expectations of citizenship or national identity. Migration that primarily moves toward opportunity may also increase the domestic differences between rural and city populations, exacerbating previously existing regional rivalries. These stressors change the political framework of how or why immigrant populations can be accepted, integrated, and, most importantly, assimilated.

This story is complex, but also simple. Potential can be used or not. The costs of immigration should not be ignored, but nor should the gains. These gains are not universal, and neither are the political consequences. Migration has the potential to unleash significant change in the world, should nations choose it.

CHAPTER 5

Recovery from Violence and the Horrors of War

Theoretical discussions of trends such as the demographic transition tend to rely on generic case studies of stable countries with peaceful histories.[1] Trend lines move up or down, even if the year-to-year variables are inconsistent. The overall picture of the relationships between youth, age, growth, and stagnation remains the same, and some cases might see an increase in democracy or even peace—the more optimistic outcomes of demographic change.

However, two phenomena can rapidly disrupt all aspects of this expected transition. In the previous chapter, I discuss one of them: migration. In this chapter, I discuss the second: war. War, more than any other spectacle known to humanity, can devastate a society and its future. It can alter a nation's most foundational frameworks—its norms, its structure, and, crucially for my discussion, its demography. War is felt and experienced not only in terms of casualties but also as a catalyst for reassessment, as wars prompt societies, families, and individuals to reconsider what they should expect to accomplish in the future. War remains even more destructive than the expected consequences of climate change, natural disasters such as hurricanes, and the ravages of plagues.

Luckily, and to humanity's credit, war is rare, even considering the recent sustained violence in Syria, Iraq, Ukraine, and Yemen. While these are all distressing examples of horror, this horror is increasingly rare on a global scale. War occurs primarily between or within developing societies; developed countries occasionally go to war, too, but with the exception of the new conflict between Russia and Ukraine, always overseas. Modern wars over territory involve poor and young countries, not old and rich ones. This general decline in warfare can be attributed to a range of factors, from the high costs of modern conflict to the rise of a dominant global power (the United States) to a combination of international and domestic changes creating less need for or even less interest in violence.[2]

FIG. 5.1. The Rise of Peace in the Modern World

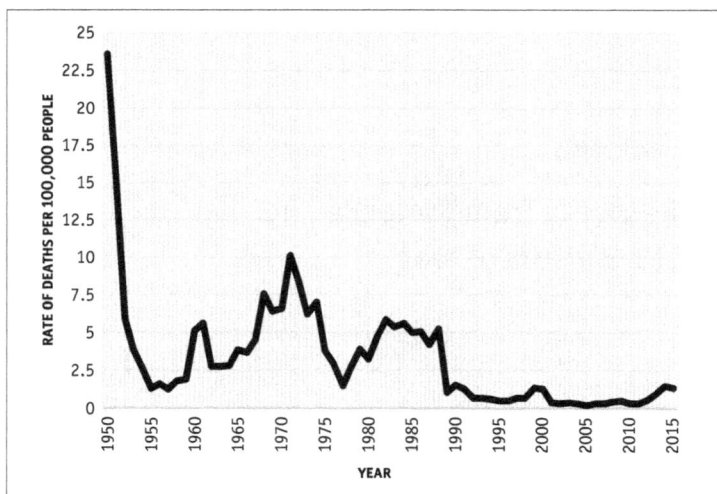

Source: PRIO Battle Deaths Dataset v.3.0; UCDP Battle Related Deaths 5.0/Human Security Report Project Dataset; United Nations, Department of Economic and Social Affairs, Population Division 2015b

As the data on battle deaths in figure 5.1 show, so much conflict in the twentieth century was exacerbated by global competition, particularly the Cold War and imperialism. [3] In this figure, spikes correspond to momentous events, beginning with the Korean War in the 1950s and the Vietnam War of the late 1960s and early 1970s. Both wars, of course, had their roots in imperialism and Cold War rivalries. The figure also shows spikes associated with a series of smaller conflicts between Iran and Iraq in the 1980s, the Soviet invasion of Afghanistan in the 1980s, and civil conflicts in sub-Saharan Africa and South Asia from the 1970s to in some cases now in 2021. The great games between major powers fueled domestic conflicts, as combatants gained access to equipment, training, and resources far more sophisticated than what they would have been able to obtain otherwise from local support. While great power involvement increased the chances that would-be rebellions could be successful, it also increased the carnage of conflicts.

Figure 5.1 shows that casualties have trended downward corresponding with the end of the Cold War and the decline of great power politics. Even the United States's post–9/11 war with Afghanistan and the subsequent Iraq War proved to be minor in terms of total casualties when compared to the conflicts of previous generations. This is not to claim that these events were not serious or bloody, only that the total number of deaths associated with them were much smaller than what would have been expected in historical wars.

Have the declines in casualties been caused by the decline of colonial domination, the end of the Cold War, and the expectation that major states will no longer wage war with each other? Or are these phenomena merely correlated? Are these declines the effects of stable international institutions that shepherd peaceful processes of resolution for national rivalries and grievances? Is this just a temporary trend, reflecting not a decline in conflict but only a decline in war between the major developed, wealthy states? Before World War II, these states regularly annihilated each other in increasingly advanced ways. Explaining this decline in conflict is one of the great questions of politics. Can this trend be trusted? Or is it a temporary condition, as we wait for the carnage that the global great powers can inflict but until now have chosen not to? Choices can change.

The declines in conflict since the middle of the twentieth century have inspired a series of major works of political science, from the concept of the "democratic peace" to an even more revolutionary idea that humans in general are moving beyond our basest violent urges. As conflict has lately been increasing (that is, as of this writing in 2021), this interesting research has again become critical for future global peace.

However, this book, dear readers, is not so much interested in war itself as it is in the aftereffects of war. Let us leave the "hows" and "whys" of war for a moment and discuss its consequences. The disrupted families, refugees, devastated medical systems, spikes in births and infant mortality, and lasting trauma that result from war all directly influence demography, and, most importantly, all will last far longer than the conflict itself. Most of the scholarly research on war has concerned negotiations between groups, the effects of aid, peacekeepers, war crimes tribunals, or even truth and reconciliation commissions. Little, however, has focused on war's generalizable demographic effects.

Violence is a choice, not a biological necessity. Humans create violence by how we shape our laws, societal norms, and shared expectations of morality. The political systems we create, the governments we accept, and the conflicts that arise between rival groups can all affect the levels of violence in our society.

Humans are not biologically wired to be violent toward each other. The archaeological record shows that in the earliest stages of human development, the percentage of humanity killed at the hands of other humans was close to 2 percent total.[4] Compared to the current murder rate estimates of less than 1.3 percent, the difference between modern humans and our ancestors is only 0.7 percent. These studies also show that the murder rate peaked at 12 percent during the fifteenth century, when a complex web of religious wars and dynastic struggles wracked Eurasia.[5] That level of carnage is genuinely shocking.

Politics and policy create the structures by which we accept violence. We, humanity, make the choice via our politics to be violent with seemingly little regard for whether that violence will facilitate lasting achievement. From personal tragedies on roads, in bars, and at work, to grandiose events such as world wars, violence is common but seems to have limited effectiveness in the long run.

Political choices can be changed, modified, and altered. Violence is not a constant, nor is the acceptance of violence. If we should expect a constant human drive for violence, then how could humanity shift from a 12 percent murder rate in fifteenth-century Eurasia to a rate of less than 1.3 percent (and dropping) today? Can peace, with all that it entails and its multitude of benefits, be made universal?

Society and Violence

War is not the only form of conflict; crime in its many forms also affects mortality rates and serves to undermine economic prosperity. This problem is seen globally, as murder rates positively correlate with group pressures to commit violent acts or to enact vengeance as a way of gaining social prestige. From Icelandic Vikings attacking well-known members of their communities, to Greek epics in which heroes listed their achievements as proof of their worthiness to fight, to drug-fueled conflicts in the United States between gangs of young people who fight under the pretense of money but often due to peer pressures— these expressions of violence are not necessarily for direct monetary gain but are instead born out of social group dynamics. Worse, if murder becomes concentrated among more prosperous community members, it undermines the overall group, as talent and investment resources are destroyed because of its their very nature. To be clear all death is a moral crime, but who dies and why they die have differing effects on the society as a whole. These choices can be changed, and violence can be abated.

While violence has declined globally over time, patterns of violence seem to differ according to geography. The Americas, in general, continue to have the highest murder rates in the world, with the only exceptions being countries in the middle of actual civil wars.[6] The United States is the most violent developed nation on Earth, even though its murder rate has dropped by half in the last twenty-five years, and parts of Central America have the world's highest crime rates, both in terms of scale and longevity. In the case of the United States, why did the murder rate fall so quickly, and why was it so high in the first place? Violence is not so clean a question as rich versus poor or violence versus peace.

Nevertheless, the Americas have seen some peace. The region was not touched by the two world wars, even though some countries sent troops overseas, and they largely (apart from the United States) missed the worry of nuclear proliferation. The Brazilians and Argentines realized the folly of nuclear development and moved away from excessive military spending. Despite extreme levels of domestic crime in the Americas, these countries have high levels of peace in the sense that their conflicts have not been so horrific as those seen in every other continent. With the notable exception of the post-Columbian era, conflicts in this hemisphere have not reached the levels of brutality that emerged in Cambodia, Rwanda, Germany, Russia, and China. This peace is not in any way perfect, but a relative peace is still more peaceful than war.

From Personal to National Violence

Comparing different scales of violence allows us to start to partial out how violence affects people's choices as they attempt to rebuild and recover from trauma. The point of the previous discussion on crime was to emphasize that in most places on Earth, casualties from war constitute only a small fraction of the total number of deaths caused by violence. This is also the case in countries that have been involved in sustained domestic conflicts. The idea is that we cannot discuss what violence does to populations through the lens of interstate conflict alone; however, considering the effects of major wars allows us to examine violence's capacity to cause foundational demographic shifts. Studies of recovery from war contextualize how recovery would work in places with similarly high death rates not due to uniforms, flags, or heavy weaponry.

All wars are not equal, and only those that cause substantial amounts of death can alter the future of a population at the fundamental level. For all its horror, the long-term consequences of crime may be to undermine development and even the stability of effectiveness of a political system.

The frequency and ubiquity of major conflicts in previous generations—ranging from civil wars large and small, to raids of rival groups, to wars of conquest—should not be understated. Humanity created civilization in brief periods of peace amid more or less continuous conflict. From Roman history to the Three Kingdoms of China; from Mongols to Huns, Anglo-Saxons, and Vikings; from colonization and imperialism to the ravages of the twentieth century, it is difficult to find a single period in human history in which a whole generation could live and die without fear of large-scale carnage. In turn, history is not only composed of stories of rivalries and empires. It also necessarily encompasses waves of recovery from successive conflicts. Human history is not one of building but one of the needs to rebuild.

I suggest that this constant need to reconstruct prior to the modern era undermined technological progress and resulted in most of humanity living lives at nearly the same rates of life expectancy, wealth, literacy, and opportunity for thousands of years. The time, treasure, and effort spent on re-creating what was destroyed and not creating new things was wasted time, treasure, and effort, as what once was and would be needed again was continually destroyed due to conflict and short-sighted violence.[7]

Before the nineteenth century, violence both killed individuals directly and disjointed economic and societal structures. Domestic instability, in turn, both increased birth rates and disrupted the provision of necessities, such as shelter and food. Without these resources, families were still plagued by the devastating effects of higher infant and child mortality rates even as fertility rates increased. This combination of increased mortality and increased fertility historically resulted in population stagnation.

Modernity and Recovery after Wars

The post–World War II era has differed from previous historical eras in several ways, chief among them the fact that populations are generally more secure. They have access to emergency food and refugee organizations, and many consider themselves to be living with at least some level of safety. After war or other significant conflicts, populations are more likely to increase, sometimes dramatically, as individuals prioritize marrying and having children. Although these increased birth rates are temporary, they have the potential to create not only a new generation large enough to make up for lives lost during the conflict but also a larger and more prosperous nation in the long run. The resultant prosperity may be even greater than what would have been expected if war had never happened. Consider the amazing growth in Western Europe, the United States, Japan, and China after World War II. This growth would not have been possible without the combination of new youthful populations, domestic peace, and the opportunity, belatedly for China, to create and grow an economy and nation.

Peace and policy are the most important factors in the fragile postwar period. The difference in the future potential of societies characterized by political disorganization, destabilization, or mistakes is that fertility can still increase but without the economic growth necessary to create the optimum combination of population and economic growth. Think about, for example, what Eastern Europe could have become had it been able to utilize its post–World War II baby boom to the extent seen in the West. If the political systems in these countries had permitted growth opportunities, the region's youthful, decently educated labor force could have reshaped these countries to a greater extent than what its postwar realities turned to be under communist regimes. China is an even more dramatic case, as so much of the nation's limited potential in the post–World War II era was wasted on failed top-down industrial policies that spoiled the potential of whole generations.

Recovery will continue to be, to my mind, a more critical part of conflict than violence itself, stretching as it does across generations. The findings in classical work on the consequences of war are often contradictory, and research is heavily weighted toward national-level studies. Early works on the horrors of World War I, Angell (1912) and Thorp (1941), suggested that the effects of wars are permanent, with economic depression as a likely outcome. If Angell and Thorp were right, how could countries have achieved development at all, given the degree to which war was such a common event in the early twentieth century? Keynes (1919) more optimistically attempted to show, far before his well-known post-Depression work, that recovery from war was possible with the help of foreign aid—a concept familiar to those who have studied Keynesian economics. Later studies, such as Kuznets (1973), supported these early assertions, while Barbera (1973) and Wheeler (1975) showed that foreign rebuilding efforts had inconclusive effects. These early studies confirmed that economic and demographic recovery from war is not easy, and how or why recovery can happen still needed a concise theory of explanation. Public policy of aid in this era was heavily based on hope rather than evidence.

With the receding of World War II and the rise of quality cross-national quantitative studies, work such as Kugler (1973) started to empirically show that countries were capable of recovery even after the most violent wars—not unlike the mythical phoenix that rises from the ashes. The term "phoenix factor" is thus used to describe the unexpected postwar advantages that translate into economic growth. Kugler's work also showed that postwar economic growth could be both faster and larger than a country's prewar economic expectations.[8] This first work on recovery helped explain the tremendous post–World War II boom in Western Europe, which saw levels of economic growth far higher than earlier scholars' expectations. How different would the world be if growth was impossible after great carnage? What if populations could never allow themselves to again work for the common good after experiencing the terror of war? Kugler (1973) hoped at the time that his theory would be generalizable to wars throughout the world—that a universal phoenix factor could be built into demographic and economic expectations.

I suggest that countries should be able to take advantage of a temporary baby boom to rebuild efficiently. Because so much of the developed world's economic system is based on old infrastructure and rebuilding, developed countries should be able to construct new and economically better systems once a war is over with relative ease. Hopefully, the timely combination of a large labor force and modern, rebuilt equipment will create growth that is more significant than expected. Such theories linking recovery to politics, economics, and demography are not unique. For example, Urlanis (1971) focused on the con-

centrations of casualties in the postwar Soviet Union and estimated the generational effects of war in the country, creating a framework for other future studies. Heuveline and Pock (2007) found what they called a "phoenix population"
in postwar Cambodia. Hill (2004) likewise showed a fertility increase in postconflict regions. Hill's work also expanded upon the previous agendas to show
that environmental work factors and access to contraception in refugee camps
creates a greater degree of nuance than the large-scale cross-national studies. We
should remember that technological advancements in contraception have altered how family planning can be arranged, and these innovations were widely
available in the second half of the twentieth century but not the first. Other
wide-ranging studies have shown that war causes perpetual harm, rapid economic growth, and possible recovery but only with the help of foreign aid.[9]

Equally important to discussions of recovery are discussions about how
to measure loss. Most conflict research focuses on casualties in terms of battle
deaths, particularly deaths of combatants. Some attempts have been made to
measure civilian deaths, and researchers use a wide range of classifications and
estimations to do so. Changing the assumption parameters changes the overall
estimates of loss, which can, in turn, change what is thought to be the scale of
the conflict itself.[10]

Some examples of accessible conflict-tracking datasets are the Uppsala
Conflict Data Program (UCDP 2016), the International Peace Research Institute Oslo (PRIO 2009), and the Correlates of War Project (2016). The first, Uppsala, originated in the early post–World War II era with "radio data." Data collection at this time was straightforward: an English speaker was hired to spend
their nights listening to the BBC World Report to collect and write down where
conflicts had been initiated, who was fighting, and often the levels of battlefield casualties in real time as it was reported primarily in the early years on
the BBC. At the time, the BBC was the largest news organization in the world,
and these news datasets gave Uppsala a single reputable source. Of course, the
data Uppsala collected was limited to where the BBC had an interest or where
an English-speaking reporter could gain access.

Limitations like these are a common characteristic of most compiled datasets. Reporting, which is vital to measurement, is primarily conducted by nongovernmental organizations. Today's data has become so detailed that it is now
geocoded, which means that the actual physical location of a death, down to
the village or even street, is part of the variable (as seen in PRIO data), or it became more interested in actions taken by one state against another (as seen in
the Correlates of War Project's data).[11] This data can be as simple as two navy
vessels following each other or some other diplomatic disagreement that does
not end with casualties. The vast majority of all difficulties between nations are
of this somewhat agitated but generally peaceful type. The latter kind of data
illustrates relationships that are conflictual but not necessarily violent, and the

former helps pull geography into the discussion. Data is critical to empirical evaluation, but it is difficult to create, maintain, and fund.

War and peace are decisions of such magnitude that, without empirical data, are at the core a gamble, a waste of money, and worse the cause of unnecessary deaths.

New work on nonviolent protests and internet mobilization helps to explain how conflict can occur off the battlefield. Postconflict surveys and more complex estimation techniques also add nuance to evaluations, but they are still limited by the scope of humans' experiences and their willingness to engage with researchers. These measurements have profoundly influenced how to study war: from interstate to intrastate conflict, from the rise of terrorism to the foundational concepts of conflict.

Much current research on conflict is concerned with how and why it starts or ends, not with its intensity or outcomes. The research has also not often considered the demographic structure of the society. Consider the case of Angola, a country embroiled by conflicts that killed at least 546,000 people from 1961 to 1994.[12] In that period, Angola underwent the first stages of the demographic transition; the size of the country doubled from 4.7 million to over 9.4 million people. A very high birth rate and low out-migration levels worked together to expand the population, even with expected high mortality due to the costs of war. When measured, the losses due to the war itself made up only one-twentieth of the estimated mortality rate, well within the rate's margin of error, meaning that the effects of the war were nearly invisible statistically. What effect does conflict have if it can be invisible in the data?

An example of how new methods of estimating casualties can alter our conception of prior wars can be seen in Hacker (2011), which compares the 1850 and 1870 U.S. censuses to shed new light on the bloodiest war in American history, the Civil War. Hacker shows via demographic estimation and assumptions of differing mortality rates that the most commonly cited casualty numbers are likely off by close to two hundred thousand lives. This vast number becomes even larger when considering the country's size at the time of only thirty-one million people, or roughly the current population of the state of California. Hacker's work suggests a new upper bound of over eight hundred thousand deaths. This new study rewrites the past, gives new context to horror, and changes the fundamental measurements of conflict. I hope this book, in turn, helps to expand and explain the outcomes of conflict.

When wartime losses are not interpreted through the lens of demography, the question of recovery becomes problematic. It creates a level of duplicity or slipperiness to the argument that a conflict's seriousness should be judged by its consequences. This situation becomes more complex when we consider that many of the countries with sustained levels of civil conflict today, such as Democratic Republic of the Congo and South Sudan, are still undergoing the first stage of their demographic transition, which combines high births, high population growth, and, most importantly, high mortality rates. What is the causal structure between these population trends and the outcomes? Does conflict that sustains a population boom but inhibits economic growth create a poverty trap? Most importantly, are the mortality rates lower than expected thanks to exogenous interventions, such as international institutions and foreign medical aid?

With all these variables in mind, creating a consensus on how to evaluate postwar recovery is important. The measurement used in this book estimates *demographic* losses, which are measured at a national level and incorporate a broader definition of loss than traditional measurements of the toll of war. Demographic loss encompasses not merely those who fall victim to direct violence but also those lost to disruptions of shelter, those who die unexpectedly because of hospital failures, the spikes in child and infant mortality rates that often accompany war, and even losses due to family disruption and subsequent birth rate variance. The estimation of loss should, I believe, include not only those lost to war itself but also those lost to what should have been the population's destiny had war not commenced. The difference between expected and actual reality increases the degree of assumption inherent to the estimation, but it allows for a higher degree of nuance.

Importantly, this method is only effective when considering cases in which large percentages of the population are lost. It cannot work in situations in which casualties are hidden in overall mortality rates, such as in Angola. This form of evaluation, like all of them, has its limitations, but I believe it is a useful method for considering the most violent of conflicts, including those close to or involving genocides and those that have ramifications over generations.

As I mention throughout this book, war is increasingly rare but still occurs with a degree of regularity in the developing world. This, in turn, means that the outcomes of conflict are also primarily seen in the developing world. In the initial stage of most conflicts, casualties are concentrated on young adult males as the combatants. If these wars stay small or are short, then that will be where deaths stay. For war to be directly seen in the demography structure with all the resulting changes, it must be only after periods of significant loss, including increased birth rates, disruption of families, and overall debilitating effects on mortality, concentrated in the very young and very old. Because postwar societies enter an expanded youth bulge with high levels of potential labor, a postwar society can, almost paradoxically, grow faster than it otherwise would have had the conflict never happened.

As I argue throughout this book, whether postwar growth occurs depends on an essential factor: politics. A postwar nation's success requires governmental stability and efficiency, the political choice to create sustained peace and, most importantly, quick action on the part of governments. If the potential of the youth bulge is ignored and not put to work after the war, a cycle begins in which subsequent governments are unable to create the necessary conditions for growth and, in turn, fail.

How do postwar youth bulges arise? It is a common effect of war for survivors to revise the number of children they expect to have. This trend has been observed in countries as wide ranging as Croatia, Cambodia, and the United States. A postwar period, particularly after a conflict, alters individuals' interests, and children seemingly become a component of the recovery process. Birth rates increase almost universally, and the four to five years immediately after war usually see significantly higher fertility rates. It is important to note that these larger birth rates are not generally consequences of wartime rape, which is clearly part of major wars; most of the effect on births are correlated instead with a rise in peace and come after the conflict not during. That difference is essential, as it exemplifies a key recovery factor: the personal actions that sustain individuals, families, and groups after the war. Rebuilding is more than physical; it is also mental, with children being a component of that rebirth.

Baby Booms and Reconstruction after War

Kugler et al. (2013) attempted to create a generalizable framework linking the postwar youth bulge to politics and economic recovery. They show that demographic recovery and population growth take place in developed societies following a conflict regardless of the nation's underlying productivity in terms of labor or government. Postwar baby booms, however, have different consequences for more-developed and less-developed societies. They can enhance the labor productivity of more-developed societies, as historical reserves of knowledge and skill are transmitted to the disproportionately young labor force, which, in turn, drives economic growth with a high level of productivity. With the help of newer, rebuilt infrastructure, these societies can outproduce their less-devastated competitors.

In less-developed societies, by contrast, baby booms add poorly trained participants to an already low-skill labor force. Rapid population growth ensures that the economic losses incurred in war are preserved. The less-developed societies endure the highest costs and are also least able to recover. As their populations explode, they cannot keep up with, much less expand on, prewar levels of human capital. Many become failed states that cannot preserve the institutions required to maintain high levels of economic performance. Foreign aid can help stem or reverse this trend but only in societies with robust, reliable political systems. Findings in economic development literature show that corruption or mismanagement of aid is a constant worry in these situations. Fisunoglu (2014) supports these results and shows additional optimistic evidence of the importance of foreign aid; in favorable conditions,

FIG. 5.2. Expected War Recovery Following the World Wars

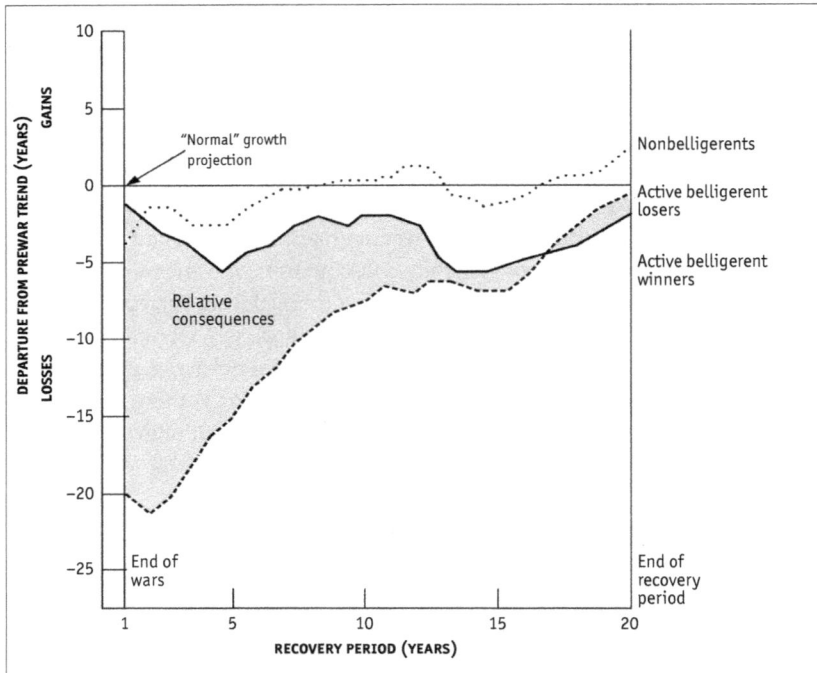

Source: World Bank (2016)

the international community may be able to help expand recovery rates, human capital, and the influence of population growth for a more sustainable, prosperous future.

Again, the scale of population loss is critical. Most conflicts, to humanity's credit, do not have the depth of horror necessary to radically alter the combatant countries' demographic profiles. Turning to a few key examples, I evaluate the recovery trajectories of a selection of countries that have suffered large-scale casualties within the last hundred years. I examine the aftermaths of international wars, civil wars, and genocides to help elucidate the different effects of these types of conflicts and illustrate their shared long-term generational consequences.[13] The earliest example of this type of investigation is seen in figure 5.2.

The first conclusion that can be drawn is that, even after the worst wars of the twentieth century, all belligerents nearly recovered demographically and economically (total recovery) within one postwar generation of twenty years. Here I define "recovery" as having reached prewar expectations of future growth should conflict have not occurred.

One remarkable finding is that some of a few highly organized developed countries seem to have improved their expected fortunes one generation out from war. That is, not only did they recover to the economic and population levels that they were expected to achieve in the absence of war, but they became even larger, more economically prosperous, and thus more powerful. Post–World War II Germany and Japan are both prime examples of this phenomenon.

This is a shocking and nonintuitive finding. Consider what remains after the devastation of war: buildings, bridges, factories, and other physical infrastructure are often gone. Trade and lives have been disrupted. Yet the population is not gone, even after real horror. So, consider again what remains in a country like Germany or Japan: a highly organized, relatively unified population, with no sustained domestic conflict. Add that to (at least in Germany's case) an extremely high level of human capital (education), and the question is not what to do after the war but when to do it. Rebuilding is not a question of how to rebuild but of what assets are available and how they can be used. In short, in countries that are relatively educated and organized, recovery creates the opportunity to build back better. Postwar recovery periods propelled both Germany and Japan to unbelievable heights of growth and solidified each country's power in the international system: Germany ascended to a regional power in Europe, and Japan became the second-largest economy in the world in the twentieth century, despite losing the bloodiest war in human history.

The stories of Germany and Japan are similar. Both countries took advantage of their new demographic worlds—characterized by a young labor force; higher birth rates; and high levels of unity, education, and productivity—and poured their populations into recovery, reinvention, and rebirth. It is likely that this trajectory is not unique to World War II recovery and that similar waves of recovery have pushed groups to higher-than-expected levels of population and economic attainment throughout history. While these stories represent destiny changed, altered, and reworked, they nevertheless still hinge on political choices.

As I mention in other places in this book, the scale of a conflict is essential to predicting the trajectory of a nation's recovery from that conflict, with high levels of casualties (near 3 percent of the population or more) radically altering the demographic nature of a country. The combination of concentrated casualties and a postwar baby boom does not merely create one larger generation—it also has the potential to ripple out, in the form of boomlets, for generations to come. China is one country that has followed this trajectory, as explained in chapter 2 and chapter 8 and highlighted in Kugler et al. (2013). These secondary booms can then grow the population beyond prewar expectations, altering a nation's expected demographic trajectory.

Postwar baby booms thus have lasting implications. They affect not merely

FIG. 5.3. A New World for Cambodia (Population in Thousands)

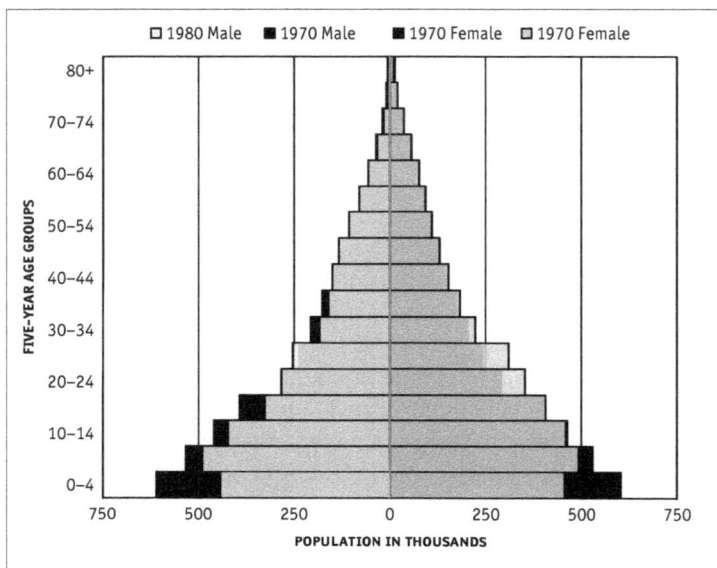

Source: United Nations, Department of Economic and Social Affairs, Population Division 2015a, 2015b

the immediate postwar generation or their children but also their grandchildren. Those generations altered by the conflict skew young to old and male to female ratios. The normal gender distribution of roughly 1 to 1.1 male to female is disrupted within that population simply because there are not as many of either gender as expected.

Figure 5.3 compares the populations of Cambodia in 1970 and 1980 to illustrate conflict's effects on age cohorts. Cambodia had the misfortune of undergoing extreme levels of violence in the 1970s, including a brutal genocide that altered the nation's future in perpetuity. When we compare the age cohorts before and after the atrocities of the decade, the difference in the total amount of males is staggering, particularly among the "conflict generation." The concentration of deaths in males is a classic finding, even if at the highest levels ever seen as our example. This has been seen cross-nationally throughout much of the literature. Males are the primary combatants and hence the primary targets of violence. What is so important about this is not only the dramatic nature of the scale of the carnage but what should also be considered is how to recover afterward. How does a surviving woman find a male partner with this level of specific male war losses? How do you rebuild if you have such difficulty in building a family?

No age cohort, meaning a near whole generation of people—in this case the youth from the early 1970s—in any country has the level of gender imbalance that the Cambodian example shows. A significant disparity in a population's numbers of men and women changes not only the possibility of future reconstruction but also the family structure needed for the rebuilding. Marriage is, very simply, based upon at least some degree of male availability. When men are "missing" from these age cohorts, a society might entertain questions of polygamy or even reconsider the social institution of marriage altogether. Conflict of this scale thus often necessitates social change.

While this example is extreme, it is not uncommon. Most conflicts produce primarily male casualties because combatant forces are generally made up of men. It is important to remember, too, that genocidal violence also targets those whom the perpetrators consider to be future threats. This often means that males, even the very youngest, are targeted. Mass killings tend to be male dominated in terms of both perpetrators and victims. Even in news reports, it seems to be a working assumption that if the dead are male, they are combatants; if they are female, they are civilians. This assumption then becomes part of the narrative and is worked into measurements of casualties. The reality of male-dominated conflict and military recruiting should not ignore that some men, even those of age, are not fighters, nor members of combatant organizations, nor even considering violent actions themselves. They can be bystanders who others happen to consider as presenting a current or future threat.

While studies have shown that nearly all developed countries have consistently achieved full recovery from war, the research is not as definitive when it comes to less-developed countries. It is thus crucial to keep the specifics of conflict cases in mind, as recovery is not a one-size-fits-all prospect. It may be the case that countries plagued by internal disunity, disorganization, and gender-specific casualties that broadly alter family structures lose the possibility of recovery. These nations are destined for a poverty trap, in which each generation is poorer than the one that came before it. These countries have lost the foundations of governance, demography, and societal peace necessary to invest in, build for, and create a prosperous future.

Successful Postwar Recovery

Figure 5.4 tracks the population and gross domestic product (GDP) of Japan before and after World War II as they relate to prewar expectations.[14] The zero line in figure 5.4 represents what would have been expected given no radical or dramatic change. This point of comparison allows for some degree of estimation as to the true costs of conflict.[15]

FIG. 5.4. Japan, an Example of the Value of Unity

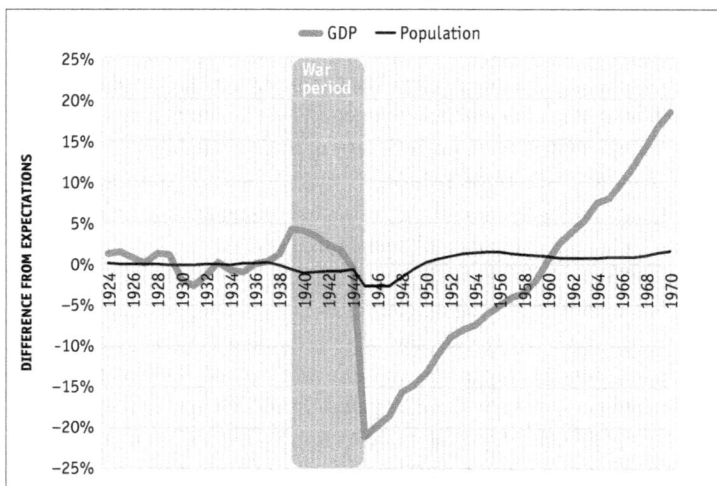

When comparing the zero-line estimation to reality in the case of Japan, the estimate is very close to actual conditions in the pivotal years of the late 1930s. The shock of conflict then undermined the nation, and by 1945, the country's economic might was a full 20 percent lower than what it should or could have been if the war had never started. While the population shows a similar fall, the percentage loss was not nearly as severe. Even this most horrific of wars did not undermine the basic demography of Japan. Population growth remained a possibility, and the population levels did, in fact, recover by 1949, likely thanks to the strength of demography and increased postwar birth rates. Even GDP recovered by 1960. Incredibly, this rapid economic growth continued far beyond expectations, showing how the war altered Japan's economic and population growth trajectory for the better.

An alternative to this tale of expansion and success can be seen in the case of Vietnam, illustrated in figure 5.5. Notice first that the length of the relevant conflict in Vietnam was far longer than World War II in Japan's case. Again, as with Japan, the comparison between the zero line and the reality shows the costs of conflict. By the mid-1970s, Vietnam's economy was nearly 10 percent weaker than what it would have been had war not occurred. Though this number is stark, it does not fully encompass the costs of that type of economic disruption, which include not only lost GDP but also lost opportunity and the stunting of individual achievement. Alongside the economic decline, however, we have an interesting rapid population growth trend.

The case of Vietnam is one of optimism. Close to 2002, over twenty years past the end of war, the economy had nearly recovered to the level that would

FIG. 5.5. Vietnam and Population Potential

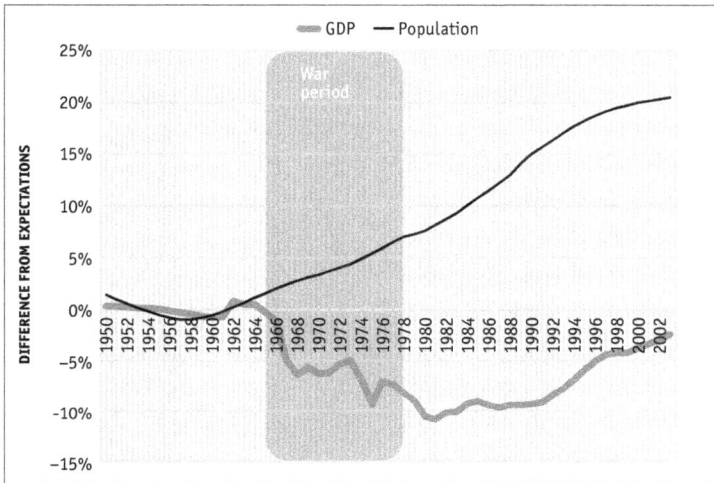

be expected if war had not occurred. The population, however, was vastly higher, showing that the influence of modest economic growth was not enough to reduce the country's birth rates and fertility. After the war, Vietnam entered a period of rapid population growth longer and larger than expected, bringing with it future possibilities. War altered the country's demographic foundation in perpetuity. But now, so many decades after the conflict, and thanks to Vietnam's large, untapped population, the country has the chance to reorganize, rework, and gain a degree of economic scale far larger than what would have been possible otherwise. Importantly, another aspect of this discussion should be the complex antigrowth policies of the government itself. Far beyond the scope of this book but what should be considered is that communist economic policies are not all that successful and are an example of lost opportunity as they caused recovery to be undermined with an interest in social engineering over sustainable economic development.

Figure 5.6 presents a case, in Mozambique, of demographic potential lost. While Mozambique's conflict itself ended in 1992, in the years since, the economy has not inspired much hope of recovery. That nuanced, complex soup of government, policy, education, and population has not yet led to economic success. Worse, Mozambique's population is soaring above zero-line estimations. Population growth without economic success can lead to the worst of all outcomes: a poverty trap, or population growth that outpaces economic growth and causes each generation to become poorer than the one before. A country in this situation cannot ever rebuild as it rapidly declines.

This poverty trap situation can be thought to be the most dangerous of

FIG. 5.6. Mozambique and the Rise of a Poverty Trap

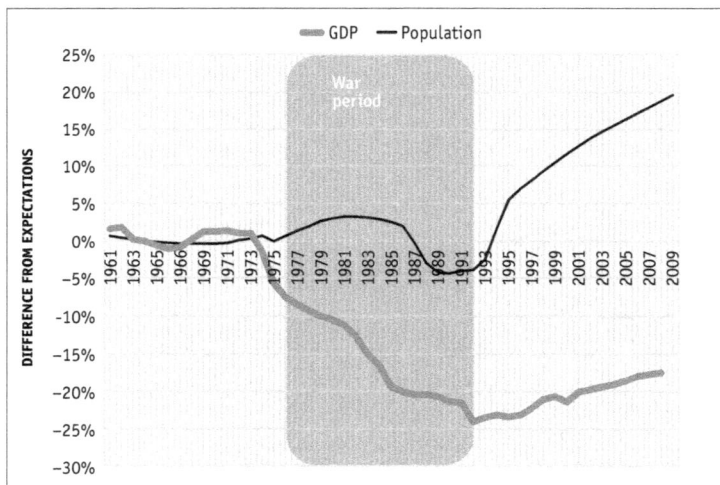

situations. It is a demographic foundation that is structurally fragile. Expectations of the future being worse than the past could lead to future conflict and again, the cycle of lost opportunity grows. Once a nation finds itself in this situation, it is foundationally more difficult to move and build upon it. The damage moves from potential to continued destabilization with a growing youthful population in continuous crisis that undermines growth and therefore perpetuates the crisis.

The point of these studies and our other discussions throughout this chapter is to remind us that the outcome of war often matters more than war itself. Conflict can disrupt, undercut, and maybe even create future potential. The effects of war remind us, in turn, that demography may not be destiny, but it is momentum. Booms in population, mass migrations, spikes in youthful populations, and, thankfully, mass casualties are all rare occurrences. These alter what should be the expectations of the future, expectations that are not destiny, but for most people, they have an equal effect. These futures can be growth periods, destabilization, or stagnation. They are all trends and what we expect can alter or undermine our own futures.

CHAPTER 6

Nationalism, Equality, Groups, and Demography

Equality is not only a moral good but also an economic imperative. Discrimination in any form undermines individual and group gains. The reason why is simple: discrimination involves spending time, effort, and money to undermine the lives of others within one's own group even if we do not acknowledge that they are part of it. It weakens their potential to create, build, and expand upon the future. Nothing can be more damaging to a society than discriminatory policies, whether based on gender, religion, race, ethnicity, class, geography, or all the above. The reasons for discrimination are less important than its effect, which decreases the overall ability to create, to build, and to grow as resources and time are spent undermining our shared future.

Group Identity, Progressivism, and the Rise of Nationalism

In recent years, countries around the world have seen a rise in nationalist and populist politics. These movements are not new; they often appear when domestic populations oppose waves of immigration or reject changes to the status quo.[1] Antitrade, antiglobalization, and even antichange politics are moving from country to country with an increasing degree of popularity. The causal framework of these movements is less important than their outcomes, which may include hostility toward immigration or widespread attempts to reset social mores to those of an earlier, often idealized, time. Trends toward openness are just that: trends. As I note in earlier chapters, societies are not necessarily destined to grow in a progressive direction over time. Humanity has gone through stages of development and regression, from periods primarily characterized by cultural acceptance to those noted for their zealotry and isolationism. Humanity is not on a clear, one-dimensional path toward a post-Enlightenment, neoliberal, utopian vision.

While globalization has had apparent benefits in economic growth and interconnection, it is far from universally popular. The divergence between globalization's (un)popularity and its effects can increase the attractiveness of policies likely to result in stagnation or degeneration, even by groups who have benefited from today's globalized world. Yes, globalization creates winners and losers; for example, while major, cosmopolitan cities have reaped globalization's benefits, rural environments have declined. This divergence has had clear political and societal implications, as generations of youth have moved to the cities, rural populations have grown older, and seemingly whole industries no longer reach large, rural sections of countries. Of course, modernity is not without consequences, and this should not be ignored or downplayed. Nevertheless, what is important is that connection to the world is the source of future opportunity, and as people isolate themselves, they lose access to the possibilities that will be afforded to future generations.

It is a common misconception that we, as humanity, know, understand, or even like our current condition as individuals. This information gap is not an indictment on the human condition! Only an important component of how decisions are made, particularly in democracies in which the votes matter, even those made with little to no specific evaluation of the issues or politicians being voted upon. Individuals are busy; they have lives, children, jobs, social activities, and interests that can be on more stimulating topics than the specifics of economic development or the success of policies. Some of the population, of course, is interested in the issues of the day or has a detailed understanding of history, but most do not. No matter our economic status, life expectancy, or other quantifiable attributes of human existence, how we consider ourselves matters more than the specificity of measurements and statistics. It is a regular occurrence for people to vote against their own economic self-interest, the current interests of the country, and the interests of future generations. It does not matter why only that it is a commonality. Knowledge of events, groups, national politics, race, ethnicity, and gender are based on the random chance of friends, family, and personal interests. Growth and development are only one part of the human condition, and individuals are often concerned with other kinds of achievements.

The unity of citizens within nations is a remarkably important question, and a unified nation may be an alternative to one that single-mindedly pursues economic expansion. However, the pursuit of unity raises the question: Can the existing generation trust the next one that might look differently, act differently, and visibly represent change? Unity is a necessary condition for long-term economic growth, but it remains remarkably tricky to create. How, precisely, is unity built? Is it best built through institutional norms?[2]

Let us take the importance of unified nations and link it to the ambiguity of populations belief structure and the possibility of organized states, public education programs, and propaganda. Here we have the potential expressed by so many nations that they can create new ethnic groups and nationalities to add additional foundations to national unity. Our individual components of social identity are constructs that change radically from generation to generation but even with this reality, our shared ideas of who is or is not part of a group change as well. Names, concepts, the very languages that individuals so often hold dear are malleable and can quickly be forgotten in subsequent generations. The psychology behind group creation is complex but key to human and societal development. Humanity requires groups to exist, but those groups themselves are not predestined.

Notably, most attempts to define new national-level or majority groups leave other groups marginalized and subject to discrimination, as propaganda and reeducation campaigns often hinge on who is *not* part of the dominant group. These narratives regularly claim that an outside group causes problems or cannot be unified with the majority whole or that their subservience is beneficial to the country as a whole.

Often, the "outside group" in question is gender based and primarily women. Women remain the most discriminated against population (even though they also constitute most people), and gender discrimination can be catastrophic to the long-term potential of nations and groups that enforce it. Although this chapter considers broader questions of discrimination, policies that suppress the rights and opportunities of women are of primary concern. The scale of the female population and the level of discrimination against women demand it.

Modern nation-states create and sustain unity among their populations through any number of cultural mechanisms. Many claim that ancient historical ties legitimize their government, and nations often mobilize national oaths, songs, and even architectural styles to create a higher degree of state unity. Nations continuously rewrite their histories as their interests change, and heroes and events are created or deliberately forgotten.

For instance, in the United States, hundreds of statues of Nathan Bedford Forrest were erected in prominent locations, including in the capitals of states such as Tennessee. Forrest was a Civil War general known for his gift for cavalry strategy, but he is primarily known for founding the most significant terrorist group in U.S. history, the Ku Klux Klan. The whole point of the statues was to write in stone or bronze a more popular argument than the reality of the Confederacy, which was about and for slavery. These, and similar ones for other southern generals, became popular during periods of domestic disunity, in the 1880s, 1930s, and during the civil rights moment of the 1960s.[3] Statues became a popular way of, in those cases, not only reaffirming the narrative of the South being for whites and controlled by whites but hammered into the towns by the physical display itself. These are not statues memorializing the dead but stating or reiterating the policy positions of the dominant group in power at the time.

Changing the narrative of history by rewriting it for current policy issues can be used to reaffirm group identity for other things including things they might not like but then ignore, whitewash, and restructure to make it more palatable. This process currently is part of the modern question within the culture wars of 2021, which asks whether the United States should continue to display hundreds of statues commemorating the founder of a terrorist group that has killed more Americans than any other in U.S. history? In 2021, the answer appears to have finally started to become no with even Tennessee deciding to take down his commemoration in the state house and his grave site, with gigantic statue, moved from downtown Memphis. Many others, some on public and many on private land, remain. What they represent is how we want to look at the defining characteristics of our shared history, who is part of the group, who is not, and therein how do we consider ourselves?

The argument that culture wars over history is often discounted as a modern phenomenon, but in fact, this is not a new process. Choosing what to venerate, idealize, and ignore is an ongoing process within all countries and is central to developing a shared myth of national identity. These choices create a foundation that binds a group together based on what it believes it is or would like to be. It often creates the expectations of who should be economically successful or in positions of power. What links individuals into a population is just as important as how many people there are or will be.

Labor Market Access and Reconsidering the Group

Opportunities to get a job, enjoy career success, and build for the future are critical not only for individuals but also for the prosperity of a population. Ensuring women's access to the labor market can be transformative. Legal and cultural protections for women's rights and education facilitate women's entry into the workforce, which in turn can affect the number of children they plan to have. Furthermore, when a large proportion of the women in a society work, it has the effect of increasing the human capital in the next generation, as a wealthier family can invest more in their children's health and education. This tendency expands the population's overall labor force by expanding who is allowed to be employed, and in turn, it kicks off the start of a country's demographic transition by changing the fertility choices of the newly employed individuals, who in many cases have fewer children.

The implementation of women's rights policy may in effect be the causal lever that catalyzes development in a traditional society or sets a country on a path toward the early stages of the demographic transition.[4] This change can also contribute to both rising urbanization and higher demands for contraception.[5] Contraception is a technological innovation that reorganizes basic human household systems. These societal effects were observed well into the nineteenth-century Industrial Revolution, as rural, often highly conservative women workers moved to urban areas to work in new factory environments. Similar flows occur today in nearly every developing country—with India a fascinating case.[6] The individual-level trauma of these changes must also be acknowledged, even if these periods of migration are temporary. Even if movement is an accepted part of an individual's life, leaving everything one has known—one's social circle, friends, family, and the streets of one's youth—for something unknown is a type of trauma. Culture shocks can inflict physiological shock on a person, and it is important that we acknowledge that movement is not easy and that costs are more than just monetary.

International organizations such as the World Bank and the International Labor Organization suggest that, globally, over half of women's productive potential is ignored.[7] They suggest that should this potential be unlocked, significant double-digit economic expansion would result in countries with limited women's rights. The process by which global norms and structures could be rearranged to facilitate women's entry into the labor force is unclear, but it *is* clear that those norms are key to change.[8]

Discrimination against or the restriction of opportunities for certain groups involves more than just gender bias. Whether it stems from domestic power concerns or from inherent biases toward "others," discrimination is a constant across nations.

Even though the costs of discrimination are not borne equally on a personal level, in nations with higher degrees of racial, religious, or gender-based discrimination, discriminatory policies undermine the capacity of the population. In many countries, domestic support for such policies reflects a broad desire to reinforce the population's homogeneity via legislation; limitations on immigration or even marriage may represent attempts to preserve the "integrity" of the dominant group.

Nationalism Is Popular

The myth of nationalism is that each nation represents a strict continuation of the population from one particular region—that one's ancestors must always have been German, Russian, Chinese, Japanese, American, Canadian, and so forth. Each of these national groups now display rising nationalistic tendencies, and each is, at best, rewriting history to fit a narrative of unity and continuation. However, each is a nation of mass migration, cultural changes, and diversity in terms of race, ethnicity, language, and religion, to such an extent that myths of continuation become intentionally vague, with actual history less important than some claim of domestic superiority.

Germans, for example, originate from an amalgamation of different tribes who moved long ago to the modern region of Germany, probably from further east during the era of the Roman Empire. Germans descend from Goths, Celts, and Romans; they are part of the greater Frankish group; and they have overlapped with Slavs for centuries. Of course, Germans exist, but claims that they were birthed from what today is German soil ignore the history of the area. A similar story is true for Russians, as well. Modern Russia, with its capital of Moscow, looks not to its current territory as a point of origin but instead locates its source in modern-day Ukraine, where the older Rus people originated. This group was most likely an amalgamation of Roman, Greek, Viking, and Slav, with a host of other long-forgotten tribes as well. We see these myths of origin too in Japan: an island nation that loves to discuss the wonders of homogeneity but that, when pushed, remembers that it, too, is born from different waves of migration from diverse regions of East Asia. The indigenous Ainu, mass migration from what would become Korea, and other migrants from island chains near China gave birth to the modern Japanese. This indisputable part of Japanese history can be seen in small museums, tombs on the coast, and genetics—but not within the nationalistic stories told by supposed native sons. Nowhere are these mythical origin stories starker than in the nations of the Americas. Most nations seem to have forgotten that they are unquestionably born from both native peoples and some of the most significant migration movements ever recorded in history.

Discrimination Is Popular and Expensive

Discrimination undercuts societies by spending time and money to make a proportion of a state, country, or region less educated, less efficient, and less financially successful. How can discriminatory policies that destroy economic growth, such as apartheid or segregation, be explained? One argument could be that a country's leadership trusts only one segment of its population. What if the government gives that subgroup resources, political influence, and power to reinforce the group's loyalty to the nation? The creation of trust not for all citizens but only for the select few could be a reason for such detrimental policies to have such popularity directly within the law or in cultural attitudes expressed by how that law is implemented. Can ethnic minorities believe in fair judges, police, employers, or is discrimination undermining the basic constructs of a society?

Discrimination against women has not declined at the same rate that education opportunities for women have increased at near globally universal levels. In almost every country in the developed world (and in most developing countries, including those with limited women's rights), women are attending school at higher and higher rates.[9] U.S. college campuses routinely enroll higher percentages of women than men, with some going well past 60 percent women. Others have gone so far as to discuss if they should directly recruit men because of this type of disparity. Even though higher education has become dominated by women in some places, this is not to say that this trend holds true in every field or discipline or that there are no stark differences between gender ratios in fields like engineering and education. What is essential to consider is that in this new generation, the most-educated segments of the population in the developed world will be female, and remarkably, this most-educated part of the population will not be the most prestigious or influential. Never has this happened. On the contrary, the most educated have usually been the most powerful and the wealthiest.

The societal influences that have created this new world are complex.[10] Men are often pressured by their families to enter manual labor jobs or to put physical work ahead of education. Women, meanwhile, still retain traditional (read limited) career choices; however, due to universal public education, they gain greater public prestige when successful in terms of awards or accolades but not income. In many nations, we see the interesting contradiction that women are encouraged to pursue education (which is often a particularly expensive national investment, particularly higher education) but are discouraged from putting that education to use. While this trend is baffling from an economic perspective, it is a common one cross-nationally. This is one example of a norm that international organizations have tried to incentivize that has not necessarily translated into the expected economic growth.

Consider the worst-case scenario if women become increasingly educated to the point that they grow into the most substantial proportion of a country's educated population. If they remain restricted in terms of economic, political, and cultural opportunities, the costs would be extraordinary and, importantly, far larger than what they would have been otherwise if the women in question had never been educated. The choice for a country to invest in women—but not profit from them—is remarkably bad, but one made not as policy but by the belief that for some reason discrimination is more important even at very high costs. As universal education policies became normalized, at no point did policy makers ask what the newly educated population would do with their educations or how men and women would use them differently. Must countries that educate people also allow them to use their education? This question is the profound underpinning of universal education in practice, not in morality or ethics, and the answer is yes! Education without the ability to use it is just a cost!

Therefore, even though policies of discrimination abatement extend access to education to women, political systems must have the necessary flexibility and capacity to productively channel these newly educated women into careers or other pursuits. The reality is that many governments have not shown that they are capable of doing so. While it is reasonably easy to educate people, it is not easy to change hiring practices and family expectations.

Education Needs to Have a Point

Consider, dear reader, my discussions from chapter 2. One of the most exciting parts of development is that small changes have large effects, with education being the best example. Educating large proportions of women causes a population's birth rate to decline. This trend initiates the more dramatic process of putting pressure on a society to make use of this newly educated, hopefully more productive, labor force before an aging society becomes a problem. Aging societies that have not liberalized rapidly may miss the gains from human capital investment and be forced to confront important questions about dealing with an elderly population. Again, humans are not Pavlovian; nations do regularly attempt to increase their birth rates through policies of direct cost payments, tax abatement, propaganda, and a host of other marketing endeavors. Once women have the choice to have fewer children, they do, instead filling their time with years in the classroom or with a career.

To put this more starkly, societies do have a choice. On the one hand, they can choose to rely upon a small percentage of the population—in this case, men—for all things, and they can spend time, effort, and money to undermine a majority of the population—women. The result is less development, less innovation, less stability, and less of everything except for a higher birth rate. On the other hand, they can choose education, which lowers the birth rate rapidly, forces the liberalization of family norms and employment, and could put pressure on the need for immigration in the long run. While these choices may seem overly dramatic and polarized, but as representative examples of national policy choices, this is the world.

In amalgamated national statistics with a shared scatter plot, figure 6.1 further investigates the remarkably consistent correlation between women's years of schooling and birth rates. Consider the importance of using years of schooling, rather than educational attainment or other achievement measures, as a variable. This variable measures not knowledge acquisition but time, often a decade or more of time. When individuals expend so much of their most valuable asset (life) on higher education instead of on the other essential and fantastic aspects of humanity that they could pursue—from jobs to love and the finding of partners—it shifts expectations of relationships, marriage, and childbearing

FIG. 6.1. Policy from Correlation: Years of Schooling to Birth Rate

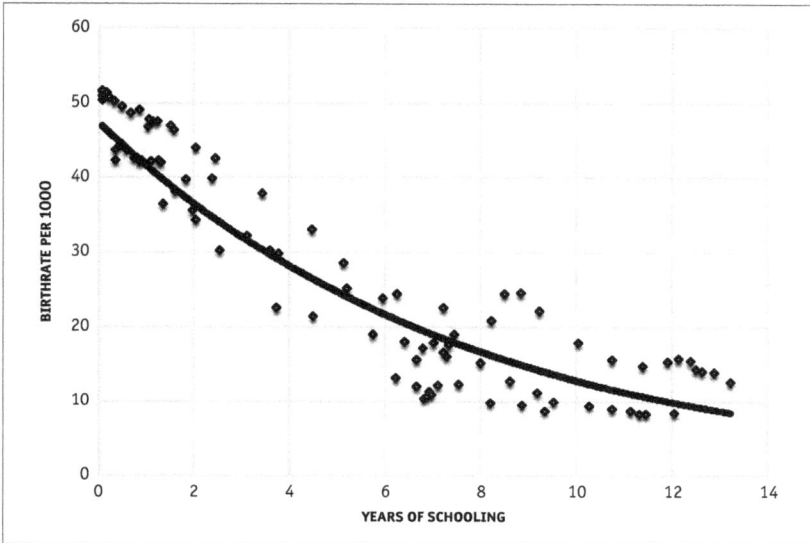

FIG. 6.1. Policy from Correlation: Years of Schooling to Birth Rate

Source: United Nations, Department of Economic and Social Affairs, Population Division 2015b;
Barro and Lee 2013

back from one's midteens (in traditional societies) to one's late twenties or early thirties. Time is finite, and nine months is a long time. So when a woman has her first child, this creates the following choices to have two or more simply because of where she is in her life and what she would like to spend time doing.[11] Combine this with the enormous investment of time required to raise children, and we can see that increased education may lead to fewer children being born not necessarily because parents have more knowledge or economic opportunity but because they have less time.

Figure 6.1 is a remarkable graphic, showing a direct negative correlation between birth rates and women's years of schooling. This correlation shapes much of today's development assistance; organizations link women's rights to microloans, cell phone access, and an assortment of similar gender-based policies in an attempt to start or accelerate development, which has the secondary effect of reducing birth rates. Currently, the most significant proportion of those living in dire poverty globally are women. With these development-oriented interventions in mind, the question becomes: Does the greater political and societal system allow newly invested in individuals to create the gains they are expected to achieve?

More Gender Bias and Employment

Gender-based pressure is not directed only toward women; it is a core component of life for all people.[12] These pressures often influence the lives and career paths of both men and women, which in turn affect how they contribute to the growth or stagnation of their societies' economic and demographic trajectories. Gender beliefs, stereotypes, and structures cannot be divorced from one another. Men are generally pressured into more violent professions—such as military service, public safety, or manufacturing jobs. We also expect women to move toward jobs perceived as more nurturing—such as nursing, teaching, or careers in human resources. These pressures arise in part from perceived differences in biology, which are profoundly challenging to divorce from societal incentives. The critical point is that, although I focus on the more problematic aspects of gender-based pressure, it is not necessarily a moral issue. What that pressure becomes or will become in the future is a normative or organizational question. Nevertheless, the existence of these pressures is constant.

Women have been limited for generations by societal doubts about their competence or capacity for leadership. To counter these assumptions, several organizations aim to create "pipelines" of qualified women candidates for political office, match women with mentors, assist with political fundraising, and even direct scholarship payments to higher education institutions. In addition, these organizations empower their members and help acclimate workplaces and employers to new expectations for women's employment.

The issue at hand connects directly with two demographic trends: first, that women will be the most-educated group in the next generation, and second, that in so many countries this next generation will be smaller. Therefore, what these educated women will want to do with their credentials, what they will be allowed to do, and most importantly, what type of education they achieve—as education creates future possibilities and sustains personal income—will radically alter what can be expected of the labor force.

These expectations are essential. Take, for example, South Korea, which has recently seen a small increase in the number of women at higher levels of management. Many of these women rose to their positions not from within South Korean firms but from within Western firms, where they contended with less overt discrimination and, more importantly, less-rigid expectations of the positions they should or could hold. The seniority-based promotion policies throughout South Korea and most of East Asia limit a female candidate's ability to move to higher career levels based on merit. This is linked to the "continuing curve" phenomenon of women's employment: women often leave their jobs in their late twenties or early thirties due to pressures of family and child-rearing, and because of that choice, they reenter the labor market in a worse career position a few years later. The combination of cultural norms and the "continuing curve" means that many of the higher-level women managers in South Korea moved to those positions first in less-discriminatory Western firms, then made lateral moves to Korean firms. While this trend represents a form of liberalization, it is based on exogenous, not domestic, effects. Change is slow but necessary, and no place needs a higher degree of productive labor than the two oldest countries in the world: South Korea and Japan.

Forced Family Planning and Gender Imbalance

Gender bias can have far more troubling effects. Prejudice in the workplace, for all its unpleasantness, is but one form of discrimination. Another involves existence itself. Gender imbalances, seen at their highest ratios in the Caucasus region, certain provinces of China, and parts of India, are a profound cultural and developmental problem. Traditionally, the literature has argued that this demographic structure is the outcome of two intertwined problems. The first is state-level, top-down family planning, and the second is a cultural preference for men over women.

The simplest way of investigating this issue is to look at the largest case: China. In China, the one-child-per-family program forcibly attempted to control (and by that, I mean decrease) the country's birth rates.[13] The idea was simple: if birth rates could be decreased, the following generation could be more prosperous than the previous one, so long as economic growth outpaced population growth. If the difference between population growth and economic growth could be enlarged, so individual economic success would increase. This plan was backed not only by algebra but also by the international development community, which helped shape and market more aggressive family-planning policies within China.[14] Combined with leader Deng Xiaoping's open-market policies, the one-child policy formed one of the two pillars of China's future economic success: reduced population and significant economic growth.

However, at no time did policy makers ask the question of how the one-child policy would affect families' and individuals' decisions to have children. The policy directly changed China's future. Yes, it likely increased the momentum of decline in the birth rate, but that change was already happening in the country, spurred by massive economic liberalization policies in the late 1970s and early 1980s. The policy also exacerbated China's demographic transition and the future aging of its population, but those effects would only become clear thirty years after the policy was implemented.

So, what would turn out to be the most dynamic, most problematic, and most damaging consequence of the policy? The selection of males over females. In a traditional Chinese family, male children are expected to support their parents' future retirement. Women, should they become wives, enter their

husband's household. Although this system was accepted and enacted to vary-
ing degrees in practice, the cultural preference for males was deep seated. Gender roles in China are densely connected to ideas of obligation to family. The
concept of filial piety is a profound one in the region.

Thanks to Chinese families' general preference for male children, the
gender imbalances in the generations born after 1980 have been extreme.[15]
In some regions of China, the ratio is as high as 120 or even 130 males to every 100 females.[16] The norm in an unaltered group is 101 males to 100 females
at birth, and the ratio slowly shifts in favor of females over time, as men have
higher mortality rates and lower life expectancies. The exact ratios differ widely
within China due to both inconsistent policy implementation at the local level
and rapid reconsiderations of the policy itself.[17] When the gender imbalance
became known, the policy shifted to a two-child-per-family policy, with either
two children allowed in some areas, or a second child allowed should the first
be a girl.

A combination of infanticides and sex-selective abortion created the gender imbalance. Some estimates also suggest that tens of millions of daughters
are undocumented by China's public education and legal documentation systems. When given a choice, families had to decide which was more important,
a son or a daughter.

While there are many traditional cultural practices around the world associated with control of women, most people in rural China do not practice
them. For example, rural Chinese do not arrange child marriages based on
price or a dowry, practice kidnapping as a marriage ceremony, engage in temporary polygamy, or fixate on virginity. So how does a country without many
extreme gender norms or expectations of group violence create a policy that
provides such a remarkable example of biases writ large?

At its core, population growth reflects the choices of women given a set of
interests. Cultural pressures, and maybe even biological needs, set the terms of
these interests. I discuss at length in this book that increasing economic opportunity and rates of education decrease birth rates, but combine that with a dramatically smaller number of actual women in society, and you get both men
who are not able to find partners and women who can be both more individually successful and far more desirable. This combination pushes marriage rates
down, and declines in births exacerbate the already existing population decline
issue.[18]

Who would have predicted that a policy designed around the wonders
of simple division could reorganize the necessary foundations of humanity in
unexpected ways, creating a future far older, smaller, and with gender issues
yet unknown in their intensity and complexity? The answer is that everyone
should have known that at the time. The damage caused is extraordinary.

Vast amounts of time, capacity, and money allowed such a sweeping policy to be implemented and supported.[19] The policy came to stand for more than just its effects; it became a symbol of government responsibility, despite the high degree of violence it has engendered and recent reconsiderations of the policy's scale. China's one-child policy is singular in size and length; almost two full generations lived under its dictates.[20] To be loyal to the policy was to be loyal to the government. It became not just a domestic affair but a cornerstone of the Chinese Communist Party's ideology.

From one to two children per family, to added exceptions and a host of other bureaucratic changes over these past forty years, what is now a cultural norm is not going to change because of a law that the government passed. Not many families are waiting for the ability to have a third child or even more children. The next part of the story is what is important: China will likely not be able to attract an immigrant population sufficient to compensate for its aging demography, and its domestic birth rates must increase.

In 2015, the one-child policy (which was never exactly that for most of the country) was relaxed to a universal two-child policy for rural and urban populations.[21] The expectation is that the number of children will increase, but most assume that this will be a temporary phenomenon. The essential core of Chinese society has changed due to economic movement and the policy itself. Why should women want to have more children, even if they are now allowed?

Policies of this magnitude are sticky. Even when abated, they continue to influence individuals' choices and concerns. The social pressures that we all deal with and that create our interests heavily influence what we want for our own family. No matter how a policy may be from a governmental or demographic perspective, policy change is not sufficient to change the fundamental core of society's interests quickly or at the level of radical change that would be needed in China to sustain its population. While a given policy may influence or nudge people toward specific actions, even that overstates policy's direct involvement in people's lives. A policy can incentivize the population, influence it, and even coerce it, but it cannot control it. The policies and actions that lead to gender imbalance or societal prejudice thus cannot be so easily diluted.

Processes that create and reinforce gender imbalances are not unique to China. For instance, the mass production of cheap ultrasound machines and continued gender discrimination in South Asia and the Caucasus have generated similar issues caused by sex-selective abortions. These regions, however, do not have the excuse of a totalitarian top-down policy. India attempted a policy similar to China's that involved forced sterilization, but it was never able to implement it to the same degree.

This diverse scope of policies worldwide threatens to create a range of future problems, with some regions seeing increased imbalances and others, such as China, showing abatement. In general, family-planning policies became more liberalized in the 1990s alongside high-profile efforts to secure women's rights around the globe. This trend was dramatically illustrated at the 1994 International Conference on Population and Development held in Cairo, where it was argued that government-imposed forced family-planning programs are at their core attacks on women's rights that perpetuate violence for the sake of expected development.[22]

Continued Policy Influences of Malthus

It seems simplistic to think that these types of policies were generated by a fanatic level of worry during the late 1960s, but fears of overpopulation leading to environmental destruction were reignited in the modern era with Paul Ehrlich's 1968 book *The Population Bomb*. This text served as a near Bible to those who believed that humanity was nearing a cliff of doom. The core of the book's argument, like that of Malthus almost two hundred years earlier, was that humanity would outeat, outconsume, and outwork Earth's ability to feed its ever-rising population. The book was of its era: a period of rapid, unprecedented global population growth. A timely combination of expanded public health programs, access to food, and an overall decline in war created massive youth bulges and growth throughout much of the world, principally the developing world. *Population Bomb* described this as a horror, not as a success. Its core thesis argued that human life is only essential when measured in total and that individual needs and wants can and should be surrendered for the estimated greater good. This "greater good," however, would in practice sacrifice the growth of impoverished families in the developing world to better the situation for wealthier Western populations.

Neo-Malthusians became the cause célèbre of new environmental movements in the 1970s. Groups such as the Sierra Club financed contraception efforts in the developing world and supported the violent family-planning policies in India and China. Although many believed that the very concept of population growth was unquestionably a problem, the process by which the total population of the Earth could be artificially reduced from billions to, at best, hundreds of millions was left to the imagination.[23]

The failure of the neo-Malthusians is the same as the failure of the eugenicists. People are not radically different from one another. They only live under different political and economic systems, and these systems can be changed. The rise of women's rights, for example, decreased the popularity of government-imposed family-planning and sterilization policies—which are, at their core, attacks on women—by the mid-1990s.[24] The groups supporting eugenics and those that created the neo-Malthusian movement were also similar in scope and scale. Race and class played as much a role in both movements as they did in which countries utilized them.[25] The concept that populations can be "bettered" via a policy of birth alternation and limitation raises the question of who and what is "better."

The tragedy of these horrific policies—of decades of forced sterilization, abortion, bribes, hidden children, and lost potential—is that the demographic transition inevitably becomes a reality anyway. The policies themselves might have accelerated declines in birth rates, but the policies did not create the declines. Birth rates fall almost instantly as economic development begins to increase. The extension of even the lowest levels of education to disenfranchised groups, particularly to women, radically decreases fertility rates and alters demographic expectations.[26] The data do not support the idea that people will never change their interests or are fixated on biological needs or the concept that innovation cannot keep up with population growth. Ehrlich's prediction of a constant population boom did not happen, nor could it have happened.[27] Most modern Malthusians, however, continue to ignore this fact.

Today, doom seems more popular than optimism. If suddenly tomorrow in the United States every person was given a half an acre of land, the whole population of the country could fit within the state of Texas.[28] Texas may have decent barbecue and a widely respected music tradition, but it is not even the largest state in the United States. The scale of this trivia fact illustrates the reality of the size of the world's wealthiest country and the scale of the planet itself. Continued urbanization trends, for example, will change what the planet can sustain, as will the outcomes of so many other choices that humans will make in the coming years. Ignoring scale or innovation is always a dangerous assumption and believing that we as humans are incapable of changing ignores so much of our basic history. The danger is pessimism: belief that change is unknown or unachievable, even if it is known and can be done. We as humans know what can be done to change our use of resources. It comes down to if we make the choice to do it, which is a far easier problem than to create the unknown.

CHAPTER 7

Foreign Policy in an Era of Demographic Change

Alongside discriminatory policies and war, a third danger threatens to upend nations' future growth and stability: an overemphasis on domestic needs at the expense of international considerations. Focusing on the European Union (EU), Japan, and select developing nations, this chapter analyzes how difficult it can be for modern nations to sustain the policy choices that contributed to their achievement of wealth and peace once these policies butt heads with powerful domestic interests. I consider both failed expansion policies reliant on conflict and, in turn, the rise of coalitions as an alternative. New trends of isolationism and opposition to international trade threaten to undermine nations' demographic potential. These ideologies ignore the realities of the demographic transition and the possibility that following the loss of a youthful workforce, a nation's economic and population growth may decline into a morass of corruption and disorganization. As I discuss in chapter 4, immigration, given the structure to help new arrivals assimilate, can expand a country's potential by enlarging its labor force.

The current international system was born from the fires of World War II and raised amid the Cold War. Its parents are the great powers of the twentieth century: the United Kingdom (UK), France, the Soviet Union, and the United States. The dominant power—the United States—created most of what we today consider to be international norms. By the late 1940s, the United States's dizzying combination of population size and productivity had propelled its economy to close to 50 percent of the entire world's gross domestic product (GDP). While U.S. GDP is today at a modern historical low, the country continues to account for over 50 percent of worldwide military expenditures. American dominance has thus had an outsized influence on today's systems of international law and the current style of trade and diplomatic relationships.

As we look ahead to what will happen next in the international system, it will be essential to consider possible power transitions, particularly as age comes to the old great powers and economic success comes to the new. Because power creates the systems of the future, how power itself is created and sustained—the concepts behind its use or loss—matter fundamentally as nations assess which policies they should pursue.

Power at its core is the ability to influence others to implement policy preferences. In every policy realm—spanning the conduct of trade, the creation of labor laws, the wonders of environmentalism, the currency used and how it is used, and numerous other considerations from outer space to the Antarctic—the interests and beliefs of the powerful matter more than the interests and beliefs of the rest. The next logical questions are: Who becomes powerful? How is power created? Where does it come from? And if we assume that power itself is of interest to nations—in other words, that nations would in fact want to be influential—why then do so many countries make choices that undermine their own ability to create a more prosperous future? Remember, although so much of power is tied to physical force, power itself primarily rests on economic influence and the capabilities of the population.

A Brief Guide to Money, War, and Marketing

The popular conception in support of violence between nations is that it is aimed at winning resources, money, and power. In the past, states relied on military policy to expand their populations, territory, and, in turn, their power on a global stage. They assumed that by covering more of the world in their own flags, they would also enjoy additional influence. The point of a nation-state's international policy was to expand its own borders.

The marketing in favor of expansion and colonization, particularly amid the land grabs of the eighteenth century, relied upon a profoundly limited proposition: that great wars could be fought, victories could be won, and in the conquest, the spoils of success could pay for all that was spent. This logic suggests that war was based upon a cost-benefit analysis, with mass death and destruction justified by profit. Would-be imperial powers, including Russia, Japan, Great Britain, France, Italy, Spain, and the United States, regularly justified military intervention throughout the world by arguing for the economic justification for owning desolate regions. If that meant invading the middle of the Sahara Desert, the tops of the Himalayas, or the most isolated of islands, so be it. All seemed to become viable targets of brutality with little regard for whether the marketing was accurate.

What is the point of control over the largest desert in the world or the highest mountains? Is ownership of pretty islands in the middle of the South Pacific genuinely important, or only important in terms of some overarching, unscrupulous concept of strategy? By the height of the empire craze in the late nineteenth century, when seemingly every European nation had overseas armies and colonies, it quickly became clear that violence can become too costly to sustain.

That is the problem with the marketing! To be economically successful, a nation needs jobs, industry, education, investment, and, most importantly, peace. The reality for most empires is that they cannot rely on invading some other defenseless nation that happens to live on a gold mine. The conquering empire needs the occupied population to work, build, create, and then be taxable. Taxes, after all, are the foundation of any economy, including that of the occupier itself. Why would an occupied population want peace in this situation? Why would they agree to work with a foreign empire at all? With this in mind, the empires' options become clear. To economically justify the imperial enterprise, most ended up moving toward one of two polarized policies: the first was massive repression, and the second was attempted integration.

The most powerful examples of imperial horror can be seen in what is today the Democratic Republic of the Congo and in Indonesia, both of which were once controlled by smaller European powers. The former was ruled by the king of Belgium, the latter by the Netherlands, and both were sites of massive export-oriented natural rubber and palm oil plantations. The colonial powers ran these industries with vast amounts of violence—pushing the populations to starvation and inflicting mass casualties—as they attempted to extract as much value from the territories as possible. The occupiers presumably had no real interest in long-term control over the territories or their people, and they enacted repression, theft, horror, and genocide all for the sake of extraction.

Imperial powers that attempted the second method of control—integration—granted populations citizenship, the right to vote, legal protections, and even some degree of say in local affairs. Investments in the economy came later with trains, universities, plumbing, justice systems, and all the rest. Colonialists justified these long-term investments as supporting their original argument that the areas they subsumed as part of their empire-building endeavors would have value in the future, whether these lands were the largest desert in the world or the shores of Somalia. Again, profit justified occupation, with increased liberties additionally important from a rhetoric standpoint; "invasion for their own good" is a common popular argument. From Algeria to the Philippines, Puerto Rico, and even Ireland, colonized nations throughout the world suffered from this combination of repression, investment, liberalization, and reconsideration during the latter half of the twentieth century.

Colonialism and conflict over resources defined the eighteenth, nineteenth, and twentieth centuries. These arguments over the importance of resources continue to be the most common marketing for war in our modern age, but like they have in the past, they continue to fail. It is simply untrue that

European empires or control over vast distances were in any way economically justified. In the long run, these policies failed and undercut the capabilities of the nation's attempting to implement them.

Winners Do Not Fight, Often

By the end of World War I, the period of direct expansionary colonialism was over. War is no longer a useful tool in today's era of dense population centers, well-organized nonstate actors, and strong nationalistic attitudes. While a few countries continue to consider attempts to expand territory, any gains in territory or population size via military action are generally too costly to justify. It is no longer possible for nations to alter their borders with impunity; these actions have consequences, and organized sanctions are common punishments.[1] Even the smallest wars are shockingly expensive and seldom lead to massive gains in either population or resources. The rate of return for war is low, at best, and war is likely to become less and less viable as a means of increasing the power of a nation.

In Norman Angell's seminal work on military power, he suggests that, before World War I, the increased military spending of Europe's great powers and the rhetoric of war's inevitability missed the essential truth that war was not financially supportable.[2] My goodness, it is hard to find a war more absurd than World War I! Major European powers killed millions of each other's citizens throughout the world, all so that, in the end, borders stayed nearly the same, a few countries were created in central Europe, and an even worse war would be fought by the next generation. All this conflict occurred primarily between countries that were similar to each other industrially, educationally, and physically, and hence were each other's closest economic partners.

Conflict in the modern era increases neither wealth nor power, only misery. Angell wrote:

> Are we, in blind obedience to primitive instinct and old prejudices, enslaved by the old catchwords and that curious indolence which makes the revision of old ideas unpleasant, to duplicate indefinitely on the political and economic side a condition from which we have liberated ourselves on the religious side? Are we to continue to struggle, as so many good men struggled in the first dozen centuries of Christendom—spilling oceans of blood, wasting mountains of treasure—to achieve what is at the bottom a logical absurdity; to accomplish something which, when accomplished, can avail us nothing, and which, if it could avail us anything, would condemn the nations of the world to never-ending bloodshed and the constant defeat of all those aims which men, in their sober hours, know to be alone worthy of sustained endeavor?[3]

Angell believed in the importance of peace and worked to proselytize its advantages. He dedicated much of his life to undercutting the argument that war was unavoidable or that the point of being a great power was to fight. He argued that these norms (he called them morals) can be changed. After the bloodiest war in human history, World War II, the understanding that war should be prevented provided much of the theoretical foundation for the new international system. Organizing nations embraced the idea that we are not cursed to follow the path of earlier generations: that new institutions and law could reorient the basic concepts of the international system.

Modern Conflict and the Cost of Military Power

The logical counterpoint to Angell's argument is that war itself is, in fact, rare. As I discuss in several of this book's earlier chapters, war in all its forms is no longer a phenomenon that most of the world will see in person. Even in the conflicts fought in Afghanistan and Iraq, those on the side of the North Atlantic Treaty Organization NATO or the coalition of the willing did not see counteractions—sea battles, devastation of cities, or hundreds of thousands of casualties—of the scale that was so common in both great wars.

Today, conflict in its truest sense is isolated from the richest and most powerful. It is on the periphery of the developed world, not within it. The idea that actual war in all its destructive horror would touch cities of the developed world has become extremely unlikely, or even impossible, thanks to the powers of alliances and even nuclear deterrence. Supporters of a more peaceful world would even point to plummeting defense budgets, since the end of the Cold War, that was the outcome of successful unity of allies. Among NATO nations, nearly all military budgets have fallen well below targeted expenditures:[4] air forces that once had hundreds of planes now consider if they should have tens; navies that once had dozens of submarines, frigates, destroyers, and even multiple aircraft carriers all now hope to have a quarter of those numbers, or even less. Money has been pulled out of militaries due to a lack of concern about new wars in Europe, the final fall of empires, and domestic political considerations about the value of war. If casualties are so damaging to elected officials' popularity, then why spend money to go to war, only to lose the next election?

Modern conflicts between major nations seem to be fixated not on power or even money but on other considerations, such as domestic propaganda or even a limited imagination. It would be challenging to suggest, for instance, that today's most powerful nation, the United States, became even more powerful or financially successful after the second Iraq invasion in 2003. Thousands of Americans died, hundreds of thousands of Iraqis were killed, and trillions of dollars were spent, and the war ended with little direct advantage for the United States. More likely, the conflict directly led to the creation of future threats to the region and the world, such as ISIS.

Even now, major politicians still claim that the wars in Iraq and later in Syria were justified because the United States "took the oil." This is a bafflingly strange belief, as the oil in both countries remains in the control of the countries themselves. Modern warfare, again, is not a Viking raid. No country can steal thousands of barrels of oil produced daily over months and then years by magic. It cannot be done—the local population itself would not allow it. Beyond that, it is against international law. Stealing a painting or looting a museum is not credibly the same as large-scale industrial mining over decades because, given the costs of any modern conflict, it would be impossible to somehow pay for the war from looted nations. The most overly optimistic arguments for the invasion of Iraq were based on some misconception that, after the occupation, the United States could just extract oil to pay itself for the costs of the conflict. Worse, oil is the cornerstone of the Syrian and Iraqi economies and accounts for much of the governments' budgets.[5] It beggars belief that tens of millions of Iraqis or Syrians would just ignore empty schools, broken water and electric infrastructure, cracked roads, and no police, fire, or emergency medical services, all caused by an invading army, and do nothing. Yes, oil is important, but access to oil is more important than control of it. Who is more important: the country that must sell oil to have an economy, or the country that buys oil from that seller, but could choose to buy it from others?

Similarly, can the Russians be called more powerful based on their annexation of Crimea? As so often is claimed, Russia gained full control over a warm water port on a peninsula whose primary purpose in the twenty-first century is to be the old Soviet version of central Florida: a region of retirement homes with the elderly living out their golden years near the sea. This seems to be nineteenth-century politics. What could be the value of abandoned, decade-old ports and retirement communities? Considering the costs associated with sanctions after the annexation, the need to militarily protect the territory, the later investments and bridge building to then make the annexation "worth it," it is as if Russia ignored the failures of prior European empires and tried their policies again.

On paper, this form of military action is financially unjustified. It is a failure from the moment it starts and, worse, could cause greater conflict in the future. Now, as this book is being published the worst case for the Russians has been realized with their expanded invasion of Ukraine. As of July 2022, it would seem to be one of the worst foreign policy decisions of the twenty-first century. It has directly expanded NATO with both Finland and Sweden being fast tracked into the alliance. It has forced Western European democracies to no longer assume that territorial conquest via war is no longer a part of the European experience, and now, they are expanding their military expenditures in direct defense from Russia. This new lack of trust with Russia is now under-cutting the only major export Russia still has, which is its energy exports, and their primary market, which was reenforced from decades of infrastructure investment in Western democratic wealth in Europe. Since the fall of the USSR, Europe in general has moved to attempt to normalize relationships with Russia and the former USSR states. The direct possible conflict between NATO and the Warsaw Pact is a part of history. Economic trust became part of the normalized diplomatic relationship and with it money flows from real estate in London to luxury goods sold in Moscow. The new peace saw rapid declines in military expenditure throughout Europe as who they were defending from became unthinkable. This diplomatic myth of Russia as a country that can be part of the expected norms of how developed nations act to one another has been heavily undermined by the first interstate conflict between developed nations since World War II.

What then is the future: a vastly more Western Ukraine, millions of refugees that might lose the ability to return and hence not be allowed to rebuild, mass reeducation attempts to force Russian culture on non-Russians, policies that would seem to be ethnic cleansing but hopefully without the mass killing of civilians? While these things seem extremely unlikely, Ukraine is a technologically advanced nation with nuclear technology. Wars tend to make nations reconsider if the most extreme choice of a nuclear deterrent is needed. I would like to say again that this is the last policy I would expect of a nation that is attempting to join the EU, but one that could be done. They have the technological capacity but hopefully will choose a different path. What then could this mean for the Russian regional hegemony? Are Central Asian countries that cannot think of their borders as being safe going to move to the embrace of China? China is again increasingly in influence with Russia itself as it becomes a central source of modern commercial products and a market for energy exports. Worse for Russia, now they are dependent on those sources no longer able to access the technical production of the West or its markets fully. Single source supplies are dangerous.

This all leads to claims that all this disaster was the attempt by the Russian government to gain additional support from the population by looking tough against foreign foes. The war markets supposed international success to a population that might not know the difference with the news so heavily controlled by the central government.

In each case, neither the United States nor Russia was motivated by what Angell or I would consider true concerns. A "true" war is one that can be lost while trying to win, one that devastates large percentages of the population and one that has consequences for the basic foundations of nations, demography, and economics.

Consider both modern Russia and China, two of the most influential nations of the twentieth century. As I discuss throughout this book, China's growth can be attributed to domestic changes and increased access to world markets. However, seemingly for propaganda reasons, it continues to spend time, effort, and money undercutting the remarkable gains it has achieved by engaging in small territorial disagreements over barren islands or the tops of mountains. Worse, these disagreements have become so popular among the population as a whole that, should China reach negotiated settlements with India over the borders in the Himalayas and with every South Asian country in the South China Sea, it would be politically tricky domestically and could undermine popular support for the government. Much of the government's legitimacy among the public has been built on an idea that only *they* can protect the nation of China from returning to the years of betrayal and occupation by foreign would-be colonial powers—such as Japan, Germany, the UK, France, and Russia prior to World War II—an era of foreign invasion, civil war, territorial loss, and, to Chinese nationalists, humiliation. Continued support for violence on China's borders by the Chinese population itself could pressure the government to escalate aggression beyond what is controllable to a serious conflict between large, organized nations. This kind of conflict has not been seen since the World Wars. It is astonishing to think that lines on mountain ranges or useless specks of sand in the ocean may cause such escalation.

War over the disputed islands in the South China Sea would not increase China's power in the international sphere, only its domestic popularity. China is no more economically assertive by building artificial islands in the South China Sea; it gains nothing from a resource standpoint that it could not have already gotten by simply engaging in trade. If anything, the potential costs could be enormous. These island disputes disrupt China's relationships with neighboring countries, all of whom are now playing complex games of international law and shoring up their militaries. Vietnam is rearming with new Russian Improved Kilo-class submarines, Bastion-P shore batteries, and maybe aircraft such as the SU-30/35 or proposed SU 75. It is even attempting to improve its relationship with the United States in the hope of negotiating a subsidized purchase of F-16 fighters. Malaysia is moving toward new aircraft and new Gowind frigates from France. Indonesia is purchasing from a wide range of countries, including fighters from the United States and France, armored personnel carriers from Ukraine, Sigma corvettes from the Netherlands, and U209 submarines from South Korea. Again and again, we see the same patterns, from Singapore to Japan, South Korea, and India. Militaries have thus been heavily fortified on three-quarters of China's borders, all as a result of China's own policies. Now, the possibility of violence by accident or mistake is higher than it would have been otherwise, and the economic costs of even the smallest conflict would be vast.

China's actions threaten to undermine decades of attempts to normalize relations with its neighboring nations, public discussions of China as a
new brand of great power, and even its Confucius Institute partnerships with
American universities. For years, China has claimed that it would be a great
power that would not make investments in other countries contingent on those
countries changing their domestic political arrangements. Nations could be
democracies, dictatorships, monarchies, or any other form of government, and
to China it would not matter. They claimed that all that was important was investment and support. This approach made them seem like a useful alternative
to the United States or Europe, both of which have tended to link economic
support with shared concepts of governance since the Cold War.

China has massively increased trade with light manufacturing countries,
such as Pakistan, Bangladesh, Kenya, and Nigeria. Whole economies have been
pulled into China's orbit not only because they can buy finished products from
Chinese companies but also because they can produce pieces of finished products. These pieces are most often assembled in China, making the integration
between China and these countries a global manufacturing network. They
need Chinese manufacturing to continue to buy but so do those manufacturers
themselves as they do not have alternative production. Both sides buy goods
from each other, both sides produce those same goods, and both sides would
be remarkably harmed by a disruption in business. The linkage is bidirectional.

All of this convoluted merging of industry and policy is sticky to a point.
Politics has the ability to change faster than production lines. In worrying examples of how international policy can cause disruption, recent riots in Vietnam and public protests in Malaysia have been fueled by attacks on fishing
boats by supposedly independent Chinese seaborne gangs. It is believed that
these attacks are linked with the new Chinese governments seaborn militia
and could not have happened without the support of the Chinese government
itself.[6]

The interests of domestic populations are not divorced from foreign policy. Continuing business relationships may be acceptable to countries' elites
but not to the populace. By aggressively courting a more nationalistic policy
position, China reinforces preexisting anti-Chinese sentiments in other countries. The outcome could be violence: not only between nation-states but also
against Chinese ethnic minorities in other countries, particularly in Southeast
Asian states.

Showing the inconsistency in Chinese foreign policy, China is engaged
in a long-term diplomatic attempt to increase its business and political relations across Eurasia through a series of investments called the Belt and Road
Initiative. China's overarching plan is to create a diverse, expanded transportation infrastructure in central Asia to facilitate the large-scale, complex transportation of goods between countries. This new infrastructure, combined with

new pipelines for energy exports, will integrate central Asian and even Western economies directly with China itself. The political motives are clear, and the costs are extraordinary.[7] Even with massive investment, shipping via rail is close to five times more expensive than sea-based bulk transportation. This initiative faces problems not only with connecting rail lines but also with standardizing them, as older, almost collapsed Soviet rail lines use a different gauge than modern Chinese rail lines.

In financial terms, these infrastructure projects must be genuinely immense for China to recoup its investment, a prospect made even more challenging by the fact that the projects run through several countries whose governments have transparency issues, making conflict a real possibility. China does, however, hope that the projects will accelerate the regional expansion of its political influence, a consideration that may explain its choice to invest even if the projects are unlikely to be highly successful and profitable from a financial standpoint. China will face some tough choices in the coming years when domestic expenditures become stressed. Will it be worth it to continue these expensive infrastructure enhancement policies?

World Wars and Nuclear Weapons

While war is, on the whole, incredibly rare in today's world, even the unlikeliest of actions is still a possibility. Nations often have made choices that seem beyond the pale or without reason. The most important technological invention in the history of mankind in terms of our ability to destroy is the invention of nuclear weapons. Although nuclear weapons have only been used twice, no other technology has ever had so much destructive potential.

Nuclear war seems to be an almost mystical consideration in modern policy discussions; it is more often understood as a Cold War myth or a plot in an apocalypse film, theoretically able to inflict conflict on so large a scale that even attempts to justify its awfulness are nothing more than a fiction of mathematics. The consequences would be so enormous as to defy estimation, and even a limited war using these weapons would be more extensive than the World Wars. The continued existence and even expansion of nuclear capabilities should continue to be worrisome because of the scale of the potential damage. Conflict is deferred until it is not, and a war fought for some forgotten reason has the potential to lead to devastation unprecedented in human history, erasing cities and whole countries from the map. Nuclear war would thus be genocide as foreign policy.

This book does not deal directly with issues of global military powers, nuclear proliferation, or rising possibilities of escalation beyond acknowledging that they exist and should always be a consideration. A low likelihood of nuclear war is not zero. As with war in general, it is rare until it is not. Conflict is primarily about grievances, norms, arguments, and resources. The issue with nuclear weapons is that they recalibrate the concerns of force. They cannot be realistically used to deescalate. Worse, a massive attack aimed at destroying the possibility of a counterattack would be the most likely scenario to arise between nuclear armed states, and that would mean the infliction of substantial deaths. This first strike is why entering the game of nuclear weapons is so dangerous. For these weapons to be used effectively, they must devastate such a high percentage of the opposition that the resultant casualties would be beyond the scope of any war in modern history. Consider, dear reader, the concerns. Once a nation has these weapons, the only way to "win" a war against it is to destroy the nation. Is that a scenario you would like to exist in? What would be worth risking the totality of everything a nation is and ever could be?

Alliances and Power Projection

States commonly forge alliances with other countries to expand their ability to influence others and hence increase their power—in this case, absolute, as opposed to relative, power. These alliances are primarily military or economic and are limited in terms of the actual integration of states. They are restricted in scope and not meant to be the foundations of a new nation-state, differentiating them from organizations that may be a first step down that integration path. NATO, which focuses on cross-national military cooperation and defense, is one example of a restricted alliance. The United States–Mexico–Canada Agreement (USMCA), formerly the North American Free Trade Agreement (NAFTA), for comparison, has no military aspirations and specializes only in trade concerns in North America. The World Trade Organization WTO is larger in size and narrower in practice and focuses on limited free-trade arrangements and neutral arbitration of trade disputes. Each type of alliance does have an importance for the dominant nation within the group, as this nation can exert a greater degree of influence over both members and nonmembers. This is not to make the claim that all members of the alliance agree, but that these types of alliances, once made, reinforce the dictates of the most influential member. In the cases of NATO or USMCA or even the WTO and UN, the dominant power globally has been the United States.

While international alliances are the most common tool used to mobilize power outside of the national paradigm, they are designed to be limited and can be unreliable. Even the most stable alliance still depends on its member nations' willingness to adhere to their treaty obligations. Should a NATO member be attacked, its allies must still choose to protect it willingly; there is no coercion within the organization that can force a member country to send military troops.

Nations have historically been reluctant to intervene in other countries' conflicts because their primary concern is self-security.[8] Alliances have a built-in free-rider problem that inevitably emerges when the issue contested is less valuable to one ally than it is to another.

Military alliances, also called collective security organizations, are used not merely to enhance a state's capacity but also to deter other nations from acting against any one of the alliance's members. The scale of an alliance itself can change the mathematics of conflict between nations. In this way, alliances can influence policy simply because they exist.[9] NATO is a classic example of such a successful organization, with thirty member nations (as of 2021) that represent a wide range of economic activity, levels of technological advancement, and population size. NATO has also continued to influence members' military expenditures to such a degree that, even after the Cold War and the subsequent rapid declines in defense necessities, it retains the ability as an alliance to not only project force but also defend. The latter is the most expensive component of a military force.

NATO was initially created in 1949 by the major Western powers as a bulwark against the Soviets. It eventually became more than just a treaty; it is now an organization designed to facilitate communication, training, and technological linkages between member states. NATO helps members understand each other's capabilities and tactics—along with the complex systems and standardizations that are necessary for actual combat—so that all members can be prepared to fight together (and hopefully win) in times of crisis. From something as critical as ammunition to communication datalinks and even the methods by which armor is evaluated, NATO is designed to limit alliances' problems by creating lasting, direct, efficient, and stable norms.

Alliances such as NATO, however, are often plagued by issues of funding. Each member of NATO is expected to contribute 2 percent of its total GDP toward the maintenance of the alliance, and only seven nations out of thirty achieve that level. Those seven nations, in turn, become the most important, as their higher levels of financial commitment signal that they are willing to take a greater degree of risk. The end of the Cold War stimulated cultural changes within European countries that undermined their contributions to NATO. With the threat of the Soviet Union no longer imminent, these countries intuited that their defense expenditures would no longer, maybe, be used for the defense of their own countries but for the training and equipping of military resources that would never be used—or worse, only used overseas. That has limited the success of the alliance as a whole. Now, new conflicts in Ukraine and Syria and increased migrant flows to the Mediterranean region have altered some of that discussion, with defense expenditures increasing globally and within NATO nations themselves. The belief that Europe will remain substantially safe, with conflict well away from its borders, cannot be supported. NATO is an example of an overall successful alliance but still one with free riders, disagreements over foreign policy, and the realization that as the group increases in size, issues increase with it.

Global Power and Institutions

Another tool that perpetuates the power of dominant nations is the institutional foundation of global politics. The intergovernmental organizations that make up this foundation are not direct security arrangements but ones based on the creation of law or on reinforcing group interests. Organizations like the United Nations (UN), the World Bank, the International Monetary Fund, and many regional organizations provide glue among partners with shared preferences. They help reinforce common interests and serve to stabilize the members themselves across leadership changes from country to country. For instance, WTO advocates free trade, the UN Security Council supports the interests of great powers, and the World Health Organization (WHO) works to create cross-national medical services to act against infectious disease. Leading nations have taken advantage of this institutionalism to perpetuate their preferred norms, relying heavily on satisfied allies to preserve them.

Yet, as challenges to the world's dominant nations—the United States and its European allies—emerge, the interactions between institutions and responsiveness decline as stability and national self-preservation become significant focuses of foreign policy.[10] Do the organizations themselves have the ability to retain influence when the nations that created them no longer have it? In all multilateral actions, issues of both trust and reasonableness dictated by loose articles within a treaty arrangement come into question when they run counter to member nations' self-interest.

The great question is: Are intergovernmental institutions themselves important? Or are they only significant as a means to advertise, or even enforce, the interests of the United States and its Western allies? These systems are largely a happenstance of the post–World War II period, and the underlying institutions may be forced to alter their interests should the combination of the United States, Europe, and Japan lose the global influence necessary to sustain them.

Power aggregation by institutions is a weak replacement for national power. While many regional groups have emerged in the last fifty years, the supranational community of the EU is most visible and apparent. The EU has achieved labor and partial monetary union, but it has not yet reached a stable security arrangement. Based on its current levels of productivity, the EU-

27 could become the dominant international power now if it wanted to do it. Though it has the globe's largest GDP, organizational issues, problems of disunity, and member nations' unwillingness to act in a coordinated manner have undercut the organization's efficiency and challenged prospects that world power could be reorganized around such a loose confederation. In order to be truly powerful, some argue, the group would need an agreed-on foreign policy or even a unified military. The inefficiency of the union's many member countries pushing different industrial ambitions or public disagreements on significant issues undermine the considerable potential power of the whole.

From Multinational Empires to Independent Nation-States and Back Again?

Those inclined to take a historical perspective look at the issues plaguing the EU as something the world has seen before: the old pre–World War I European empires. Most were built on a murky combination of conflict and mergers of family dynasties. These empires introduced the notion that borders, citizenship, and even law could radically change at any moment due to diplomatic decisions connected to birthrights and blood, which the citizens themselves had no control over. The Hapsburgs are a classic example. Their reign ended with a range of ethnic groups under one unified political power, including Croatians, Slovenians, Hungarians, Transylvanians, Czechs, Germans, Poles, and many others, from Ruthenians to Armenians. Seemingly none of these groups were given a true democratic vote on their new political allegiances. That last great central European empire ranged from the poorest of communities, living lives that looked unchanged from medieval times, to the highest societies of Vienna and Prague, major cities with abundant wealth.

The Hapsburgs are often written as hapless elites who failed upward from generation to generation. Jokes about gigantic hereditary jaws caused by inbreeding cloud what can be thought of as an alternative history within Europe: the creation of a stable extranational country with a shared sense of citizenship and loyalty to a central government, one that lived in the light of liberalism and did not care about religion or ethnicity. Notice that this sounds near to a Europhile's dreams for the EU: to create something larger than individual nations that can harness the untapped power of Europe, one lost or hidden behind borders or historical accident.

These origins were lost thanks not only to the fires of World War I but also to the Hapsburgs' inability to create and institutionalize a cross-national unity relying on loyalty to the empire as opposed to loyalty to the Hapsburg family itself. This mistake created more conflict as ethnic groups gained and lost in opposition to each other. World War I thus marked the end of an often-forgotten part of European history when the continent was more ethnically and religiously diverse than it was at any other point in the twentieth century. World War and ethnic-cleansing campaigns in the 1920s, 1930s, and most horrifically the 1940s decreased Europe's diversity significantly. The inability for new nation-states to seemingly regain unity created modern Europe, which became a region of ethnic specialization rather than diversity.

We are left to wonder whether a new, reformed Hapsburg Empire would have fared better than the horrors of war that followed World War I. Perhaps a unified multiethnic state with some form of a democratic system could have harnessed efficient markets, technology, and culture to create a greater degree of human success in the region. Unification creates true gains from scale and could have kept alive the possibility of a major, stable state in the region, rather than smaller states whose later history was characterized by invasion, occupation, and a lack of independence from far larger, more powerful countries. Unity, once lost, is far more difficult to re-create than reform.

Brexit, or How Countries Still Make the Same Mistakes

The 2016 Brexit vote turned the EU-28 into the EU-27 with little understanding of the consequences. Imagine a popular referendum, only won by a tiny percentage of votes, that devastates the single largest economic unit in world history. Not only that, but the arguments as to what would happen afterward oscillated from devastation to destruction, with little reliable analysis suggesting that it would be better for Britain to be isolated than to remain connected. The UK, the country that in fact created free trade, in the end voted against it. Worse it would seem that the sheer necessity of having an agreement with their largest trading partner, the UK, will in turn force them into a situation in which they have less control over the rules that govern that trade undermining the whole point of Brexit. What could be the only good thing from the Brexit crisis is that it will help institutionalize the EU among other EU members or at least create a greater degree of agreement on the organization's goals. Should they be more or less economic, political, or cultural? Add the return of interstate war and being an EU member has greater meaning.

The most optimistic result of Brexit would be further integration of the remaining EU members, not only in terms of politics but also in terms of culture, law, and, perhaps most important, their militaries. Consider the electoral ramifications of this hypothetical change. Any casualties of war would be lost to individual nations while serving as part of a new EU defense force under an EU flag. Would this decrease antiwar sentiment or the domestic electoral effects of war? It seems unlikely. However, one upside of combined EU armed forces would be a greater degree of military efficiency. The smaller militaries of European states have been unable to buy supplies more cheaply in large amounts, meaning that the militaries are individually more costly than they likely would be if they combined forces. Many attempts at unified procurement have heretofore failed because of international rivalries or concerns about production in one country or another.

Integration in the Twentieth Century

Many EU advocates once dreamed that the EU would become "the United States of Europe"—an association of nations with reasonably close political systems, laws, and even the possibility of similar attitudes or cultures. Indeed, the EU has a complex history, but it has also had, excepting the breakup of Yugoslavia, sixty years of peace. It has bridged divided cultures and helped to heal historical wrongs. Is it possible that this group could become institutionalized into a new nation-state, one that could finally take advantage of its opportunities and become the dominant power on the international stage? Is this a dream that ignores why nations exist? Maybe. Is it a dream rooted in questions of power? Indeed.

Similar weaker attempts at integration, such as USMCA in North America or MERCOSUR in Latin America, are examples of agreements with limited horizons. They focus on financial transfers or unified customs but do not address issues of labor mobility and security. While these and other intergovernmental structures could eventually emerge into federated bodies—like the United States, Brazil, or Russia—that express consistent foreign policy preferences and optimize power potential, such steps are speculative.

From a power perspective, supranational organizations unified to such an extreme degree would restructure the international system. For example, a USMCA federation that expanded to the whole of the Americas would increase the population size of the dominant power in the region, the United States, from four hundred million to nearly a billion by 2050. This population and its productivity would match or exceed the expected population size and anticipated productivity of any existing state. Indeed, a federation that combined America's North, Central, and South populations could even exceed the population of China and approach India's projections. Provided that China and India did not themselves choose to unite with each other, a federated American state would be sufficiently large to compete directly with the Asian giants. That said, this possibility is likely to remain forever speculative. The near impossibility of unification across such a diverse range of nations would certainly undermine what could be a reasonable argument: that if power, or even economic efficiency, is the goal, then size is needed. If culture is the goal, then it is not. This, more than anything, darkens the dreams of Europhiles.

Wealth, Power, and the Limitations of Money

Yet another approach to explaining changes in power potential assumes that wealth translates into political power. This focus minimizes the role of populations and focuses on nations' financial capabilities. Proponents note that dynamic changes in the global economy are at the root of our current transitional period in international politics. Privatization and technology transfers have led to increased economic convergence, most easily gauged by the rise of the BRICS nations (Brazil, Russia, India, China, and South Africa).[11] The liberalization of domestic economic policy in these countries has led to increased productivity, driven mainly by the size of these newly created market economies. In many cases, the domestic policy choices are reasonably straightforward: allow the population to compete in the marketplace by increasing the degree of economic freedom, relax investment regulations and profit repatriation policies to encourage investment in physical capital, and expand access to educational opportunities. Such regulated but relatively open domestic markets have been and continue to be causes of dramatic economic change.[12]

The BRICS countries offer interesting case studies of how domestic economic development can intersect with the possibilities represented by youthful populations. Referring to Brazil, Russia, India, China, and South Africa, the catchphrase "BRICS" has become shorthand for "economically rising nations."

While the BRICS countries have designs on future greatness, the realities of each country's population size and trajectory may undermine their expectations of expansion. The BRICS phrase is memorable, but it does not detail the likely growth trajectories of the countries themselves. They are not within the same categories of development and combining them obfuscates the differences between them. Worse, the BRICS label has been used by some almost as an alternative to the G7 or the UN Security Council to suggest that these countries will be the world's future great powers.

For example, Brazil and South Africa have increasing industrial bases, with Brazil moving into aerospace and becoming a world leader in bioscience. Both countries have also had significant domestic political disturbances dealing with impeached and arrested presidents, massive corruption scandals, political assassinations, and continued domestic unrest. In terms of population size, they are both only a small fraction of the size of either India or China, and still smaller than the EU or United States, limiting their total potential for growth. Worse, the demographic transition is already upon Brazil, and South Africa has had difficulty integrating its population and finding solutions for its sustained, chasmic income inequality nearly three decades after the end of apartheid. Should we look elsewhere on the African continent for demographic potential with a greater degree of political stability, Kenya, or Nigeria, could have higher aspirations than South Africa. Brazil at least has no comparable rivals within its region should it retain its stability.

Russia is an aging society with a large military, some decent innovation in that area, and significant oil exports. It would not seem to have the fundamentals necessary for high sustained future growth. Economic investment is low in Russia, infrastructure is frequently disrupted, and, most importantly, Russia's demography matches that of a nation well into the final stages of its demographic transition. Unless Russia begins to allow substantially higher levels of immigration from central Asia, it will not have the same potential as the other BRICS nations.

Of the group, only China (which I have already discussed at length) and India can lay any claim to possible great power status. These countries have all the requisite characteristics necessary for economic growth, including population potential, organization, technological competency, and total geographic size. If anything, the BRICS group really should just be called the CI or the IC, accounting for the only two billion people nations on Earth (so far). Population, yet again, offers a better measurement of power than policy: the power of these countries was built from their domestic demographic potential, and each country depends on the choices it makes domestically, not on the aspirations of international rivals.

Who Will Decide the Future of the World, and Why

Today, the large, heavily populated developing societies of Asia continue to accrue wealth (and, hopefully, the population-rich countries of Africa will soon follow). These economic gains have translated into increased political influence on the international level. The framework of the international system, built after World War II at Bretton Woods and continued today in the form of organizations such as the G7, is now under stress. While today's most affluent nations are still relatively rich and continue to grow, they are losing ground relative to developing societies' economic gains.

The lead story, then, is of the rapid economic development of the world's less-affluent societies.[13] Population growth provided the demographic "window of opportunity" for societies like China, Brazil, and India, whose fertility rates first rose before rapidly declining. These countries now have large, active populations ready to absorb technological gains from globalization and economic openness. In developed societies, by contrast, growth rates and the active proportion of the population declined slightly over the same window of time. These countries have shrinking populations that can still sustain balanced growth, but they cannot radically change their populations' size or productivity. Simple increases in fertility, given the costs of adding human capital, would not be enough to compensate for relative power losses.[14]

The international system, however, may begin to complicate this domestic story of development, as many countries turn away from free-trade policies toward protectionist policies. Yes, development is driven by access to capital, laws that facilitate investment and ownership, and demography that is conducive to growth, and each factor is an essential part of the successes seen in the developing world. Nonetheless, these domestic concerns are still connected to international trade in all its complexity, created and sustained by those very same postwar institutions that rely on the older powers for their authority.

I discuss China, a classic example, but not a unique one, at length in the next chapter. We have also seen the importance of international trade in the cases of Taiwan, South Korea, and India. Although development in many countries is directly linked with domestic growth, this growth, in turn, is often due to exports. This means that those very same intergovernmental institutions that could be losing influence are the enforcers of the economic stability that has facilitated the expansion of the newer, rising powers. Many countries developed export-oriented industries based on the idea that to grow is to trade—a real cornerstone of the postwar international system. The policy has been generalized to newly growing South and Southeast Asian countries and countries in Africa. As these societies shift from selling raw materials or agricultural products to light manufacturing, they will hopefully continue to move up the human capital and technological manufacturing pathway toward prosperity.

We have seen the trade-as-growth story of development again and again both in theory and in reality. Even if the causal relationship between trade and societal wealth is more murky than direct, the correlation is still valid. Troublingly, trade is in decline or near stagnant globally, a fact that lends a higher degree of uncertainty to any society's future estimation of its worth. Even when discussing trade, we focus on goods instead of services. The latter is more directly linked to the formation of human capital, and the former is heavily influenced by total labor force and per-unit costs.

Considering this distinction within the United States, we have seen a near stagnation in terms of goods imported to the country. While the total value of these goods increased from $1.9 trillion in 2007 to $2.2 trillion in 2015, this increase of almost 14 percent took place over eight years. Contrast that with the period from 1999 to 2007, which had a fantastic import growth rate of 47 percent.[15] This dramatic difference mirrors general declines in global trade.[16] Most upper-income countries now see the same dollar value of import volume as they had in 2008. Most countries saw a drop of over 10 percent between 2014 and 2015, which was nearly unprecedented in a period of rising economic growth in the United States and most of Europe. China is, as of 2021, the world's largest trading partner, as it now trades with more countries than the United States does. Trade is thus decreasing even as growth (albeit limited growth) continues. This exciting and complex puzzle for economists directly influences the developing world.

Access to the world's most affluent markets is an essential and problematic issue. Trade is becoming limited globally even as it becomes more important. WTO members adopt an average of nineteen new trade restrictions per month.[17] Over 2,800 such measures have been adopted since 2008, and only a small percentage have been repealed via negotiations under free-trade policy. And these are restrictions among countries that are supposed to be free-trade adherents! These statistics are unlikely to be new information to trade scholars or those who have taken political development classes, but they are still seemingly ignored in terms of the expected outcomes of the story of development. The popular media has discussed this matter to some degree, but I think the more important points are still to be evaluated.[18]

Questions of how to develop in a nontraditional way will become more important if the classical international market-oriented strategies are altered. Development as we know it has required that nations use their demographic dividend to create a new technological foundation, and, in the past, this transition has required access to investment capital housed in international financial markets. As mentioned earlier, domestic organizations of markets, investment, entrepreneurship, and education are the most important policies for facilitating development—but all countries are still a part of the world. The world's technological know-how, organizational experience, and investment capital are all fuel that, once linked with a young, organized population, can cause substantial success. China's success, for example, came only after both domestic reforms and international realignment. It would have been interesting to see what could have happened with either one or the other, but that is a story for another book and another day.

The catch with all of this, again, is that aging continues once it has started. Worse, an unfulfilled youthful population could cause conflict should investment and personal growth opportunities not be available. Lost opportunities in the international market could undermine expected domestic growth patterns and cause a generation or more to lose the individual income gains that they would have otherwise expected. This is a dangerous proposition, but it could be one of the greater consequences of trade protectionism in the developed world.

That this stage of development will no longer have the same influence that it had in China or historically in the more-developed countries is a highly troubling prospect. Alternatives for employing the young, urbanizing, informed, and wanting population have not yet been imagined.[19]

Middle-Income Countries Must Act Now!

Dear reader, let us take a step back and examine those nations that can be grouped together as "middle-income countries." These nations constitute nearly three-quarters of the world's total population and include all those countries that have the right combination of demography and government to allow for substantial growth possibilities if they act quickly. It should be said that humanity's successful future growth depends on the decisions of these countries, as dramatic as that sounds.

Figure 7.1 builds a case that many of these middle-income countries are starting to display demographic profiles that look like those of their more-developed neighbors. The middle-income countries will hit the 30/40 point I discuss in chapter 3—with a median age of thirty years and 40 percent of the population under age twenty-five—at roughly 2025. Importantly, by this point, the countries would not have had enough time to become fully advanced, suggesting that they will face problems to some degree as care for aging populations becomes a more substantial component of their domestic spending. The ensuing trends are akin to those seen in the high-income countries, with rapid aging leading by 2050 to an average age close to what we currently see in the developed world.

The possibility of a world with less interest in trade changes the development trajectory of those areas that have not yet enjoyed trade's fruits, primarily South and Southeast Asia and Africa. All three regions include members of the BRICS group (South Africa and India, respectively), and all three regions are seeing inflows of foreign direct investment and the early adoption of highly labor-dependent industries (primarily textiles but other forms of light manufacturing as well). This combination of some manufacturing with preexisting agricultural and resource-based industries would look to be the start of traditional development paths. The next steps in the development process would be to combine this industrial mix with a youthful population, a hopefully higher degree of government stability, and economic freedom, and then start to make the move from unskilled labor-based industries to higher-tech, education-oriented, and subsequently higher-paying work. Think of the move from making sneakers to ships and cars to finally world-class aeronautics and software. We have seen this story in South Korea, Japan, Taiwan, and China. Development and trade can be linked by countries doing manufacturing work that wealthier countries no longer want to do: low-paid, labor-intensive, and dangerous work of the kind seen in textile plants, agriculture, mining, and light manufacturing of goods such as toys or electronics. Trade and investment were so easy to access in the later years of the twentieth century, and it had been assumed that easy access would continue. By 2021, however, that is no longer a

FIG. 7.1. Middle-Income Countries' Growth Potential and Demography

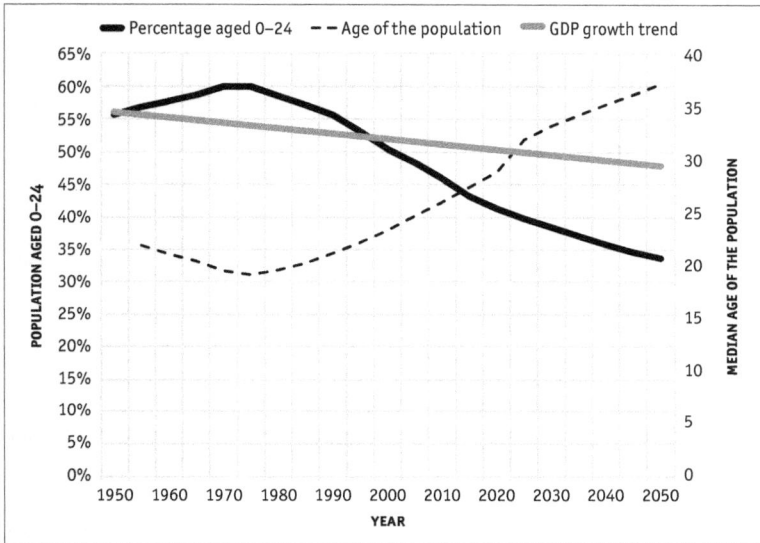

Source: United Nations, Department of Economic and Social Affairs, Population Division 2015b; World Bank 2016

sure assumption. Middle-income nations have not been able to make the move to products that are compatible and competitive with products of wealthier nations because of trade protections, which has limited their access to those markets. The fact that these protections may have caused these countries to miss their demographic boom is, without question, a fundamental concern.

Back to Politics and the Global Hierarchy!

Let us look now at some examples of nations changing in terms of age and political power. The demographic structures in the following examples will help highlight the complex nature of forecasting and potential. Remember from chapter 1 that growth comes from a combination of fertility rates, immigration, declines in mortality, increases in life expectancy, and, most importantly, growth from within the demographic structure itself. Each of our examples is undergoing different changes, mostly because of increasing age but also due to immigration policy.

Table 7.1 compares the medium population forecasts from the United Nations until 2040 with population forecasts that include zero migration. The zero-migration version is an unlikely but essential point of comparison and

TABLE 7.1. Creating Future Age

		Average age of the population	
		2040	
	2015	Medium	Zero migration
China	37	47	47
USA	38	41	43
Germany	46	50	52
UK	40	43	45
France	41	43	44
Japan	46	53	53
Saudi Arabia	28	35	35
India	26	34	34
Brazil	31	41	41
Russia	38	43	41

assumes that both forms of migration—out and in—are at zero. It allows for a critical comparison with medium projections that assume (or are close to a valid assumption of) policy consistency.

Remember again just how quickly countries are aging and how age is correlated with GDP growth. Countries such as China, Japan, and Brazil show no change in average age between the medium population projection and the zero-migration projection. In China and Brazil, this is due to the limited effects of total migration on population growth. Both countries are heavily dependent on domestic influences—that is, whether their people have children or not—and international migration is only of limited importance. While both countries lose population via immigration, the numbers are far too small to change the nations' destinies. India is in a similar situation: the country's scale is so vast that immigration or emigration is lost within the population's margin of error as a whole.

In both scenarios, China is projected to be older than the United States and many Western European countries by 2040. Its demographic profile—the outcome of domestic choice—will be far older than those of even the most developed, prosperous, and isolated countries. Japan does not have these same characteristics as it has chosen to not be as welcoming to immigration as other nations and is an example of a country whose immigration rate is so low that the difference between assumed constant policy and a reduced flow is near zero; it offers an example of our aging future.

It is in the developed, older countries that our complex story starts to unfold. The dominant international actor, the United States, is projected to age to a certain degree by 2040, as are its Western allies Germany, France, and the UK. Of the three, Germany is not only the oldest but moves toward levels of age never seen before: if migration were to remain at zero, Germany's average age is projected to be fifty-two. Though this is only an increase of two years over the medium projection, it is even more critical considering that the medium projection itself is a shocking expectation: that Germany's average age will increase by four years from the 2015 average. Though this may seem like a small difference, it is a profound one. An average age of fifty-two suggests a society with high levels of elderly dependents, a reduced labor force, and even greater stress on the country's social welfare system—a system that was already expected to see great difficulty under the current projections. The UK and France also show higher ages in their medium and zero-migration projections, but neither are as extreme as Germany.

In this difference, we see some residual demographic strength within France that can be attributed to its slightly higher level of youth, some greater gains via momentum, and at least some capacity to retain growth potential. Notice that these ranges are not a given for all countries one way or another—for instance, the UK could introduce zero-migration legislation while the rest of the world might stay consistent. Instead, they represent a series of potential domestic decisions that can be made independently of each other. These different possibilities, in turn, depend on the domestic choices within each country's electorate. How those domestic arguments end is yet unknown, but the potential outcomes and possibilities are clear.

Now consider Table 7.2, which compares projected total population across the same set of countries. These statistics are critical: they represent the scale of potential to countries, nations, and economies. This scale, more than any other variable, creates the future and the bounds of national ambition; the total population of each country thus gives form and function to the world. The difference between scenarios of zero migration and the current norm is a key concept, as it changes the heights that countries with high levels of immigration can reach and shows the effects of policies that restrict people from coming and going. The ranges presented here are fantastic but have similarities with the average age projections. Should nations such as the United States and the European countries choose to undermine their inward flows and restrict migration to zero, they would lose massive amounts of population. The United States would incur the largest loss of the bunch, with over thirty million fewer than the medium projection (a group the size of the state of California). This choice would create a tremendous potential loss for future generations.

In Europe, the choice to restrict inward flows would knock off 2.5 million from the medium projection in France and close to 5 million from the medium projections in the UK and Germany. These numbers are potentially staggering in the context of struggles for regional dominance among Western European powers.

Are nations making the choice to undermine their own relevance by limiting the capacity and size of their future populations, causing a historical end to regional power changes, making a forgotten consideration of policy and the

TABLE 7.2. Population (in Millions) and Potential Futures

		Medium	Zero migration
China	1,376,049	1,394,715	1,404,077
USA	321,774	373,767	341,825
Germany	80,689	77,300	72,671
UK	64,716	72,840	67,215
France	64,395	69,931	67,310
Japan	126,573	113,788	112,215
Saudi Arabia	31,540	43,136	41,311
India	1,313,816	1,633,728	1,645,584
Brazil	207,848	236,015	235,883
Russia	143,457	132,892	129,446

outcome? I would suggest the answer is very much yes. A zero-migration policy is being discussed by major parties in each of our examples; these are not purely theoretical, even if taken to the extreme.

One possibility is that the UK could become the largest country in Western Europe if it retains large-scale international migration. Because each of our example European countries are so similar in terms of education, rights, and efficiency, this population advantage would then give the UK the largest economy and hence the most influence or power. Another possibility to consider is that if UK had kept its immigration policy consistent with migration rates just prior to Brexit, this "Rise of Britain" could have been the reality by 2050. What, then, will be the effects of Brexit or anti-immigration in general? While the UK will lose unfettered access to the world's largest single global market, more importantly for Brexit's nationalist boosters, it will also lose the potential to be more powerful than Germany.

Should the UK lose its chance to become the premier economic power in Europe because of its choice to reduce migration, the competition for most powerful nation would shift to Germany and France. The French traditionally have had higher levels of immigration but have had difficulties assimilating new residents from international sources. The Germans have seen large waves of refugees in the last few years, and these flows have had their own associated issues; these new populations seem unwilling to move to the eastern part of the country, where demand for labor is large and there are few remaining local sources. Both countries must contend with domestic concerns about how to retain their competitive edge in a world of countries many orders of magnitude larger than they are. But, in all cases, the size, complexity, and strength of their economies are based on, at their core, the size, complexity, and capabilities of their population; with all things being equal, more is better. The UK's future potential hinges on the choice between aiming to be 20 percent larger or believing that smaller is necessarily better. This translates into a choice between being the largest in Western Europe or forever second (or even fourth!).

The story outside of Western Europe remains complicated. China grows in a situation of zero migration, as does India, with Russia in decline. Russia's foundational demographic difficulties stem from a higher-than-expected mortality rate and continued problems with both public health and infrastructure. In either of our two projections, it loses about ten million people. Russia's demographic profile is like that of a developed country in terms of total population decline, aging, and dependence on a shrinking labor force, and the country in turn must figure out ways to increase its productivity to compensate for population losses. How or even if this can be done will be a useful guide to other countries dealing with the similar problem of being not quite wealthy but saddled with a population that has the characteristics of a wealthy one. These great questions are seen globally and are not unique.

In the case of the United States, difference between policy outcomes is large. In economic terms, a difference of thirty million people equates to a nearly 20 percent larger GDP. Amazingly, the United States stands nearly alone in the developed world in that it still expects a rising population even with immigration being undercut, at least as of 2021. Its slightly higher-than-expected fertility rates (compared with other developed countries) will help sustain the nation to the middle of the century but not far beyond. Immigration is still the most important component of population growth, and the differences between individual nations are important considerations.

Policy Change, Freedom, and Demographic Outcomes

The story of political change built on economic and demographic foundations is also a story of action taken over decades. It is not a temporary or short-term story but one on the scale of generations. However, demographic change is still as relevant as the series of crises plaguing the world today, from conflict to plague itself.

Demography may not always or often be a joint consideration of policy, but its effects are powerful and should be evaluated. The future power potential of a country is built from its demographic foundation. Tables 7.1 and 7.2 show us countries that can change if they choose to maneuver their immigration policies (the United States, France, and the UK), countries that are locked into a far more likely destiny due to their scale and past population choices (China and India), and countries that would have to radically change their basic concepts of immigration and assimilation to change their futures (Russia and Japan). All are under some level of demographic stress, but they do not have the same range of choices available to shape their futures.

Let us now turn to the most practical means to augment the potential power available to developed societies: immigration policy and labor market expansion. As I discuss in earlier chapters, policies that improve fertility rates and life expectancy, welcoming immigration policies, and policies that increase the opportunities available to women and disenfranchised minorities all facilitate the full employment of populations, which provides the foundation for underlying growth in stable societies.[20] If most of a country's labor force is productive, educated, employed, and engaged in their profession for a longer time span, economic growth will follow.

Human rights, broadly defined, drive economic growth.[21] A state gains legitimate power from the consolidation of productive individuals satisfied with their political rights.[22] States use the political power of their growth potential, which is embedded within their demography, to influence the international system. Thus, the power dynamics of the international system have domestic foundations. Domestic policy choices with demographic effects, in turn, have implications for a country's power on the international stage. Domestic choices, in short, create international realities.

Growth for Growth's Sake?

In sum, nations seeking to be global leaders need to be larger, technologically more advanced, and more productive than their competitors. How this can be done, or whether it should be done at all, are two questions that need to be addressed. The first is a logical outcome of increased rights that result in a reduction in fertility, hence, the dramatic morally problematic policy choice of reducing rights to increase population. This dangerous logical progression may lead to women being forced from the workplace, which would limit education opportunities as well as innovation. If it were enforced over years, however, it might eventually increase fertility rates. The damage to society, particularly a developed one that depends on women's employment, would be vast, but this policy is one that could hypothetically be enacted. The classic alternative would be to attempt to reduce a country's fertility rate: decreasing the population growth rate is a means of increasing the per capita levels of economic success, all other things being constant.[23] This policy change is highly suspect from an international political perspective because it affects a nation's overall size and population composition. However, due to both changing incentives for the population and declining population growth rates among poor societies, it can lead to moderate economic success. The demographic transition is a well-established pattern and a key driver of growth in both rich nations with declining populations and developing nations with expanding ones.

These restrictions on who can participate in the labor force also have a marginal rate of decline, raising questions of stagnation. While economic growth creates political power, gains in power, in turn, are constrained by a nation's population size. Following this trend, the expanding populations of the developing world are gaining both economic and, more importantly, political influence. However, the demographic transition that drives today's baby booms in the least-developed nations is completed in developed societies and near completion in most of the developing world.[24] While fertility declines are nearly constant, they are not destiny, and they must be a part of conscious conceptions of our future.

Population booms and demographic dividends have been seen and spent, respectively, in most fast-developing countries in the past twenty years.[25] The advantage of these time periods is that economies can create capital and then reinvest it without diverting substantial expenditures to sustain large elderly populations. As populations age, so too does this advantage.[26] The current economic boom within the developing world is based upon the youth of these nations, and their outsized labor force is temporary. All nations at all levels of development need to discuss how growth can be sustained after this stage of development is over or, worse, if it has been wasted.

Throughout the book, I argue that immigration is, to my mind, the last policy that can radically reorganize global power with simple increases in population size. The challenge, however, is that immigration policy is not universally accepted, and it cannot be universally implemented to achieve consistent results. To enact it, a nation must have societal and institutional systems for assimilation, a history of previous migration flows, and political will. All three are rare in the international system.

While some Western European and North American countries have most of the right conditions to encourage immigration, all of these nations are under continued domestic stress and rising disagreement within their populations about the value of immigration. This raises a critical question. If immigration is the last valid policy that can create power, why is it ignored? Of equal importance is the dynamic nature of the interaction between domestic policy and global power. Domestic choices create the international system.

CHAPTER 8

The United States, China, and Immigration versus Population Control

The story of the twenty-first century will depend heavily on the decisions made by China and the United States over the last hundred years. Wars, immigration restrictions, exile, isolationism, xenophobia, forced population control, economic liberalization, economic restriction—all have at one time or another played a significant role in the domestic politics of both countries. The outcomes of these political choices, most made generations ago, have affected world politics throughout the past century and have had a hand in creating the political system of the world today.

The power of the United States is based on neither destiny nor democracy.[1] Immigration and geographic expansion built the United States into the dominant political actor on the international stage, and it is this very national ability to take immigration and turn it into development that was ignored and restricted for most of the twentieth century.[2] We must be clear: domestic U.S. fertility is in decline. Current rates of population growth are caused by immigration, and it is only in immigration that many of the future economic problems of the country can hope to be abated.[3]

Xenophobia and Anti-Immigrant Sentiment in the United States: A Cautionary Tale

Historically, immigration has a checkered record in the United States. Periods of proimmigration policy have alternated with times of anti-immigrant law and sentiment. For most of its early history, the United States was a nation of immigrants with high, steady levels of migration flow. Intermittently, however, the country enacted some of the most restrictive anti-immigration policies in the developed world. Examples of particularly harsh policies are the 1882 Chinese Exclusion Act, the Emergency Quota Act of 1921, and the Immigration Act of 1924.[4] All three restrictive policies were motivated by anxieties about the ability of new migrants to assimilate, often defined as conforming to a Protestant, Western culture. The popular "science" of eugenics and xenophobia also lurked behind these policies. At different times, assimilation was declared by media pundits, academics, and occasionally the government itself to be "impossible" for Germans, Poles, Catholics, South Americans, Mexicans, Central Americans, Chinese, Japanese, Jews, and Italians.[5] In the mid-nineteenth century, racial and religious riots on the East Coast targeted Irish and French Canadian Catholic communities, while violence in the West was aimed at Chinese settlements. It is, in fact, difficult to find a single immigrant group that has always been openly accepted throughout American history.[6]

In response to xenophobic tensions among the American public, the government created overt racial classification systems to restrict the immigration of selected groups. Even the Immigration and Nationality Act of 1952, which sought to organize what had previously been a dispersed set of immigration laws into one statute, was a clear continuation of the policies that began in the 1880s: it replaced the earlier exclusion acts and granted Asian migrants a pathway to citizenship, but it kept quota restrictions on Asian groups in place to ensure that the number of migrants of Asian descent would be limited. While all other groups were classified by national citizenship, Asians were defined racially so that no matter their country of origin (keeping in mind that Latin America has significant Chinese and Japanese populations) the entry of someone of Asian descent would still count toward the Asian quota.

Changes to immigration law in 1965 reversed specific discriminatory policies that controlled population flows. Family became the key factor in accessing visas. Originally, policy makers believed that this new system would simply continue the old quotas in practice while creating a more legally equitable immigration system, but unexpected changes in broader migration trends actually did translate into a more ethnically diverse population of newcomers. Traditional flows from Asia and Europe gave way to increased migration from the south, including from Latin America and Africa, as a direct result of the 1965 liberalization policy. The move to a more equitable and less racist system may not have been the intention of those who crafted the policy, but the benefits have been vast. Modern U.S. immigration policy has opened new possibilities for industry, opportunity, and national growth.

The consequences of these anti-immigration policies are evident—and distressing. In the 1970s, the U.S. foreign-born population hit all-time historical lows. Remember policy changes involving population cannot radically change a country the size of the United States quickly. They need years and millions of immigrants for an effect to be visible. This restricted flow of new-

comers, limited both in percentage and total numbers, contributed to the decline in U.S. power that is now underway. By my estimations, without anti-
immigration policies (see figures 8.3 and 8.4), the U.S. population could have
reached 350 million people by 2013—nearly one California worth of people
larger than the country's actual population in 2013.

Increasing constraints on labor flows and a lack of consensus among U.S.
political parties on what level of immigration reform is acceptable have increased the enforcement of border restrictions and reduced levels of legal immigration. Stagnant, yet stringent, immigration laws have encouraged many
people to try to enter the country without documentation. Throughout the
1980s and 1990s, an estimated half million undocumented migrants entered
the United States each year, and many were absorbed into an underground
economy that contributed to increased economic growth. Migrants took jobs
in industries dependent on hardworking but low-skill labor, such as hospital-
ity, construction, and agriculture, and their willingness to work for lesser pay
rates both increased the profitability of those industries and decreased prices
for American consumers on everything from vacations to homes.

The influx of less-expensive labor decreased total income for those in the
least-educated labor bracket, but it translated into economic advantages for
people with higher incomes. Consider your own economic situation. Do you
buy goods and services from people who work "unskilled" jobs? Or do you
work an "unskilled" job yourself? If the former, paying unskilled workers even
less would decrease your own costs. If you are in the latter group, then immigration undercuts your income by increasing competition. Immigration has
thus induced economic anxiety among unskilled workers—an important consideration that has had deep and significant political consequences.

A greater degree of opportunity could have been created overall by allowing a larger number of people to enter and work in the United States legally. Unfortunately, policy choices since the early 1990s and during the recent
Trump administration have tended toward increased restrictions and reinforced border security. Although there is no clear answer to the question of
what to do about the millions of undocumented immigrants already living in
the United States, vocal proponents of reducing, restricting, and restraining
new arrivals seem to guide current immigration reform efforts. These anti-
immigration forces, whether focusing on all immigrants or specifically undocumented workers (whom they often criminalize with the label "illegal"), claim
that they are acting in the interests of native-born workers or the economic
security of the nation. The past offers few examples of this nativist, closed-
border stance being beneficial to either. Reducing immigration flow instead
holds long-term negative consequences for national power. In addition to stok-
ing societal xenophobia, it undercuts the many advantages of immigration,
whether documented or not.

The American Dream While Being a Second-Class Citizen

Policies that limit the ability of foreign-born Americans to gain citizenship cause as much damage as those that limited marital and property rights in the 1920s. Barring racial groups from citizenship, as the United States once did with Asian migrants, holds negative consequences not only for members of that group but also for the economic futures of the regions and communities in which they live. Whereas today there are fewer limitations on property ownership for noncitizens in the United States, in the early twentieth century, state-level alien land laws prohibited noncitizens from owning land, which posed a significant barrier to the accrual of wealth in immigrant communities. Immigrants from non-European groups also faced greater difficulties bringing over spouses before 1965. Similarly, antimiscegenation laws before 1967 prevented people from marrying outside of their race, limiting the ability of citizens to act as immigration sponsors for their spouses in the case of mixed-race partnerships. These couples faced the possibility that their marriage would not be recognized in all states.[7] These laws were successfully designed to create second-class citizens, and they ultimately altered the makeup of the nation and lessened the possible gains from immigration. Nothing, with the exception of a complete closing of the border, can be more detrimental to immigration than restrictions on marriage, citizenship, or ownership of property.

The interconnectedness of systemic racism and anti-immigrant policy is difficult to understate. I would suggest, in fact, that much of how the United States as a society defines race is deeply enmeshed in its history of anti-immigration legislation. Notably, the Chinese Exclusion Act, later expanded to the Japanese, was the first and only immigration restriction that employed definitions of race for screening purposes.[8] The quota systems that followed, while not explicitly race based, had clear racial implications, as nationalities deemed racially less desirable faced the most extreme limitations. Even the family-centered immigration reforms of the 1960s could be justified in terms of racial exclusion, the thought being that if previous waves of population were restricted by race, then subsequent waves of family members would likewise be confined to a limited number of races.

A country's ability to assimilate and utilize its population is essential to its prospects for power expansion. A recent Organization for Economic Cooperation and Development OECD publication, "International Migration Outlook 2013," addresses the issue of assimilation in the United States in detail. The report shows that immigrants to the United States have employment rates nearly equal to those of native-born Americans and that the first generation born in the country is generally financially successful. Over multiple generations, descendants of immigrants report dramatic increases in economic status. By contrast, most European countries fail to incorporate their immigrant populations to the same degree and do not report comparable convergence among immigrants and natives. A similar assessment by the Pew Research Center suggests that in terms of income, work, home ownership, and English language ability, second-generation populations in the United States are nearly equal to what could be considered native-born populations.[9]

The United States is uniquely equipped to support this story of generational change because the scale of its economy can incorporate a great variety of employment interests. The United States has the advantage of being the largest economy in the world, and, more importantly, it is one that relies on many types of labor and hence can gain from both skilled and unskilled workers. Additionally, the country has some of the highest rates of employment opportunities for immigrants. The need for labor is virtually continuous in industries as varied as agriculture and high-energy particle physics; therefore, the United States can continually attract and employ immigrant labor without regard to where it comes from or why it has arrived.

A long-term perspective is required to envision how immigration eventually transforms into national power. Regardless of their fundamental skills, immigrants contribute to the expansion of subsequent generations. From an economic perspective, the children and grandchildren of foreign-born immigrants are more important than the newcomers themselves because they add directly to a country's youth population with the same capabilities, productivity, and education levels. The children of immigrants, who have presumably assimilated into the broader population, are projected to achieve median levels of education, skills, income, and fluency with American culture, and they will also have a lower fertility rate than their parents. These assimilated populations fuel the power potential of the country. Thus, immigration dividends are not simply the gains from the first generation, they include gains across generations. This story has not always proceeded as anticipated; certain groups have seen reductions in economic success once they reach third-generation status, while others have not ascended as quickly as expected. There is thus variation in the story of assimilation that should not be ignored or oversimplified into the suggestion that each generation has more success than the one before it.

The temporary gains accrued from limited increases of new, highly skilled employees are not the primary benefits of immigration; immigration is valuable because it catalyzes dynamic, generational change. Immigration is thus the unrecognized competitive advantage of the United States: the country can expand its population by assimilating people from throughout the world into a stable, unified whole.

The United States was once nearly unique in its ability to assimilate diverse groups under the banner of a new national identity. This advantage, however, has been undercut at times by domestic politics. The systemic anti-immigration

FIG. 8.1. Foreign-Born Proportion of Population and Growth Rates

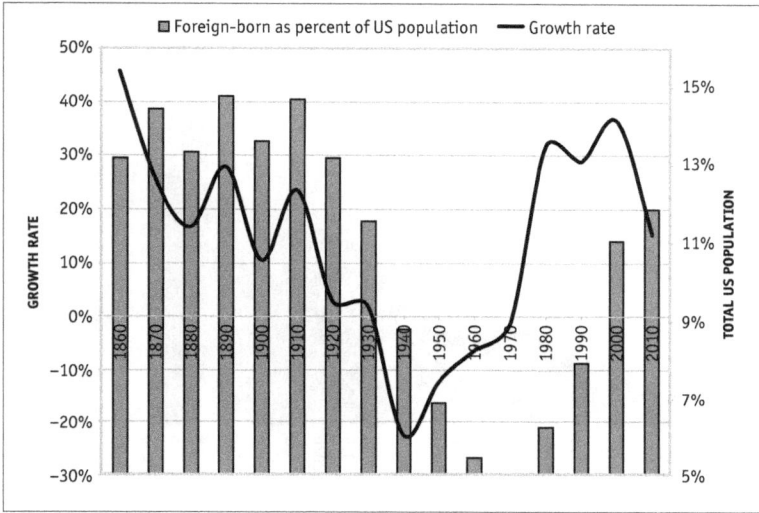

Source: U.S. Census Bureau 2016b

movements in 1920s America had dramatic, long-term implications for the power hierarchies of the international system. Yearly total immigration to the United States in 1921 dropped by more than 95 percent, and it only recovered to 1921 levels in 1988. This period of decreased immigration reduced the nation's expected total population and produced a much older cohort distribution. Immigration reduction policies have thereby diminished what could be the status of the United States today by not only limiting the contributions of immigrants themselves but also forgoing the benefits that their children may have brought.

As figure 8.1 shows, the proportion of foreign-born people in the United States hit a historical low in the early 1970s and only recovered to pre-1920 levels in the late 1980s. This dramatic drop in the proportion of foreign-born Americans was profound and historically unique. The United States experienced its least-diverse era in the late 1960s and early 1970s, as self-isolation limited the country's interactions with the world. Restrictive immigration policies undercut what could have been the third-greatest wave of migration in U.S. history: the post–World War II emigration of displaced peoples from Europe. It is remarkable to think that those waves of people, some of the largest ever, did not have the opportunity to move to the land that would have given them the best opportunity for growth.

Figure 8.2 shows that, had immigration stayed at its 1860–1920 median levels throughout the twentieth century, the United States would by 2015 have

FIG. 8.2. Lost American Future: Immigration Policy as a Constant

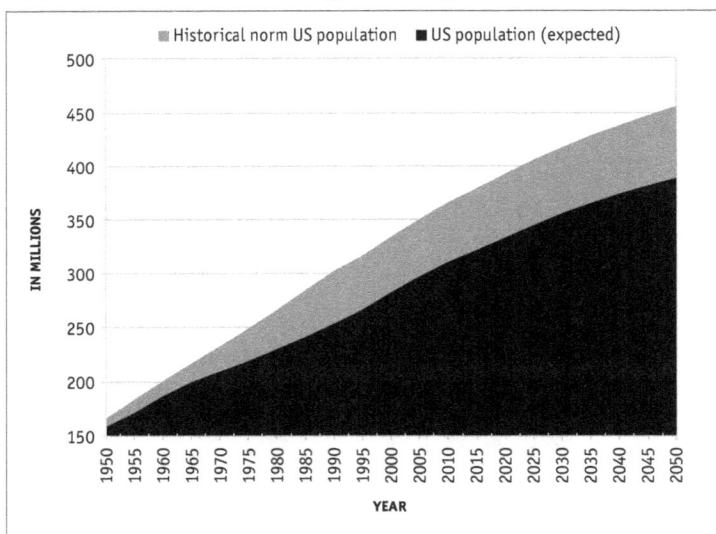

Source: UN Population Division 2015b; and author-constructed estimations

had a population of over 360 million—a full 50 million more than present estimates.[10] The lower levels of immigration for most of the twentieth century have thus reduced the potential size and global influence of the United States.

The estimates in figure 8.2 do not consider the likelihood of increased global population flows after World War II. There is little question that, given a more lenient immigration policy, the postwar United States would have seen not simply the effects of the baby boom but also far higher-than-expected immigration because of postwar and postcolonial refugee flows. This estimate only attempts to evaluate how the population would have grown assuming the foreign-born population stayed at the historical norm. The true scale would have been far higher.[11] The implications of a much larger United States should pop from the page. Every foreign policy decision is somehow based on the scale of the country; should the United States have been larger by 20 percent or even more, there is no telling how its foreign policy and position in the world would be different today.

Immigration Trends and the Alternative
Futures of the United States

If current immigration trends continue, the United States can expect to gain fifty million people over the next thirty years, resulting in a population approaching four hundred million in 2050. Forecasts are necessary, but they are always unreliable. They allow us to evaluate what could happen, but they cannot control for the possibility of the unforeseen. This means that major errors in projection are possible. Malthus, as I discuss throughout this book, famously assumed that population growth would outpace agricultural production, leading to mass famine and the destruction of society. Neo-Malthusians working with the idea of the "population bomb" had similar concerns in the 1970s and forecasted mass devastation by overpopulation within that decade.[12] Other prognosticators—worried that the Earth had hit a peak level of oil production in the 1980s—anticipated that doom would follow the peak. The apocalypse sells.

I do not subscribe to such doomsday predictions, especially in cases of absorbing larger populations. The problem with these doomsday scenarios is that they fail to account for innovation. In the first two examples, agricultural production more than kept up with population growth, causing food prices to crash. Furthermore, fertility rates plummeted due to changing incentive structures for women, driven by political factors and the influence of economic growth.[13] The idea that more income would result in more children turned out to be wrong. Instead, modern, affluent societies have reduced their fertility rates to the point that they are now actually below a stable, self-sustaining level. Likewise, oil-doomsday predictors failed to anticipate changes in technology. Higher oil prices translate into more money to invest in efforts to extract it, and, each year, the amount of recoverable oil has grown. Moreover, other energy sources, such as natural gas, have supplemented oil around the world, and still other sources (including hydrogen, solar, and even nuclear) loom on the horizon. All of this may seem simplistic, but this history does suggest that innovation will likely overtake demand with necessity often a fruitful reason for invention.

Using population projections from the United Nations' (UN) Population Division, we can see that fears of a "population bomb" overtaking and dooming the United States are overblown if not outright wrong. Figure 8.3 shows high, medium (status quo), and low population projections based on high, medium, and low levels of immigration. The medium projection is roughly equivalent to assessments by the U.S. Census Bureau that assume immigration policy will remain generally constant.

The differences between these estimates are important, and the potential influence of what would be the size of the country on power is wide. The low and high projections show a difference of roughly one hundred million people by 2050, or the equivalent of nearly $10 trillion in total gross domestic product (GDP; constant 2000 U.S. dollars).[14] Even maintaining the status quo choice reduces the potential of the country by over fifty million people.[15]

The significance of this estimate cannot be overstated! In the United States

FIG. 8.3. Expected U.S. Population Growth Estimations (in Millions)

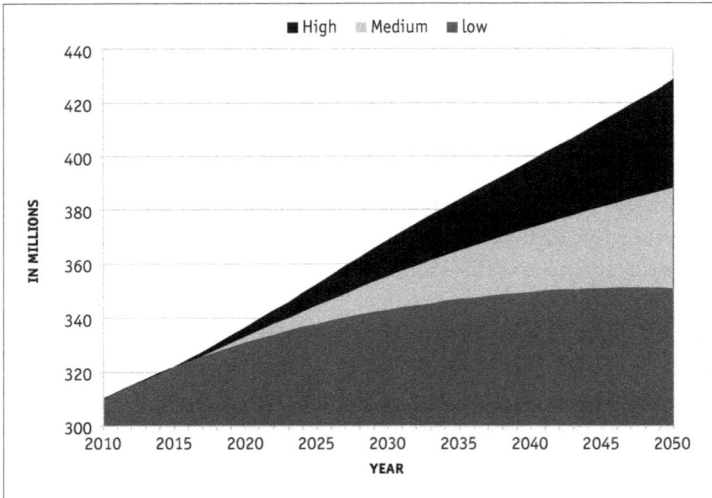

Source: United Nations, Department of Economic and Social Affairs, Population Division, 2015a, 2015b

today, the rate of population growth due to children born from the stable population (that is, "natural increase") is relatively low compared to growth that comes from net international migration, that is, the difference between immigration to and emigration from the country. Immigrants, despite their relatively small numbers, are responsible for over half of the total U.S. population growth forecasted in the next four decades.

In Figure 8.4, the ratio of net migration to natural increase is projected to grow from 0.50 in 2015 (meaning half a migrant for every natural-born person) to over 1.50 around 2045. Migration is not only a moral issue but also, more urgently, an issue of power, as it almost singlehandedly can determine the scale of the country and its ability to influence the world. For most of the Western world, migration has become the key variable for population growth and the only method by which a labor force can be sustained in the second half of the twenty-first century.

This is a clear domestic policy choice that will be the making of the future of the country. In the United States, maintaining immigration at its current rate will allow close to three-quarters of a total year's population growth to be made up of immigrants. If we assume that the United States continues its status quo and admits over a million immigrants per year for the next fifty years, the population outcome is reflected in the gray estimate. Conversely, if the U.S. government were to restrict immigration, the outcome would look like the black estimate, which reflects the natural rate of population growth alone. Recall that

FIG. 8.4. Sources of U.S. Population Growth

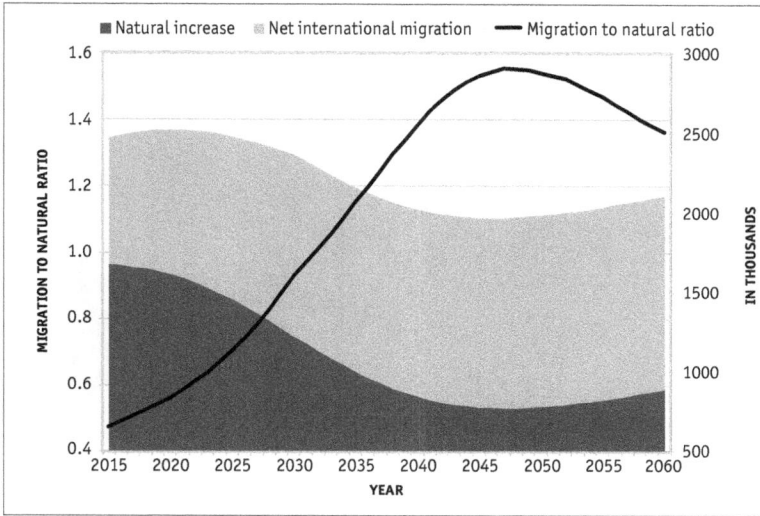

Source: U.S. Census Bureau 2016b

between the 1920s and the 1990s, U.S. immigration was two to five times lower than it is today and two to five times lower than rates of immigration before the 1920s. The U.S. Census Bureau assumes immigration policy as a constant. However, the assumption that both domestic and international conditions will remain stable for decades ignores the possibility of a national change in policy preference or an exogenous change in the pull of economics.

Alternative Futures and Repeated Histories in China

While immigration has the potential to sustain the United States as one of the world's great powers, what about its rival, China? Will immigration alleviate the potentially detrimental old age burdens seen in China's future? Can China adopt an effective policy of assimilation?

Let us consider a forecast of the likely power dynamics between China and the United States through 2055. The prevailing consensus is, as you would expect, that China will continue to rise. The only questions are to what degree it will do so and whether that growth can be sustained.[16] Projections vary, of course, but two of the critical determinants of when China will overtake the United States are the size of the countries' relative populations and their productivity. These two measures determine the gap between the two countries.

Figure 8.5 evaluates and maps several elements of American and Chinese

FIG. 8.5. International Power: Expected Transition

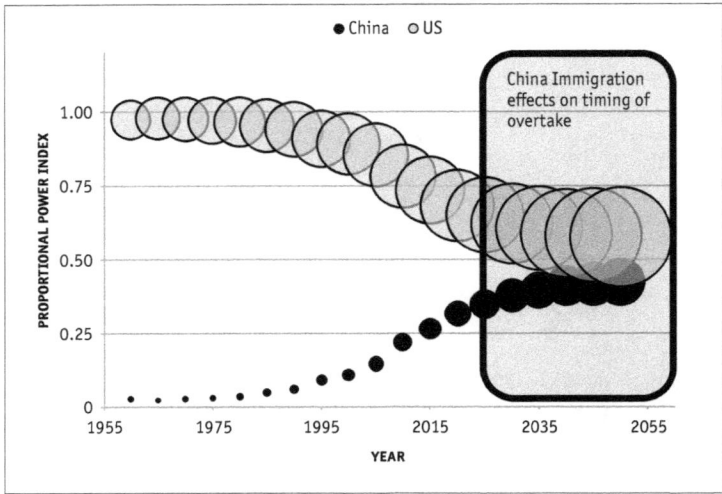

Source: United Nations, Department of Economic and Social Affairs, Population Division, 2015b;
O'Neill and Stupnytska 2009; World Bank 2016; author-constructed variables
Notes: Medium population projections and GDP (constant 2000 US dollars)

power. The size of the bubbles indicates GDP per capita (using constant 2000 U.S. dollars); the vertical scale indicates the relative strength of the two nations, based on the medium estimated population trajectory; and the horizontal scale extends from 1955 through 2055. The idea is to combine several measures of economic success for the sake of comparison.

The transition period starts and ends at 90 percent of rival total GDP. With low population growth, the period is projected to begin in 2030; with medium growth, in 2035; and with high growth, in 2055. The difference is immigration expansion of the United States that reduces the capacity of the Chinese to reach the transitional period.

Figure 8.6 explores the complex interactions among immigration to the United States, population growth, and rising China. The figure presents three possible alternatives: medium projected growth in both China and the United States (the light gray bars), medium projected growth in China and low projected growth in the United States (the dark gray bars); and medium projected growth in China and high projected growth in the United States (the black bars). In all three scenarios, it is likely that China will hew to medium population and economic growth projections. Unlike the United States, China does not have a viable policy option to increase its immigration rates, and China is overwhelmingly dependent on natural rates of population growth. The United States has a greater degree of possible variance, as illustrated using these three UN projections. The medium scenario is closest to what the U.S. Census Bureau

FIG. **8.6.** Comparison between the United States and China

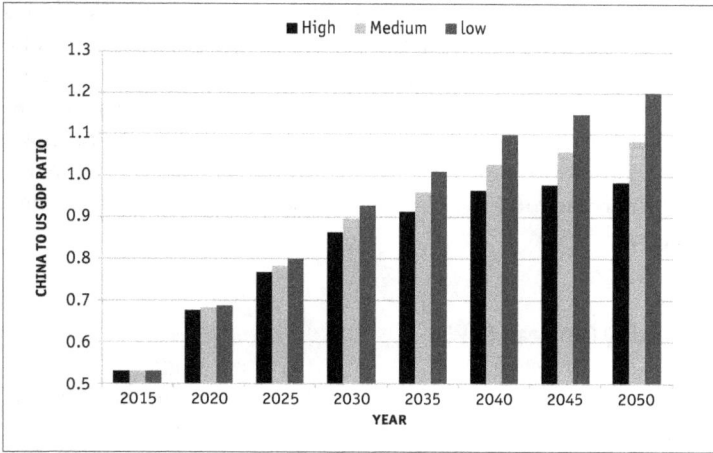

FIG. **8.6.** Comparison between the United States and China

Source: United Nations, Department of Economic and Social Affairs, Population Division, 2015b; O'Neill and Stupnytska 2009; World Bank 2016; author-constructed variables

Notes: High, medium, low U.S. population projections, medium China population projections and nominal GDP

predicts, assuming policy as a constant. The low scenario assumes restricted immigration rates, so the population growth rate is nearly at the natural rate of growth. U.S. economic growth is held as a constant but low number in line with expectations of development and growth. Most important in this figure is the ratio of total Chinese to U.S. GDP. In it, we have the following considerations.

Consider what would happen if the United States were to reduce immigration and accept the low population projection. China would equal U.S. nominal GDP by roughly 2035 and surpass it by 2040.[17] If the United States maintains its immigration policy at the current level and hews to the medium projections, China will equal the United States approximately at the midway point of the century. If immigration increases to the highest level projected here, China's overtaking is postponed until 2055. Higher rates of immigration to the United States would clearly allow for the possibility of postponing this transition, but they would not prevent it indefinitely. The increased population growth in the United States, driven by immigration, would help to stabilize the power dynamics between the two countries. Now China can only surpass the U.S. total GDP by increasing its economic growth rates and closing the gap in per capita productivity. As this chapter asserts, and as the data confirms, the U.S. domestic immigration policy is the country's only hope if it wants to remain the dominant force in the international system. Undermining immigration will undermine the nation's future power potential.

The reader must have noted that China is not expected to have such flexibility. The reason is, again, that international migration is not a viable policy for China. Internal rural-to-urban migration will continue to dominate China's horizon for the foreseeable future, allowing fertility rates alone to determine the country's population size. As I argue, in this transition, only the United States can use domestic policy to hedge against its relative decline in relation to China. The population scale of China is simply too large for international flows to compensate for the labor losses it will suffer as its population ages. Without renewing its current youthful, working-age demographic, its population growth will stagnate. [18]

Parity in Perpetuity Can Lead to War

The transition process by which China overtakes the United States as the world's great power is expected to last twenty-five years, and if dissatisfaction persists, conflict is most likely to occur in the last decade of that period.[19] Dissatisfaction can be anything from legal arrangements for trade to the purity of rivalry of just wanting to be more important. Aggressive proimmigration policies in the United States can delay the transition period by twenty-five years, moving the likelihood of conflict from 2045–2055 to 2085–2100. Other changes, such as integration of the USMCA nations or federalization of the European Union (EU), could further alter such calculations. Most importantly, however, accepting an increased number of immigrants would expand the time that the United States has to accommodate China as the new dominant nation, and it would ensure that the period of overtaking would take place among two countries far closer in per capita productivity. I believe that economic inequality is one of the underlying reasons for dissatisfaction and arguably an essential precondition for severe conflict; so reducing such disparities would bode well for a peaceful transition.

A significant and somewhat troubling outcome of these projections is the possibility of a bipolar world emerging: a world with two nearly equal major powers and a globe divided. Although this phenomenon was discussed throughout the Cold War period, it was never truly the reality, as the Western alliance remained significantly richer and possessed far more power potential than the Soviet Union. The "equity" between the two factions was the case of both possessing nuclear weapons, not economic might. Polarity equals neither peace nor balance. It could induce continued stress on the international system, as the older hegemon (the United States, in this case) might attempt to incentivize or corral the rising power (China) through treaties and even direct payments. Such a dynamic could create lasting grievances between the two great powers.

This realty would be a true balance-of-power situation—worse, one with no end, as the two rival countries would have reasons to fight without means to win. Foreign policy decisions and massive conflict cannot change that basic arithmetic. Such a situation is worrying because, unlike my realist colleagues, I believe that the international system is created for and sustained by a hierarchy of many nations and regions that must work together. This system would not be best managed by two rival powers without the ability to push or pull policy to their ends; such a situation would create a sustained level of parity that could be far more dangerous than a scenario in which one country dominated the other.

Another possibility is that the United States might sustain its hegemonic power due to the influx of population it would gain in a high-growth scenario. This is not commonly discussed, but it would represent a radically different possibility for the international system. With slightly higher immigration flows into the United States, it is possible that a transitional period could conclude with a scenario of two closely paired powers in which the United States continues to maintain hegemony, albeit a reduced hegemony. This version of the United States may have less power, but it would still have the largest economy in the world. The rise of China may end with the nation at power parity with the United States. This story differs greatly from the more alarmist writings on the rise of China and its effects on the international community. In this scenario, the rise of China would not simply be an upward trajectory but a plateau. This demographic perspective should be a more worrying consideration. When growth stagnates or ends, growth stagnating or slowing, let alone ending, is as important as the growth itself.

The crucial point here is not about the consequences of that potential near parity but about the possibility that the United States can retain its influential global position if it embraces a more open immigration policy. To further counter some of the more dramatic popular discourse on the "End of America," even if the United States actively reduced immigration, it would then be the second-most-powerful country in the world. This would hardly be a scenario of complete decline.

Demography is not destiny. Immigration is a domestic policy choice that has implications far beyond the domestic arena, and indeed, it is the single most important policy that allows developed nations to regulate their international power.

Fertility changes also affect potential power, and China's attempt to limit its population while increasing the productivity of the smaller group provides an important case study of how developing nations can rise to the top of the global hierarchy. While these types of policies may temporarily increase a nation's growth, they may also have the long-term effect of limiting the nation's total potential. China, more than any other great country, has a future of difficult decisions ahead, with population being at the core of its likely domestic problems.

The Choice to Be an International Actor

Power matters. It creates the world in which we live. National power on the world stage remains a critical concern of any political system, and the international implications of domestic policies must be considered even if the domestic influences that create those policies would wish to ignore them. Immigration is one of the largest such domestic policies with significant international implications, but it is not the only one. Protectionism in all its economically undercutting forms, cultural nationalism, and even the belief that one's country is always right in all things and all ways are others.

Protectionist limitations have proved popular not just in the heartland of the United States but also in the farms of France and the halls of power in China. Self-imposed limitations are more dangerous than the wiles of international conspiracies because unlike those they exist in persuasive paranoid effectiveness. Isolation and internal dependence are remarkably popular, and these are the policies that undercut potential future power. Often this is the exact opposite of many isolationists claims as they seem to assume being alone and ignored, and in decline, is more advantageous.

History shows that the United States's once-restrictive immigration policies produced clear population gaps and led to a relative loss of power on the global stage. Moreover, with the global decline of territorial and population acquisition by force, continued disorganization among alliances, and political integration unlikely, immigration policy choices have gained added importance as the last comprehensive policy available for expanding national power. Fertility patterns suggest that wealthy regions will lose population, and their international influence will continue to decline relative to the developing world. Immigration policies can delay such shifts but not prevent them, as developing nations' continued vitality strengthens their economic and political systems.[20] The transition from one dominant power to another is a wave of political and power change personified. The one possible alternative to this would be the United States as it stands alone with its capability to integrate and expand its current population. Long-term growth will depend on consistent U.S. immigration policy, but a more liberal policy may be a better decision should greater economic and political power be desired.

As I discuss in chapter 7, policies that have proved successful on the global scale—be they international institutions or even large-scale military alliances such as the North Atlantic Treaty Organization NATO—may not have sustained popularity among domestic electorates. With Brexit undermining the EU and the stricter immigration restrictions imposed by the Trump administration, the choices that democracies make are critical. To many politicians and everyday people, success is not necessarily measured in terms of global power or influence but, alternatively, by perceived domestic gains. This idea strikes at the heart of the classic theory of nations working against and with each other.

The fact that some crucial domestic actors do not consider power on the international stage to be necessary or relevant must be a concern for all, as it is the state-level choices of those actors that affect what a country will do in both the present and the future. Relative international power is but one factor, or even just a by-product of other interests, in a universe of options. Domestic decisions still matter to the global hierarchy, even if they are ignored or uninteresting to the electorate.

CHAPTER 9

Challenges of Future Demographic Changes

Individual choices build societies, and it is from the complex interaction between what people want and need that our shared human history emerges. This book hopes to illustrate these fundamental building blocks of population to weave together an argument on how seemingly unrelated individual choices and governmental policies activities shape the future.

Reviewing Our Story of Population and Potential

We begin with birth itself, examining the choice to bear children. These are expensive choices that can limit families' access to income gains. Mothers still bear a disproportionate amount of responsibility for childcare in addition to the costs inherent to pregnancy. As the classic concept of economics dictates, as costs rise, demand declines. As children become more expensive, birth rates fall. Within a few decades, younger generations decrease in size, and there is general population decline. Despite these trends, however, the foundational importance of procreation remains; the youth are the future of humanity, and so how we as individuals perceive and make decisions about childbearing determines what we as a species can accomplish. Beyond individual choice, the factors that influence birth rates are numerous, ranging from limited medical technology to conflict, racial and gender discrimination, movement and migration restrictions, and timing that can correspond with disaster or devastation. Individuals are also not machines that evaluate each decision based on cost-benefit analysis. Nevertheless, population trends allow us to investigate the factors contributing to birth rates rising and falling.

Our modern age began only two hundred years ago and yet is characterized by a chasmic shift in the expectations for our lives compared with those that came before us. Modern humans survive longer than ever in human history, and when we have children, they, in turn, are now expected to live to adulthood. Traditionally, this expectation would have been a fantasy as both rich and poor could expect childhood and infant mortality rates at levels that no country currently experiences. Thus, the expectation might have been that starting a family meant future heartbreak, perhaps the death of children or the loss of mothers after birth. Humans could assume that life would be short, and we subsequently designed our societies to compensate for this. We certainly would not have expected to grow significantly in total population size, to witness leaps and bounds in technological progress, or that there would be the option to retire instead of working till our deaths. Civilizations across the globe, with some minor idiosyncrasies, could universally expect these individual traumas prior to our modern era.

Then, as if a light from the sky, arrived new technologies on food production; medical advancements such as vaccines, sanitation, the scientific method; and mass publishing to expand access to knowledge. In combination with the emergence of more efficient forms of governmental organization and transportation, this led to population booms with dramatic implications that continue to this day. Indeed, humans are still experiencing the outcome of this synergy all these decades later. The population booms of the last two hundred years fundamentally shaped our modern society. This book deals with how these inventions in technology, politics, and society have been disseminated throughout the world and, most importantly, what our future may hold in their aftermath.

The dissemination of innovations in technology and medicine throughout the world have both created opportunities previously unheard of, as well as created new after-growth issues of aging and population decline. Massive youth surges emerged first in what would become highly developed countries in Western Europe, and then in the Americas and East Asia, to finally percolate throughout the world with current epicenters in sub-Saharan Africa and South Asia. In modern times, societies that maintain high birth rates while assuming historically high levels of infant mortality are now able to delight in watching their youth survive into adulthood but must also contend with the fact that more people necessitate more organization, provide more opportunities, and generate more problems. The question turns to what then to do with these new masses of people?

This book advances that these newly surviving populations have fundamentally shaped the modern world when they have been allowed to invest, create, and grow. The freedom to make these choices is the second part of our story. As populations increase, so do the pressures to take advantage of available opportunities. New lands are cultivated, cities are built, new industries are invented, and most importantly, cultural hierarchies and norms are reconsidered. All of these outcomes are the result of individual choices. Notably, this implies the possibility that even those nations that have not seen the same near two hundred years of development, as much of the Western world has, have the potential to alter the world itself if their current youthful populations are mobilized and allowed to tap into their own potential.

Central to harnessing the potential of a growing population is encouraging economic growth. A culture of entrepreneurialism, educational attainment, with limited gender or racial discrimination combined with an efficient, likely democratic, government will outperform all other forms of human organization in the long run. Discrimination is at its core expensive as it is the choice to undermine oneself for some other less directly developmental reason. Isolationist authoritarian regimes, whether they are dedicated to an elitist power base, religious creed, or have some other reason to reduce their population's personal successes, are forced to be willing to accept being surpassed technologically or tend to rely on massed natural resource wealth. We do not live in a state of Hobbesian anarchy, but we do have competition between nations and between groups. Those that are more effective will by that very definition have more of all things from life to entertainment.

However, in these growing populations, aging quickly becomes apparent should economic growth be created, or at least expensive social, economic, and welfare programs enacted. Aging is at its core caused by success. This success comes from many factors, such as the implementation or creation of new medical technology that can expand the life expectancies of the average person. The possibility of becoming elderly is now not only for the lucky few but a commonality. This new reality is the end of the modern human experience and the beginning of the postmodern in which decline is our shared experience. We have moved from expectations of early death to individually expanded years of existence and population decline in our future.

Duality of Violence and Nonviolence

Youth to aging is as much a progression from potential to stagnation as it is from change and violence to possible acceptance and peace. As shown by Urdal (2006) and Cincotta, and I discuss in chapter 2, there is a trend of societies with a disproportionate amount of youth seeing rapid political change and increases in violence. However, intriguing new research suggests that an opposite trend is apparent in aged populations, whereas violence associated explicitly with politics declines but nonviolent protests increase dramatically. This research created by Stowell in his 2021 dissertation has remarkable but also troubling implications.

The first and most crucial point is that violence has historically tended to be more attractive to research investigations. It is only reasonably recently that in-depth empirical studies of the effects of nonviolent protests have become a part of our shared research lexicon. One explanation for this is that an aged population has at this point only been seen in highly developed states or states with large welfare programs and subsidies to the elderly. It would be hard to find an aged society without implemented policies pertaining to medical care, pensions, housing, and sustenance at various levels of generosity and cost.

That, in turn, means that an ever-increasing percentage of the total population knows that governmental subsidy is a vital part of their lives. These are lives that are no longer filled with the necessity of labor by choice but rather are characterized by physical decline. These are lives that also now allow that aging population to protest, but these nonviolent protests will have more direct policy influence, unlike those by the youth. Indeed, the so-called third rail of politics in the United States is a reorganization of Medicare—those who touch it see the end of their political careers. Some of the largest protests ever recorded in France were in response to President Macron's attempts in 2021 to change the age of retirement. Similar efforts are met with significant resistance throughout the developed world. This is a world that continuously discusses the need for assistance and medical reform but pushes it off past the next election and to the next politician. To date, no country has successfully been able to make substantive change or deal with the political consequences of a massed, organized, and activist aged population. We can expect that this is an issue that will only grow as aging only continues and will become the norm in other less-developed countries with similar political realities.

This aging stagnation to policy reform further illustrates the necessity to implement policies while being a young nation that can allow the old to survive but not undermine the population's finances. Where that interconnection point lies depends on the scale of the country, but no policy discussion matters more than one that can have direct financial consequences for decades and cannot be changed due to the successful activity of its population. Welfare is a need in a modern society with the type and cost, to my knowledge, not created as a sustainable system in any developed nation.

The Aftershocks of a Pandemic

COVID mortality estimations continue to be in process. Those who have died directly from COVID-19 will, in the final measurements, be less than the total casualties. This is due to the inconsistency in data collection at the municipal, state, and federal level in the case of the United States, as well as differences from country to country globally. Some will only claim a COVID-19 death if it occurs directly after a positive test, others only if it is a positive test and victims died within a small period of time (e.g., ICU stay). Still others will measure the human cost of COVID-19 by taking the overall mortality rate increase as a de facto measurement of the pandemic experience. The latter measurement is closest to the methods used in this book, and I would suggest it as the better metric overall.

Unlike many of its alternatives, this approach does not depend upon the availability of a test or the willingness of a family to allow for publication. It only looks at what would have been the expected mortality of a population in comparison to actuality. Some limitations are that this metric does depend on the production of death certificates and presumes the presence of basic bureaucracy within a government to follow the lives of its people. Luckily, of all metrics, this is the easiest to measure. Of all demographical measurements, death in a time of peace is the most accurate. It has the least number of differing definitions, the least amount of arguments to its validity, and, most importantly, it is a metric for which there is a large amount of internal and international interest in reducing and thus in tracking. Consistent databases on mortality predate the modern global system, and it is here that the true costs of COVID-19 can be evaluated.

Using this concept of excess mortality, again the amount of death higher than the expectations, the undercounting of the pandemic becomes clear.[1] There is evidence of undercounting by 30 percent in some Latin American nations, and double or even quadruple that in South Asia and Russia. Worse, the persistent concern to hide the consequences of inaction courses through the veins of politics. Diseases do not care about the timing of elections and the egotism of politicians. Still, these considerations are moving nations to pretend that COVID is over. Yet, as of February 2022, it is and continues to be the third leading cause of death in the country. Within the United States in 2021, more people died of COVID than all those who died of murder, accidents, overdoses, and every other infectious disease combined. This is a remarkable, horrifying reality that is being ignored for the sake of political expedience.

Worse, the reality of disorganization regarding community agreement on something as obvious as a mass pandemic leads to the worrying conclusion that the response to the next great crisis will be even less organized or effective. The argument made by anti-vaxxers claiming the importance of individual freedoms over group protection is now a core tenant of major political parties throughout the West. We have seen such movements in the United States in every southern state, most of which are less than 50 percent vaccinated; in Canada with its small minority of trucker protestors; and from Romania to Bulgaria, both some of the least vaccinated countries in Europe.

Reiterating, COVID is the worst pandemic in a hundred years, with death tolls so high that they challenge our expectation to reach old age and that diseases are limited to being linked with old age, personal choices, or bad luck. Neither cancer, heart diseases, diabetes, or liver cirrhosis are contagious, and these are the ailments that have shaped how we think of death in the developed world.

Meanwhile, COVID is fundamentally different from the normal wear and tear of aging. This disease forces us to seemingly newly consider what dangers lurk in merely being in closed quarters with others, and thus just in existence itself.

Yet, within living memory, tuberculous (TB) killed thousands every year; polio ravaged so many that the United States had special sanatoriums for young victims. Of course, HIV was a part of any modern generation's understanding. Have we forgotten the reality of human existence in these few years of relative safety from one of the great horsemen of the apocalypse? Lost from our memory are the expectations of family members dying far too young and disease ravaging communities with regularity.

My great worry is that this increasing choice to ignore group protection and the reality of infectious diseases will become so familiar that it becomes a devastating indictment of choice itself. In the next pandemic, if so many of our population cares not for the group, we are all forced to choose higher levels of mortality, horror, and the crisis caused by losing loved ones. Those choices can be ours, our neighbors, or our governments. Despite being our shared responsibility, this does not limit the concern that our choices themselves will cause untold suffering during future pandemics as is the evident reality at present.

Children Are Now More of a Luxury

While the pandemic and the resulting economic uncertainty may have exasperated recent trends in falling birth rates, we should reiterate that fertility has been trending down in most countries for decades. However, the level of that decline seems to have intensified since the COVID pandemic started in 2020. As it is only early 2022 while this book is being written, it remains to be seen if this is a temporary phenomenon as couples may hold off decisions about having children until more peaceful times or if this is just the exacerbation of already evident trends. Notable, however, are the stark differences in how the pandemic affected parents and those without children. Consider the realities of children being forced to stay home, with limited to no warning in many cases, fluctuations in policy for testing or quarantine, and the resulting direct damaging impact on parents' work life and even emotional stability. The costs of having children have significantly increased.

War with an Aged Population

In chapters 5 and 7, I discuss the Syrian conflict as an example of a conflict that can never be fully recovered from. The demographic characteristics of such a large number of refugee populations outflowing from the country, already without particularly high fertility rates and now with substantial uncertainty about their future, quickly undermined any potential to rebuild better what had been destroyed—being able to tap on some level into a Phoenix factor and bounce back even with the aged characteristics of the society likely decreasing the overall effect. The only other conflict recorded in the twentieth century with this same phenomenon was seen in Kosovo in 1994.

In a traditional society, large youthful portions of the population allow for high casualties while maintaining lots of potential for childbearing. An aged society loses the latter part of that equation. An older population will have lower fertility rates due to human biological realities (e.g., menopause). Now let us consider the current conflict between Russia and Ukraine, an emerging crisis at the time that this book is being written in February 2022. These are countries with aging populations that are well within their demographic transition. Former communist countries, in general, all have these same characteristics. Even if they have not enjoyed the prosperity of the West economically, they did have liberalized policies toward women and primary universal healthcare and thus saw the subsequent fertility declines. The migrational patterns of both nations are first as conduits toward the European Union, in the case of Ukraine, at best a place to move from not toward with migration primarily being out-migration, people moving away. Russia migrational pattern features a more complex interlocking of populations from increasingly economic desolate regions moving toward the major cities in the east, both from within Russia's borders and those former USSR nations in central Asia. In neither case are these population movements large enough to compensate for declines in labor. The unavoidable reality is that without domestic changes, population growth in these countries would already decline from below replacement rate fertility to high levels of out-migration and even in the case of Russia low life expectancies.

In this context, every causality due to this conflict will cause an irreplaceable loss. The conflict between aging societies is one that cannot be recovered. The scale of a conflict between organized nations with Russia's and Ukraine's means has not been seen since the Yugoslavian civil war in the 1990s, Iran-Iraq wars in the early 1980s, or even further back to World War II. Hundreds of thousands of troops with modern equipment and training in combat with the possibility of cities with populations in the millions under siege is a sight that should scare the souls of us all. The potential level of violence of a full-fledged war between these nations would far exceed that seen in Iraq or during the Syrian civil wars, where small, poorly armed militias could undermine their nation's governments. This war could be at a scale that would endanger the future of Ukraine to a degree that is unlikely to be recovered from, both due to direct casualties as well as the resulting refugee waves.

NOTES

Introduction. Why Population and Politics Matter

1. Fertility is measured as a rate representing the number of children born to a woman if she were to live to the end of her childbearing years and bear children in accordance with age-specific fertility rates of the specified year. The World Bank and cross-nationally census collections use this standard definition.

2. Birth and death rates are the number of births in a given year per one thousand of the population or deaths in a given year per one thousand. Subtracting deaths from births gives the natural rate of growth, which is the population's expected expansion or decline without immigration. Baby booms and youth bulges are similar to each other. They consist of either or both higher level of births and those births surviving to adulthood. They can be associated with changing medical care or societal attitudes after wars, such as happened with U.S. servicemen returning after World War II and the resulting increase in U.S. birth rates, hence, the baby boom.

3. The worst-case scenario for a country's development is often referred to as a poverty trap. In this case, population grows faster than economic growth so that each generation is poorer than the generation before on a per person basis. Using a per person measurement of economics, most often GDP per capita, as a de facto development measurement leads to policy prescriptions in which changing the basic mathematics of division, if possible, can alter growth itself—in this case forcing population growth down to increase economic per person development. Division thus becomes a foundation for policy.

4. Parity means close to equal levels of political and economic power, the ability to have and mobilize resources for a political policy gain. Two nations may be on par even though one is larger than the other in population, because the smaller one is more productive and technologically advanced.

Chapter 1. Demography, People, and Nations

1. The literature on the international dynamics of nation-states is vast and well beyond the purview of this book, starting first with Organski (1958) and the genesis of power transitions and moving to Tammen et al. (2000), who argue that stability comes from power preponderance and alliances arise and persist from a combination of the status quo and a limited ability to change. See Waltz (1979) for a guide to realism. Also, Waltz (1997) offers a key guide to the intricacies of realism, neorealism, and balance of power. See also Mastanduno (1997) on U.S. strategy in a unipolar world; Walt (2009), which helps to establish the issues associated with power as a concept and polarity on institutionalism; and Jervis (2009) on the intricacies of unipolarity.

2. The interaction between domestic and international systems is a continuing research agenda. An extensive overview of the interdependence approach and institutionalism in general can be seen in Farrell and Newman (2014). They make the case that a multitude of diverse research agendas and foci need to be linked from domestic to international and developed for the Global South and developing nations. The mechanisms of politics are still to be developed, and this paper hopes to move to an underdeveloped research agenda as a way to expand upon our understanding of politics as a whole.

3. See Wohlforth (1999a) for an evaluation of the measurements of polarity and Wohlforth (1999b) on the interaction between realism and the end of the Cold War.

Chapter 2. Feast or Famine

1. Malthus 1976, 20.

2. Vaughn 2015.

3. In another example of a popular film motivated by a Malthusian plot, the 2011 Pixar Animation Studios/Walt Disney Pictures film *Cars 2* (Lasseter 2011) is a comedic spoof of British spy films from the 1960s and 1970s that takes place in a world entirely populated by anthropomorphic cars. The villain Sir Miles Axlerod seeks to undermine public faith in electric vehicles and alternative fuel. To do so, he recruits his underlings from the ranks of lemon cars: vehicles that are marginalized because they have manufacturer defects and commonly need replacement parts. The henchmen lemon cars' motivation for aiding Axlerod in his plot is the promise of a world in which they will no longer be mocked or economically exploited. While the conflict is resolved with the villain exposed, the social hierarchy facilitating the subjugation of lemon cars remains intact. *Cars 2* peddles a familiar story, one in which a government coopts a marginalized population and turns it against another, undesired population.

4. Russo and Russo 2019.

5. Even his willingness to torture and kill his adopted daughters is portrayed as part of his ideological purity.

6. Ideas of the superiority of some races and the inferiority of others were first popularly conceived by Francis Galton in 1883. Galton, a cousin of Charles Darwin, created an intellectual fervor with his book *Inquiries into Human Faculty and Its Development*, which coined the term "eugenics" and linked new ideas such as the theory of evolution with the first real attempts at comprehensive nation-building policy works. Galton connected the supposed inherent capability of individuals to the future success of nations and humanity. If, in the natural world, some variations within a species are bigger, faster, or fly higher than others, then could those very same differences be measured, evaluated, and then maximized within humanity? The disciplines of anthropology and biology took on the task of "measuring" humanity itself as discussed in Field (1911). More importantly, then simple cross-racial measurements would be societal. The poor were evaluated not on questions of access to public education or health but on their very basic biological makeup, and poverty itself was considered the outcome of biological destiny. Evolutionary theories as the base of future public policy thus became real (Rosen 2004; Bashford and Levine 2010).

7. Eugenics-based programs themselves provided proved extremely popular. These

aggressive family planning initiatives are seen throughout the developed world within countries as wide ranging as Canada, Sweden, Russia, Brazil, and the United States. Please see Kevles (1995); Adams (1990); and Broberg and Roll-Hansen (2005) for a comprehensive look at policies within these states and overviews of their influence globally. Lombardo (2008) looks at the case of Buck v. Bell in the United States, which is a foundational court case supporting the use of eugenics policies as a basis of forced sterilization. Eugenics itself was even still taught in university-level biology classes as late as the 1970s in the United States, as discussed by Glenna, Gollnick and Jones (2007).

Futurist human maximization policy continues to spark the imagination of scholars. Some argue that a contemporary form of eugenics must be continued—that even if it was unscientific at its height, new policies could be created based on modern genetic studies (Caplan, Glenn, and David 1999).

While this idea may once have seemed squarely in the realm of science fiction, as the prospect of actually modifying the human genome moves from fantasy to reality, so too do questions of capacity. If these policies become practical or even a question of medical necessity, must we then not change our terminology? (Duster 1990).

8. Criticisms of eugenics are not new and were argued in detail at the height of the movement. Even the basic idea of a "European race" is fundamentally flawed and was argued against in *We Europeans*. The book illustrates the massive waves of migrations that had populated the whole Eurasian continent, thus limiting the ability for populations to claim some form of localized superiority based on supposed historical isolation. All people are the outcomes of generations of intermarriages resulting from continuous movements (Huxley, Haddon, and Carr-Saunders 1935).

9. Forecasting data can be found at the UN Population Division with alternatives at the U.S. Census and other demographical organizations. Few, if any, have radical disagreements on aging with at least the developed world and this is discussed at length in the following chapters.

10. Teitelbaum 1975; Becker 1992.

11. Bhrolcháin and Dyson 2007.

12. The concept of higher incomes leading to, or maybe even causing, declines in fertility was discussed as early as Carr-Saunders (1936). He championed investigating the demographic structures of nations to evaluate where or when great powers would be put under pressure by population growth and, in turn, become more susceptible to international conflict and even world war. Consequently, he dedicated much of his life and career to stopping international war both before World War I and after, an early example of social science research being used for policy goals, and one that with World War II was unsuccessful.

13. The full name and variable are the "age dependency ratio," which is the ratio of dependents—people younger than fifteen or older than sixty-four—to the working-age population—those ages fifteen to sixty-four. Data are shown as the proportion of dependents per one hundred working-age population (World Bank [2016], using UN Population Division data).

14. Using the World Bank (2016) definition, a labor force comprises people ages fifteen and older who supply labor for the production of goods and services during a

specified period. It includes people who are currently employed and people who are unemployed but seeking work as well as first-time job seekers. Not everyone who works is included, however. Unpaid workers, family workers, and students are often omitted, and some countries do not count members of the armed forces. Labor force size tends to vary during the year as seasonal workers enter and leave.

15. Longevity is primarily composed of life expectancy at birth, which indicates the number of years a newborn infant would live if prevailing patterns of mortality at the time of its birth were to stay the same throughout its life again from World Bank (2016), using UN population definitions.

16. As a reminder, fertility is the estimated number of children born to a woman in her life for that population. Roughly 2.1 is the amount needed to be at a stable state of growth called replacement rate or near zero population growth. Two children replace the two parents, hence replacement rate. Normally, a fertility rate is thought to be slightly higher at 2.1 because it is easier to factor in expectations of losses due to accidents and early mortalities.

17. The economic change is intrinsically linked to demography. Density is mainly caused by urbanization, which itself is a product of increased population and labor. As workers consolidate in cities, they move toward one another, creating new industries or even allowing them to exist. These new industries, in turn, reinforce the importance of cities and alter the basic fabric of humanity—from a population that is rural and linked to agriculture to one that is urban, moving from an industrialized economy to a service-oriented economy as technology advances.

18. During conflict and humanitarian crises, fertility is disrupted and the youngest are the first people affected by the collapse of medical systems and access to food. Prior to this modern age of mass-produced medicine and humanitarian aid, the disruption could be vast.

Chapter 3. The Outcomes of Youthful and Aging Populations

1. Cincotta and Doces (2012) focus on the expectations that youthful population would be more motivated to change a government with a special focus on those living under authoritarian regimes. Urdal (2006) considers that this same youthful population, a "youth bulge," could also be linked to violence and the start of sustained civil wars. In both cases youth seem to be more risk acceptant and willing to make major changes to society. This change does not necessarily lead to positive outcomes.

2. Bloom, Canning and Sevilla (2003); Lee and Mason (2006); and Dyson (2010) are all foundational texts on the concept that the age structure itself is a deterministic component of economic growth. The idea manifests in the term "demographic dividend" and, much like the youth bulge, this describes a youthful population as one of potential because a large amount of youth means large amounts of labor. As labor is the core of an economy, growth can be created.

3. World Bank 2016.

4. According to the World Bank, high-income countries are classified as the following: Andorra, Antigua and Barbuda, Aruba, Australia, Austria, the Bahamas, Bahrain, Barbados, Belgium, Bermuda, British Virgin Islands, Brunei Darussalam, Canada, Cayman Islands, Channel Islands, Chile, Croatia, Curacao, Cyprus, Czech Republic, Den-

mark, Estonia, Faroe Islands, Finland, France, French Polynesia, Germany, Gibraltar, Greece, Greenland, Guam, Hong Kong Special Administration Region of the People's Republic of China, Hungary, Iceland, Ireland, Isle of Man, Israel, Italy, Japan, the Republic of Korea, Kuwait, Latvia, Liechtenstein, Lithuania, Luxembourg, Macao Special Administrative Region of the People's Republic of China, Malta, Monaco, Nauru, Netherlands, New Caledonia, New Zealand, Northern Mariana Islands, Norway, Oman, Poland, Portugal, Puerto Rico, Qatar, San Marino, Saudi Arabia, Seychelles, Singapore, Saint Maarten (Dutch part), Slovak Republic, Slovenia, Spain, St. Kitts and Nevis, St. Martin (French part), Sweden, Switzerland, Trinidad and Tobago, Turks and Caicos Islands, United Arab Emirates, United Kingdom, United States, Uruguay, and the U.S. Virgin Islands.

5. Connelly 2008.

6. Kahl 1998; Winckler 2002; Goldstone 2010.

7. Winckler 2002.

8. United Nations, Department of Economic and Social Affairs (UN DESA) 2015a.

9. Mason 2001.

10. Bongaarts 2006.

11. Swift 2005.

12. Swift 2005, III.10.197; Kugler 2017.

13. Balter (2006) discusses building from a dramatic concept of the low fertility spiral, which is a concept of the economic dissolution of the state and has led to movements to attempt to incentivize more births.

14. Committee on the Long-Run Macroeconomic Effects of the Aging U.S. Population 2012.

15. Chinese Exclusion Act of 1882; "America's Demography Is Looking European" 2021.

16. Sitting on the more numbers-based and certainly not apocalyptic side are works such as Teitelbaum and Winter's *The Global Spread of Fertility Decline: Population, Fear, and Uncertainty*. This text evaluates fertility declines cross-nationally and investigates the time needed for the changes to happen. As mentioned later, much of the more problematic financial crisis is projected to occur within twenty years.

17. Bowdler 2010.

18. Hedge and Borman 2012.

19. Jackson and Howe 2012; Yoshihara and Sylva 2012; Haas 2007.

20. This problem of success is increasingly universal (Teitelbaum and Winter 2013).

21. People in more-developed countries live four years longer at age sixty-five and three years longer at age seventy than people in less-developed countries. These differences are larger when comparing life spans in the more-developed and least-developed countries, at five and four years, respectfully.

22. Policy importance is critical. Age-specific life expectancy provides a motive for immigration: someone might migrate for the chance to live longer, primarily caused by increased security at a younger age, not at the earlier stages. These numbers are the visual example of development within the world. Should a person survive in a more dangerous area, directly aspects of life are down to a reasonably small number of three to five years. These numbers have been surprisingly consistent for decades, with similar

differences seen in the 1950s, even with much higher differences in average total life expectancy due to vastly improved youth mortality statistics.

23. Differences will be reduced to three years of life.

24. Oeppen and Vaupel (2002), for instance, offer just one of a multitude of attempts to evaluate our biological limits, and a common characteristic of the others was that they were proven wrong by our decades of increased life.

25. Moving from expectations of the low seventies to the high eighties is an extreme number of years added to pensions and the fabric of society.

26. UN DESA 2015b.

27. In terms of total life expectancy.

28. The political power of Japanese farmers continues to affect everything from military actions toward the Chinese to the negotiation of international trade treaties; the latter continually proclaim that one of the most protected industries in the world, Japanese agriculture generally and rice specifically, must be opened up to trade—a move that the elderly, costly, and powerful rice industry in Japan rejects.

29. Vanhuysse and Goerres 2012.

Chapter 4. Movement

1. Hobbes 1909, from 1651 edition, 96.

2. Hobbes 1909, from 1651 edition, 110 (with a small paraphrase).

3. Locke 1824, 387.

4. Rousseau 1984, 109; Rousseau 1913, 207.

5. Hume (1777) can be found in an exact facsimile of his original published edition at Hume Texts Online (davidhume.org) (Other Collections [OC], 24, Mil 475).

6. Hume 1777, OC, 27, Mil 476.

7. The middle-income trap is a topic of current debate and worry in China. The continuation of the one-child policy and the *hukou* system of restricting internal migration are problematic for long-term potential with both having seen significant change in the last twenty years. See Fan (2002) for more on intra-Chinese migrations. In the *hukou* system, the government designates each individual from birth as either "rural" or "urban" and assigns restrictions on movement. Vollmer et al. (2013) illustrate possible growth potential. Despite such obstacles, China still has remarkable capacity for future growth centered on traditional development strategies that prioritize education and infrastructure. The move from labor-intensive to physical capital industries will allow or could allow for the expansion of services and the mechanization of agriculture, all of which are difficult. The likely outcome is continued economic growth but with marginal declines inherent to the system.

8. A nation is caught in a poverty trap when its population growth exceeds the growth of its per capita productivity.

9. See Yoshihara and Sylva (2012) for an evaluation of demographic change and great power politics; see also Weiner and Russell (2001). A focus on declines in the total population available for military service is an interesting contribution. Some new sources suggest that the U.S. military is changing its rules on visible tattoos due to their high popularity and the detrimental effect that previous policies had on their ability to recruit an ever-larger proportion of the total population. This change is a seemingly

small one caused by an interest in body art, but it is also due to difficulties with recruitment in general.

10. See Hatton and Williamson (2005); Hatton and Williamson (2002) look at the fall of authoritarian states, domestic limitations on emigration, and the possibility that the reasons for migration will decline due to domestic economic growth and the alternative possibility of massive increases due to economic growth, which in turn allows population to afford to migrate.

11. See Massey (1988) and Mayda (2009), who have written extensively using cross-national systemic studies of migration flows via gravity models.

12. Western Europe here includes Austria, Belgium, France, Germany, Luxembourg, the Netherlands, and Switzerland.

13. The 1965 immigration reforms in the United States matter because of their unforeseen outcomes. Coinciding with the civil rights movement, it was no longer socially acceptable to demonstrate clear racial preferences in immigration. Initially, the reforms were designed to gauge people by human capital, ignoring racial classifications. Later, and with limited analysis, family sponsorship would be added. The former attempted to increase the economic gains of immigration by limiting the entry of those thought to have less of an effect on the labor market, with efficiency gained by education being a primary concern. The latter began as a small moral argument in favor of family reunification. Both were not originally thought to have direct effects on racial restrictions. At the time, skill was thought to reside primarily in the same groups that had been supported by the quotas: northern Europeans. After forty years of quotas, it was thought, the family allocation and reunification would simply add people of similar characteristics, in effect perpetuating the same system without the overt nature of the previous systems. This turned out to be a miscalculation, as over time a more racially diverse population was able to take advantage of this new system. New high-human-capital migrants can take advantage of the family allocation policy, in effect diversifying the country via a combination of merit and opportunity. Currently, over three-quarters of total immigrations to the United States are via family sponsorships, and people are often permitted to enter after spending years waiting. The total number of visas allowed is still restricted without regard to the total amount of immigrants legally allowed.

14. The measurable effectiveness of this type of policy is, as far as I know, unsupported. It is important to consider that, although the average immigrant story is based upon assimilation in the second or third generations, certain subgroups whose movement is allowed because of refugee status can have differing histories. Economic and forced migration likely cause differing incentives for emigrating to the new host country. Additionally, certain subgroups have needed more than two generations to see similar median levels. The level of cultural isolation that is needed to remain unassimilated, at least in terms of economics, is profound but not impossible.

15. Much of demographic transition research links its subject of study to migration. See Balter (2006) and Preston (1984, 1986). How a country can support its elderly given declines in its labor force is an interesting question and heavily researched, with all three works being good examples.

16. See Gratton (2012) for an extensive overview of immigration policy.

17. Most of the current debate on immigration reform seems to simply devalue the

importance and decrease the numbers in immigration allocation based upon family and increase those based upon skill sets, with low-skill labor given temporary visas.

18. Organization for Economic Cooperation and Development 2013.

19. "Migration in the Gulf" 2016.

Chapter 5. Recovery from Violence and the Horrors of War

1. Lee 2011.

2. The field of global security studies has made remarkable advances over the past sixty years. The Uppsala Conflict Data Program (UCDP), starting with its "radio data," the Correlates of War Project, and Peace Research Institute Oslo (PRIO), have all allowed for increasingly detailed analyses of casualties (Gleditsch et al. 2002; Ghosn, Palmer, and Bremer 2004; Lacina 2009). The victims and victors, the complex webs of relationships in multiactor civil war, and the influences of terrain (mountain, jungle, desert, etc.) have all been the focus of a multitude of influential studies (Horowitz 1985; Cunningham, Gleditsch, and Salehyan 2009; Fearon and Laitin 2011; Weidmann 2009; Hendrix and Salehyan 2012). Deterrence, game theory, agent-based models, and rational choice theory have all used (and demanded) ever more detailed and complex data, furthering the systematic investigation of war (Organski and Kugler 1980; Levy and Thompson 2010; Cederman, Gleditsch and Buhaug 2013). Geocoded data and even the possibility of real-time analysis via satellites (or social media) are two additional avenues of current research (Satellite Sentinel Project 2012). Pinker (2011) and Goldstein (2011) both give interseting discussions of rising peace in the modern era.

3. Figure 5.1 was constructed using an amalgamation of three sources: the PRIO Battle Deaths Dataset v.3.0, the UCDP Battle Related Deaths 5.0/Human Security Report Project Dataset, and United Nations population data. PRIO and UCDP define what constitutes a battle death somewhat differently. I attempted to use the wider definition that includes both military and civilian casualties. There is some disagreement between both PRIO and UCDP. For the years 1989–2015, I used the UCDP data, which is lower in total numbers then the alternative. For the UCDP data, some relevant citations are Gleditsch et al. (2002) and Melander, Pettersson, and Themnér (2016). The data can be found at USDP, Dataset Download Center, http://ucdp.uu.se/downloads/. PRIO data can be found at International Peace Research Institute (PRIO), Data, https://www.loc. gov. Lacina, Gleditsch, and Russett (2006) discuss the decline in battle deaths, and International Peace Research Institute (2009) offer an introduction to the PRIO dataset. I used the United Nations population data to create the rates per one hundred thousand in the graphic.

4. There is some disagreement on this number. Fry (2012) and Gómez et al. (2016) support 2 percent of people murdered in the hunter-gatherer era. Pinker (2011), however, considers the modern era to be fundamentally different from the past and argues for 15 percent casualties in the hunter-gatherer era. The depths of history are often not straightforward, and differences are expected in the archeological record.

5. Gómez et al. 2016.

6. United Nations Office of Drugs and Crime 2019.

7. How and why populations change is a great question of humanity. Worse, why are

the advent of urbanization and increased political unity correlated with higher rates of violence in human history?

To be "civilized" is often imagined as a concept driven by considerations of peace. However, civilization is not necessarily about creating peace but about creating efficiency. Civilized, educated, and efficient societies are also the ones most capable of barbarity due to their higher degree of competence.

8. Organski and Kugler 1980; Koubi 2005.

9. Paris and Sisk 2009.

10. Seybolt, Aronson, and Fischhoff 2013.

11. Jones, Bremer, and Singer 1996; Palmer et al. 2015.

12. Kugler 2016.

13. This section is based upon Kang, Kugler, and Kugler (2016) and this note has literature background text from Kugler et al. (2013) and Kang, Kugler and Kugler (2016) on the process of estimations as to where the nation would have been should the conflict never have happened. In those papers, we apply a variant of the Overlapping Generation (OLG) Growth Model, which was introduced by Samuelson (1958) and Diamond (1965) and elaborated on by Lucas (1988). Galor and Ryder (1989), Azariadis and Drazen (1990), and Galor and Weil (1996) extend the number of economic factors. This work is heavily influenced by Feng et al. (2008), who first incorporated political factors such as relative political capacity. My model is based on these works. The OLG Growth Model is selected because it captures nonmonotonic dynamics during the postwar recovery. Further, the model allows multiple steady states that at one extreme allows for rapid recovery and at the other extreme permits a postwar collapse leading to a poverty trap.

Developed by economists, the typical OLG Growth Model includes investment, population, human capital, and technology. I follow Feng, Kugler, and Zak (2000), who show that political capacity affects growth and demographic changes. This formulation allows the incorporation of insights by Kuznets (1973) and other researchers who share his conclusion that political factors shape the rate of growth.

Let me now outline the core argument formally. The dynamics of capital accumulation in a recovering economy are defined as follows:

$$k_{t+1} = \frac{a\beta A(p)}{1+n}\left[\ln(1+k_t) - \frac{k_t}{1+k_t}\right] (2)$$

where
k capital per capita
a human capital
n population growth
$A(p)$ economic effectiveness of political capacity
p political capacity
β saving propensity

The outcome of the estimation is the future expectations when compared to a traditional (Solow 1956) model. Again in Kang, Kugler, and Kugler (2016), the economic effectiveness of political capacity is intertwined with human capital and the propensity to save. In that paper, we argue that capable governments can more effectively implement crucial policies in the recovery phase. Capable governments will provide infrastructure and maintain political stability. They will also enforce laws and contracts far more vigorously than less capable governments. Capital infusion from foreign or domestic sources remains a major component of recovery.

The importance of this would be to show how recovery can be forecast given the political constraints of a country's domestic system. The influence of foreign aid and the types or practices of how peace was established are both topics for further study.

14. I use the work of Kang, Kugler, and Kugler (2016) and Kugler et al. (2013) as a base for this discussion. In my previous work, my colleagues and I used classic economic growth forecasts based upon the Solow model to give a raw but helpful illustration of expectations. We expanded upon this early work by adding the importance of education, the demographic characteristics of population growth, measurements of political efficiency, and the choices of individuals, such as savings.

15. A much less complicated system of linear estimation is used for the population expectations.

Chapter 6. Nationalism, Equality, Groups, and Demography

1. Inglehart 1997; Norris and Inglehart 2009, 2016.

2. Consider the use of Japanese Shintoism in the late 1800s after the restoration of imperial rule under Emperor Meiji. Shintoism is a religion closely connected with the local traditions and interests of the Japanese, but it also maintains that the primary political entity (the emperor) is a direct descendant of a god. Divinity affords the emperor legitimacy and helps to create a myth of unity, which in turn created the political foundation for modern Japan.

Under the rule of the Meiji government, a unified Japan transformed from one of the most isolated countries in the world to a global power within two generations. Japan industrialized at an unprecedented clip by breaking away from a feudal caste-based system that had hampered its population potential for generations. Before Japan's turn toward development, previous regimes had invested in a system of population controls that divided people among five levels: noble, samurai, farmer, merchant, and untouchable. Each caste was restricted in terms of occupation, permitted actions, and potential for achievement by both law and societal norms. Japan explicitly created this system to enforce peace, under the assumption that domestic change was dangerous and that innovation undermined governments. As the nineteenth-century international system began to embrace imperialism, Japan realized that its policy of isolationism was no longer tenable and that change would either be forced upon them from without, internationally, or from within, domestically. Similarly, from Henry V of Great Britain to the Roman emperors and the pharaohs themselves, religion has acted as a unifier of state control, with belief being a requirement for membership in the more influential group.

3. Southern Poverty Law Center 2022.

4. Bloom et al. 2009.

5. Bailey 2006.

6. Goldin 2006.

7. International Labour Office 2010; Morton et al. 2014.

8. Mammen and Paxson 2000.

9. Barro and Lee 2013.

10. Goldin 2006.

11. Jejeebhoy 1995.

12. Mammen and Paxson 2000.

13. Banister 1987.

14. Greenhalgh 2008.

15. Sen 2003.

16. Note, however, that the imbalance is more severe in some parts of the Caucasus region than in rural China.

17. Zhu, Lu, and Hesketh 2009.

18. Ding and Hesketh 2006.

19. Wang 1999.

20. White 2006.

21. Xinhuanet 2015; Phillips 2015.

22. Halfon 2007.

23. Popular culture, too, embraced these ideas. In the classic science-fiction movie *Soylent Green*, the population has destroyed the planet and left humanity with nothing more than the ability to consume itself. Even the plot of the modern movie *Kingsman*, as discussed in chapter 2, is built around the concept that we as humans are a disease; we create global warming, and hence to fix the problem, we must fix the population. These movies argue that we as humans are too far gone to rectify our mistakes peacefully, and the only recourse we have is massive slaughter. In *Kingsman*, much like eugenics would suggest, the rich are kept safe, and the poor are made to destroy one another.

24. Bashford 2014.

25. Hansen and King 2013.

26. Pritchett 1994.

27. Lam 2011.

28. It is an example for illustration purposes and should not be thought as a policy recommendation. Texas has 171 million acres of land, and the population of the United States is 332 million as of 2022.

Chapter 7. Foreign Policy in an Era of Demographic Change

1. The recent events in the Crimea notwithstanding, the cost is still ongoing both in the civil war to the east of Ukraine and in the extensive sanctions on Russia.

2. Angell 1912.

3. This is Angell's (1912, 362) ending argument.

4. The current baseline by 2030 was to be 2 percent of total gross domestic product.

5. The continued belief that it would be acceptable to "take" Iraqi's oil as a form of spoils ignores practicality, law, or even how markets work. Then president Trump regularly stated this and even mentioned it as reason by him to stay in Syria. Johnson 2016.

6. Nguyen and Ton 2019.

7. Center for Strategic and International Studies 2016.

8. The literature on alliances is complex and nearly as vast as that on the dynam-

ics of nation-states. See Walt (2009) on the complex and yet unknown relationships between unipolarity and alliance formation. The bandwagon effect and the dynamics of changing power are two other key components to the stability of alliances. The continued importance of alliances after the Cold War is also up for debate. See Levy and Thompson (2010) for additional evaluations of the reasons for alliances in terms of a possible balance against the United States.

9. Johnson 2016.

10. The issue of retrenchment is heavily debated. The importance of the United States to the current international system is highlighted and evaluated in Brooks, Ikenberry, and Wohlforth (2012/2013). Their position is that the sheer gains to the United States by being heavily involved at the highest levels of the international system outweigh the costs dramatically.

11. See Beckley (2011/2012) for a critique of the importance and concept of the rise of China. See Schweller and Pu (2011) for an evaluation of a potential balancing effect after the rise. See MacDonald and Parent (2011) for alternative policy choices of the United States that could lead to relative decline but also possible retrenchment.

12. See Beach and Kane (2007) for an index to economic freedom and Gwartney, Lawson, and Holcombe (1999) for its theoretical underpinnings. See Kugler and Swaminathan (2006) for a linkage of economic growth, population, and power.

13. See Feng et al. (2008), which links freedom to economic growth. Lucas (1988) evaluates economic development, with Solow (1956) being the classic originator of the concept and model. The latter is one of the most heavily cited articles in social science history.

14. Feng et al. 2008.

15. U.S. Census Bureau 2016b.

16. World Bank 2016.

17. World Trade Organization 2016.

18. Appelbaum 2016.

19. Rodrik (2013, 2014, 2015) discusses this.

20. See Bloom, Canning, and Sevilla (2003) for a complex evaluation of the linkages between female labor force participation and the demographic dividend. Policies related to fertility are an additional influence on growth as well as a long-term consideration toward the demographic transition.

21. See Brander and Dowrick (1994), which again expresses the important connection between population and economic growth in a cross-national study.

22. International immigration is highly profitable to most of the developing world because investment in both physical and human capital is abundant. Continued reorganization of economic freedoms improves the potential to increase the GDP per capita.

23. See Becker, Glaeser, and Murphy (1999), who also link economic growth to fertility.

24. Demographic transition is a profoundly important topic, and a good starting point is illustrated in Canning (2011) (and of course in previous chapters of this book).

25. See Bloom et al. (2009) again on the possibility of population growth having a long-term economic benefit via the demographic dividend.

26. See Bongaarts (2006, 2008) for extensive evaluations of life expectancy, economic growth, and the dynamics of developing nations.

Chapter 8. The United States, China, and
Immigration versus Population Control

1. Dyson 2010; Lucas 1988; Mason 2001.

2. Current research suggests that a significant number of immigrants who once settled in the United States have "boomeranged" or flowed back to their origin countries, both due to current economic issues in the United States and due to reductions in their ability to gain from success such as local prejudice. It is hard to suggest that increased hostility to undocumented workers is not associated with increased hostility to documented workers as well.

3. O'Neill and Stupnytska 2009; National Intelligence Council 2012.

4. These, and other local and federal acts, are often lumped together as "Alien Exclusion Acts" for simplicity's sake. It is important to remember that these policies oscillated for nearly thirty years before solidifying behind the 1924 act and significant quota-based restrictions.

5. Koven and Götzke (2010) offer a particularly useful guide to the intricacies of modern immigration policy and historical precedent.

6. For an alternative view on American liberalism and migration, see Moses (2009). In it, he postulates that the early acceptance of migrants was due to the radical individualism of the founding fathers and that the increased restrictions in the twentieth century were due to the acceptance of more constrained European ideas of nations.

7. Because antimiscegenation restrictions were primarily concerned with interracial marriage and interaction that involved "Whites" (notably no longer categorized in terms of European descent), these policies permitted marriage between other races. This led to complex multiethnic and racial groups and a new type of multiethnic identity that predated those commonly seen today. Antimiscegenation restrictions became law in the 1920s and persisted in part until the 1960s.

8. After the Chinese Exclusion Act of 1882, the Immigration Act of 1924, or Johnson-Reed Act, and the Asian Exclusion Act and National Origins Act 1924 were passed.

9. See Pew Research Center (2013). This is also observed in various surveys of values.

10. It is likely that in-migration population flows would have been far higher due to the turbulence caused by the end of World War II and the following fall of colonial empires. This is likely a low estimation.

11. Figure 8.2 also suggests the future ramifications of these restrictions by using the UN Population Division's median population projections for the United States. These estimates assume that the current semirestricted flows will remain in place. To compensate for the lows in the foreign-born population as a percentage of the U.S. population in the early 1920s to 1990s, I have used the UN's population growth numbers from 1990 to forecast up to 2050. Notice that the loss of fifty million still appears, but further losses are avoided.

12. See earlier chapters again on neo-Malthusianism and eugenics, Ehrlich (1968) for the original population bomb, and Goldstone (2010) for a modern reconsideration.

13. Organski et al. (1984) is one of the first books written from a political science perspective that connected systemic evaluations of population to power dynamics.

14. Estimations are constructed from O'Neill and Stupnytska (2009); UN DESA (2015b), and author's estimations. For ease of notation, O'Neill and Stupnytska (2009) will simply be called "Goldman Sachs" and the UN DESA, Population Division (2015b), as detailed in the *World Population Prospects 2015*.

15. Using Jones et al. (2016), let us consider the complexity of how Americans think about immigration. One highlight from this report is the concept of nostalgia: the idea that the past was better than the present or, more importantly, would be better than the future. This is an important point to consider when questioning why people vote or who they vote for in elections. The population's beliefs about the success or failure of national policy, or how that policy is connected to them, influence not only domestic politics but also international politics. Figure 8 in this report summarizes survey responses to a key question about nostalgia. Paraphrased, it is, do you think the American culture and way of life has mostly changed for the better or for the worse since 1950? Responses range widely and seem to show a high degree of distinction along lines of race, class, and age. The White working class and White evangelical Protestants lead the way in terms of nostalgia, with only 34 percent and 25 percent, respectively, saying that the country is in a better place today than it was in 1950. Those two groups are also the least likely to be foreign-born, have seen radical changes to political power and maybe even economic stability, and—if we consider world politics a zero-sum game— are the losers. They also make up a substantial part of the total U.S. population and have a powerful voice when it comes to immigration policy. The size and increased anti-immigration rhetoric of this subgroup consistently undermines political attempts to reorient current U.S. policy. Interestingly, this same survey suggests that Americans are split on the question of whether newcomers to the country are a benefit: 44 percent say that they "strengthen our society," while 46 percent say that they do not.

16. See Tammen et al. (2000) and National Intelligence Council NIC; (2012) for projection evaluations. The NIC's series of reports was periodically used to give light to what they consider future considerations of global politics. Demography is increasingly, and rightly, a part of that concern.

17. One complicating factor with predictions is the consideration of what type or component of GDP is being projected. The most common is GDP at purchasing power parity (PPP), with PPP thought to be close to an ideal method of evaluating an average person's ability to buy, considering vast differences in costs in different countries. This allows the popular press, and some academics, to make extreme claims about the rise of China. My one minor problem with this consideration is the outcome of convergence. A higher relative growth rate not only pushes two countries toward one another in terms of overall buying power but also causes the resulting goods to become increasingly similar. Convergence should be bidirectional, considering total growth as well as similarity of purchasing power. Traditionally, when working with projections of GDP, it is assumed that PPP would be a constant for the decades involved in the projections. I find that a bit difficult to continue, as, with the rise of China, the increased necessity

of importing goods and the increasing standardization of goods means that the basket used to estimate PPP should, in turn, become increasingly similar as development grows. Currently, China enjoys nearly 1.5 times U.S. nominal GDP in GDP PPP. In the next forty years, convergence should decrease the differences between the United States and China from eleven times GDP per capita to only three times, assuming that a fixed basket causes that difference to be dramatically overevaluated. That, in turn, means that also using real GDP has clear consequences in reduction of actual spending. It should allow for a greater degree of projection ability as those reductions are reduced by time and growth. PPP as a constant would overstate the transition by well over a decade or even two.

If we consider expenditures such as those on defense, GDP at PPP is a strange measurement to use. Some small difference might be expected due to lower labor costs for the construction of naval vessels or even aircraft, but I would suggest that this difference is not as significant as it would be between the prices of Big Macs or soda across countries. The Chinese do not get a discount for buying Russian equipment, and not much of one when they make it, so why assume that GDP at PPP is a good measurement of power? Or even a useful measurement for comparison purposes at all at this level?

18. Constructed using the UN Population Division's medium population projections, supplemented by economic forecasts provided by O'Neill and Stupnytska (2009).

19. Organski and Kugler 1980.

20. Jackson and Howe 2012.

Chapter 9. Challenges of Future Demographic Changes

1. Karlinsky and Kobak (2021) give a snapshot of the crisis and compile the estimates or mortality by nation, COVID claims, and total mortalities for ninety-four nations and territories. This research paper although not yet peer reviewed will be the type needed for future pandemic measurements. The dataset in question is the World Mortality Dataset: Tracking Excess Mortality across Countries during the COVID-19 Pandemic.

WORKS CITED

Adams, Mark B., ed. 1990. *The Well-Born Science: Eugenics in Germany, France, Brazil, and Russia*. New York: Oxford University Press.

"America's Demography Is Looking European." 2021. *Economist*. January 2. https://www.economist.com.

Angell, Norman. 1912. *The Great Illusion: A Study of the Relation of Military Power to National Advantage*. New ed. London: William Heinemann.

Antero-Jacquemin, Juliana da Silva, Geoffroy Berthelot, Adrien Marck, Philippe Noirez, Aurélien Latouche, and Jean-François Toussaint. 2015. "Learning from Leaders: Life-span Trends in Olympians and Supercentenarians." *Journals of Gerontology: Biological Sciences* 70 (8): 944–949.

Appelbaum, Binyamin. 2016. "A Little-Noticed Fact about Trade: It's No Longer Rising." *New York Times*. October 30. http://www.nytimes.com/2016/10/31/upshot/a-little-noticed-fact-about-trade-its-no-longer-rising.html?smprod=nytcore-iphone&smid=nytcore-iphone-share.

Azariadis, Costas, and Allen Drazen. 1990. "Threshold Externalities in Economic Development." *Quarterly Journal of Economics* 105: 501–526.

Bailey, Martha J. 2006. "More Power to the Pill: The Impact of Contraceptive Freedom on Women's Lifecycle Labor Supply." *Quarterly Journal of Economics* 121 (1): 289–320.

Balter, Michael. 2006. "The Baby Deficit." *Science* 312: 1894–1897.

Banister, Judith. 1987. *China's Changing Population*. Stanford, Calif.: Stanford University Press.

Barbera, Henry. 1973. *Rich Nations and Poor in Peace and War: Continuity and Change in the Development Hierarchy of Seventy Nations from 1913 through 1952*. Lexington, Mass.: Lexington Books.

Barro, Robert, and Jong-Wha Lee. 2013. "A New Data Set of Educational Attainment in the World, 1950–2010." *Journal of Development Economics* 104: 184–198.

Bashford, Alison. 2014. *Global Population: History, Geopolitics, and Life on Earth*. New York: Columbia University Press.

Bashford, Alison, and Philippa Levine. 2010. *The Oxford Handbook of the History of Eugenics*. Oxford: Oxford University Press.

Beach, William W., and Tim Kane. 2007. *Methodology: Measuring the 10 Economic Freedoms*. Washington, D.C.: Heritage Foundation.

Becker, Gary S. 1992. "Fertility and the Economy." *Journal of Population Economics* 5 (3): 185–201.

Becker, Gary S., Edward L. Glaeser, and Kevin M. Murphy. 1999. "Population and Economic Growth." *American Economic Review* 89 (2): 145–149.

Beckley, Michael. 2011/2012. "China's Century? Why America's Edge Will Endure." *International Security* 36 (3): 41–78.

Bhrolcháin, Máire Ní, and Tim Dyson. 2007. "On Causation in Demography: Issues and Illustrations." *Population and Development Review* 33 (1): 1–36.

Bloom, David, David Canning, Günther Fink, and Jocelyn Finlay. 2009. "Fertility, Female Labor Force Participation, and the Demographic Dividend." *Journal of Economic Growth* 14 (2): 79–101.

Bloom, David E., David Canning, and Jaypee Sevilla. 2003. *The Demographic Dividend: A New Perspective on the Economic Consequences of Population Change.* Santa Monica, Calif.: RAND.

Bongaarts, John. 2006. "How Long Will We Live?" *Population and Development Review* 32 (4): 605–628.

——. 2008. *Fertility Transitions in Developing Countries: Poverty or Stagnation?* Working Paper No. 7. Washington, D.C.: Population Council.

Bowdler, Chris, ed. 2010. "The Economics of Ageing." *Oxford Review of Economic Policy* 26 (4): 581–734.

Brander, James A, and Steve Dowrick. 1994. "The Role of Fertility and Population in Economic Growth: Empirical Results from Aggregate Cross-National Data." *Journal of Population Economics* 7 (1): 1–25.

Broberg, Gunnar, and Nils Roll-Hansen. 2005. *Eugenics and the Welfare State: Norway, Sweden, Denmark, and Finland.* East Lansing: Michigan State University Press.

Brooks, Stephen, G. John Ikenberry, and William Wohlforth. 2012/2013). "Don't Come Home, America: The Case Against Retrenchment." *International Security* 37(3): 7–51

Canning, David. 2011. "The Causes and Consequences of Demographic Transition." *Population Studies: A Journal of Demography* 65 (3): 353–361.

Caplan, Arthur L., McGee Glenn, and Magnus David. 1999. "What Is Immoral about Eugenics?" *British Medical Journal* 319: 1284.

Carr-Saunders, Alexander Morris. 1936. *World Population: Past Growth and Present Trends.* Oxford: Clarendon Press.

Cederman, Lars-Erik, Kristian Skrede Gleditsch, and Halvard Buhaug. 2013. *Inequality, Grievances, and Civil War.* Cambridge: Cambridge University Press.

Center for Strategic and International Studies. 2016. Reconnecting Asia—Mapping Continental Ambitions. October 25. https://reconnectingasia.csis.org/.

Chen, E., C. Schuetze, and B. Novak. 2021. "World Is Facing First Long Slide in Its Population." *New York Times.* May 23, A, 1.

Cincotta, Richard P., and J. Doces. 2012. "The Age-Structural Maturity Thesis: The Impact of the Youth Bulge on Advent and Stability of Liberal Democracy." In *Political Demography: How Population Changes Are Reshaping International Security and National Politics,* edited by Jack A. Goldstone, Eric P Kaufmann, and Monica Duffy Toft, 98–116. Oxford: Oxford University Press.

Committee on the Long-Run Macroeconomic Effects of the Aging U.S. Population. 2012. *Aging and the Macroeconomy: Long-Term Implications of an Older Population.* Washington, D.C.: National Academies.

Connelly, Matthew. 2008. *Fatal Misconception: The Struggle to Control World Population*. Cambridge, Mass.: Belknap Press of Harvard University Press.

Correlates of War Project. 2016. Militarized Interstate Disputes (v4.1). http://cow.dss.ucdavis.edu/data-sets/MIDs.

Cunningham, David E., Kristian Skrede Gleditsch, and Idean Salehyan. 2009. "It Takes Two: A Dyadic Analysis of Civil War Duration and Outcome." *Journal of Conflict Resolution* 53 (4): 570–597.

Diamond, Peter. 1965. "National Debt in a Neoclassical Growth Model." *American Economic Review* 55 (5): 1126–1150.

Ding, Qu Jian, and Therese Hesketh. 2006. "Family Size, Fertility Preferences, and Sex Ratio in China in the Era of the One Child Family Policy: Results from National Family Planning and Reproductive Health Survey." *British Medical Journal* 333 (7564): 371–373.

Dong, Xiao, Brandon Milholland, and Jan Vijg. 2016. "Evidence for a Limit to Human Lifespan." *Nature* 538: 257–259.

Duster, Troy. 1990. *Backdoor to Eugenics*. New York: Routledge.

Dyson, Tim. 2010. *Population and Development: The Demographic Transition*. New York: Zed Books.

Ehrlich, Paul R. 1968. *The Population Bomb*. New York: Ballantine.

Fan, Cindy C. 2002. "The Elite, the Natives, and the Outsiders: Migration and Labor Market Segmentation in Urban China." *Annals of the Association of American Geographers* 92 (1): 103–124.

Farrell, Henry, and Abraham L Newman. 2014. "Domestic Institutions beyond the Nation-State: Charting the New Interdependence Approach." *World Politics* 66 (2): 331–363.

Fearon, James D., and David D. Laitin. 2011. "Sons of the Soil, Migrants, and Civil War." *World Development* 39 (2): 199–211.

Federal Highway Administration. 2016. Highway Statistics, 2014. Washington, D.C.: U.S. Department of Transportation.

Feng, Yi, Jacek Kugler, Siddharth Swaminathan, and Paul Zak. 2008. "Path to Prosperity: The Dynamics of Freedom and Economic Development." *International Interactions* 34 (4): 423–441.

Feng, Yi, Jacek Kugler, and Paul Zak. 2000. "The Politics of Fertility and Economic Development." *International Studies Quarterly* 42 (2): 667–694.

Field, James A. 1911. "The Progress of Eugenics." *Quarterly Journal of Economics* 26 (1): 1–67.

Fisunoglu, Fahrettin Ali. 2014. "Beyond the Phoenix Factor: Consequences of Major Wars and Determinants of Postwar Recovery." Claremont, Calif.: Claremont Graduate University.

Fry, Douglas P. 2012. "Life without War." *Science* 336 (6083): 879–884.

Galor, Oded, and Harl E Ryder. 1989. "Existence, Uniqueness, and Stability of Equilibrium in an Overlapping-Generations Model with Productive Capital." *Journal of Economic Theory* 49: 360–375.

Galor, Oded, and David Weil. 1996. "The Gender Gap, Fertility and Growth." *American Economic Review* 86 (3): 347–387.

Galton, Francis. 1883. *Inquiries into the Human Faculty*. London: Macmillan.

Ghosn, Faten, Glenn Palmer, and Stuart Bremer. 2004. "The MID3 Data Set, 1993–2001: Procedures, Coding Rules, and Description." *Conflict Management and Peace Science* 21: 133–154.

Gleditsch, Nils Petter, Peter Wallensteen, Mikael Eriksson, Margareta Sollenberg, and Håvard Strand. 2002. "Armed Conflict 1946–2001, a New Dataset." *Journal of Peace Research* 39 (5): 615– 637.

Glenna, Leland L., Margaret A. Gollnick, and Stephen S. Jones. 2007. "Eugenic Opportunity Structures: Teaching Genetic Engineering at U.S. Land-Grant Universities since 1911." *Social Studies of Science* 37 (2): 281–296.

Goldin, Claudia. 2006. "The Quiet Revolution That Transformed Women's Employment, Education, and Family." *American Economic Review* 96 (2): 1–21.

Goldstein, Joshua S. 2011. *Winning the War on War: The Decline of Armed Conflict Worldwide*. New Nork: Penguin [Dutton/Plume].

Goldstone, Jack A. 1994. *Revolution and Rebellion in the Early Modern World*. Berkeley: University of California Press.

———. "The New Population Bomb." *Foreign Affairs*. December 1. https://www.foreign affairs.com.

Gratton, Brian. 2012. "Demography and Immigration Restriction in American History." In *Political Demography: How Population Changes Are Reshaping International Security and National Politics*, edited by Jack A. Goldstone and Eric P. Kaufmann, Monica Duffy Toft, 159–175. Oxford: Oxford University Press.

Greenhalgh, Susan. 2008. *Just One Child: Science and Policy in Deng's China*. Berkeley: University of California Press.

Gómez, José María, Miguel Verdú, Adela González-Megías, and Marcos Méndez. 2016. "The Phylogenetic Roots of Human Lethal Violence." *Nature* 538: 233–237.

Gwartney, J. D., R. Lawson, and R. G. Holcombe. 1999. "Economic Freedom and the Environment for Economic Growth." *Journal of Institutional and Theoretical Economics* 155: 643–663.

Haas, M. L. 2007. "A Geriatric Peace? The Future of U.S. Power in a World of Aging Populations." *International Security* 31 (1): 112–147. https://doi.org/10.1162/isec.2007 .32.1.112.

Hacker, J. David. 2011. "A Census-Based Count of the Civil War Dead." *Civil War History* 57 (4): 306–347.

Halfon, Saul E. 2007. *The Cairo Consensus: Demographic Surveys, Women's Empowerment, and Regime Change in Population Policy*. New York: Lexington.

Hansen, Randall, and Desmond King. 2013. *Sterilized by the State: Eugenics, Race, and the Population Scare in Twentieth-Century North America*. Cambridge: Cambridge University Press.

Harris, Marc, Robert Dixon, Nicholas Melin, Daniel Hendrex, Richard Russo, and Michael Bailey. 2014. Megacities and the United States Army—Preparing for a Complex and Uncertain Future. June. Chief of Staff of the Army, Strategic Studies Group, U.S. Army.

Hatton, Timothy J., and Jeffrey G. Williamson. 2002. *What Fundamentals Drive World*

Migration? Working Paper No. 9159, Washington, D.C.: National Bureau of Economic Research.

———. 2005. "What Fundamentals Drive World Migration?" In *Poverty, International Migration and Asylum*, edited by G. J. Borjas and J. Crisp, 15–38. Hampshire: Palgrave Macmillan.

Hedge, Jerry W., and Walter C. Borman. 2012. *The Oxford Handbook of Work and Aging*. Oxford: Oxford University Press.

Hendrix, Cullen S., and Idean Salehyan. 2012. "Climate Change, Rainfall, and Social Conflict in Africa." *Journal of Peace Research* 49 (1): 35–50.

Heuveline, Patrick, and Bunnak Pock. 2007. "The Phoenix Population: Demographic Crisis and Rebound in Cambodia." *Demography* 44 (2): 405–426.

Hill, Kenneth. 2004. *War, Humanitarian Crises, Population Displacement, and Fertility: A Review of the Evidence*. Roundtable on the Demography of Forced Migration, Committee on Population, National Research Council and Program on Forced Migration and Health at the Mailman School of Public Health, Columbia University. Washington, D.C.: National Academies Press.

Hobbes, Thomas. 1909. *Leviathan*. 1651 ed. Oxford: Clarendon Press.

Horowitz, Donald L. 1985. *Ethnic Groups in Conflict*. Berkeley: University of California Press.

Hume, David. 1752, 1777. *Essays, Moral, Political, and Literary, Part 2*. Hume Texts Online. https://davidhume.org.

Huxley, Julian, Alfred Cort Haddon, and Alexander Morris Carr-Saunders. 1935. *We Europeans: A Survey of "Racial" Problems*. London: J. Cape.

Inglehart, Ronald. 1997. *Modernization and Postmodernization: Cultural, Economic and Political Change in 43 Societies*. Princeton, N.J.: Princeton University Press.

International Labour Office. 2010. *Women in Labour Markets: Measuring Progress and Identifying Challenges*. Geneva: ILO. https://www.ilo.org/global/lang—en/index.htm.

International Peace Research Institute, Issuing Body. 2009. The Battle Deaths Dataset. Composed by Bethany Lacina and Nils Petter Gleditsch. Oslo, Norway: PRIO. https://www.loc.gov.

Jackson, Richard, and Neil Howe. 2012. *The Graying of the Great Powers: Demography and the Geopolitics in the 21st Century*. Washington, D.C.: Center for Strategic and International Studies.

Jejeebhoy, Shireen J. 1995. *Women's Education, Autonomy, and Reproductive Behaviour: Experience from Developing Countries*. Oxford: Clarendon.

Jervis, Robert. 2009. "Unipolarity: A Structural Perspective." *World Politics* 61 (1): 188–213.

Johnson, Jesse C. 2016. "Alliance Treaty Obligations and War Intervention." *Conflict Management and Peace Science* 33 (5): 451–468.

Jones, Daniel M., Stuart A. Bremer, and J. David Singer. 1996. "Militarized Interstate Disputes, 1816–1992: Rationale, Coding Rules, and Empirical Patterns." *Conflict Management and Peace Science* 15: 163–213.

Jones, Robert P., Daniel Cox, Betsy Cooper, and Rachel Lienesh. 2016. *The Divide over America's Future: 1950 or 2050? Findings from the 2016 American Values Survey*. October 25. Washington, D.C.: Public Religion Research Institute (PRRI).

Kahl, Colin H. 1998. "Population Growth, Environmental Degradation and State-Sponsored Violence: The Case of Kenya, 1991–93." *International Security* 23 (2): 80–119.

Kang, Kyungkook, Jacek Kugler, and Tadeusz Kugler. 2016. "Economic Consequences of Conflict." International Studies Association, Atlanta. SSRN eLibraryhttp://SSRN .com/abstract=1900761.

Karlinsky, Ariel, and Dimitry Kobak. 2021. "Tracking Excess Mortality across Countries during the COVID-19 Pandemic with the World Mortality Dataset. *eLife* 10: e69336. https://doi.org/10.7554/eLife.69336.

Kevles, Daniel J. 1995. *In the Name of Eugenics: Genetics and the Uses of Human Heredity*. Cambridge, Mass.: Harvard University Press.

Keynes, John. 1919. *The Economic Consequences of the Peace*. New York: Harcourt, Brace and Rowe.

Kirk, Dudley. 1996. "Demographic Transition Theory." *Population Studies* 50 (3): 361–387.

Knorr, Klaus. 1970. *Military Power and Potential*. Lanham, Md.: Lexington Books.

Koubi, Vally. 2005. "War and Economic Performance." *Journal of Peace Research* 42 (1): 67–82.

Koven, Steven G., and Frank Götzke. 2010. *American Immigration Policy: Confronting the Nation's Challenges*. New York: Springer.

Kugler, Jacek. 1973. *The Consequence of War*. Ann Arbor: University of Michigan.

Kugler, Tadeusz. 2016. "The Demography of Genocide." In *Economic Aspects of Genocides, Other Mass Atrocities, and Their Preventions*, edited by Charles H. Anderton and Jurgan Brauer, 102–124. Oxford: Oxford University Press.

———. 2017. "Demography and International Relations: Politics, Economics, Sociology and Public Health." In *Interdisciplinary Approaches to International Studies*, by Steve A. Yetiv and Patrick James and, 229–262. London: Palgrave Macmillan.

———. 2020. "Europe: A Nationalist Dream and the Effects of Zero Migration on Political Power." In *The Rise of Regions: Conflict and Cooperation*, edited by Ronald L. Tammen and Jacek Kugler , 103–114. New York: Rowman and Littlefield.

Kugler, Tadeusz, Kyungkook Kang, Jacek Kugler, Marina Arbetman, and John Thomas. 2013. "Demographic and Economic Consequences of Conflict." *International Studies Quarterly* 57 (1): 1–12.

Kugler, Tadeusz, and Jacek Kugler. 2012. "Political Demography." In *The International Studies Encyclopedia*, edited by Robert A Denemark. Oxford Reference. https:// www.oxfordreference.com/view/10.1093/acref/9780191842665.001.0001/acref -9780191842665.

Kugler, Tadeusz, and Siddharth Swaminathan. 2006. "The Politics of Population." *International Studies Review* 8 (4): 581–596.

Kuznets, Simon. 1973. "Modern Economic Growth: Findings and Reflections." *American Economic Review* 63 (3): 247–258.

Lacina, Bethany, and Nils Petter Gleditsch. 2005. "Monitoring Trends in Global Combat: A New Dataset of Battle Deaths." *European Journal of Population* 21 (2–3): 145–166.

Lacina, Bethany, Nils Petter Gleditsch, and Bruce Russett. 2006. "The Declining Risk of Death in Battle." *International Studies Quarterly* 50 (3): 673–680.

Lam, David. 2011. "How the World Survived the Population Bomb: Lessons from 50 Years of Extraordinary Demographic History." *Demography* 48 (4): 1231–1262.

Lasseter, John, dir. 2011. *Cars 2*. Los Angeles: Walt Disney Pictures and Pixar Animation Studios, 2011.

Last, Jonathan V. 2013. *What to Expect When No One's Expecting: America's Coming Demographic Disaster*. New York: Encounter.

Lee, Ronald D. 2011. "The Outlook for Population Growth." *Science* 333 (6042): 569–573.

Lee, Ronald D., and Andrew Mason. 2006. "What Is the Demographic Dividend?" *Finance and Development* 43 (3): 16–17.

Levy, Jack S., and William R. Thompson. 2010. *Causes of War*. Newark, N.J.: Wiley-Blackwell.

Locke, John. 1824. *The Works of John Locke in Twelve Volumes*. 12th ed. London: C. Baldwin.

Lombardo, Paul. 2008. *Three Generations, No Imbeciles: Eugenics, the Supreme Court, and* Buck v. Bell. Baltimore, Md.: Johns Hopkins University Press.

Lucas, Robert E., Jr. 1988. "On the Mechanics of Economic Development." *Journal of Monetary Economics* 22 (1): 3–42.

MacDonald, Paul K., and Joseph M. Parent. 2011. "Graceful Decline? The Surprising Success of Great Power Retrenchment." *International Security* 35 (4): 7–44.

Malthus, T. R., and Thomas Robert. 1976. *An Essay on the Principle of Population: Text, Sources and Background, Criticism 1766–1834*. New York : Norton.

Mammen, Kristin, and Christina Paxson. 2000. "Women's Work and Economic Development." *Journal of Economic Perspectives* 14 (4): 141–164.

Mar, Lisa Rose. 2010. *Brokering Belonging: Chinese in Canada's Exclusion Era, 1885–1945*. Oxford: Oxford University Press.

Mason, Andrew, ed. 2001. *Population Change and Economic Development in East Asia: Challenges Met, Opportunities Seized*. Stanford, Calif.: Stanford University Press.

Massey, Douglas S. 1988. "Economic Development and International Migration in Comparative Perspective." *Population and Development Review* 14 (3): 383–413.

Mastanduno, Michael. 1997. "Preserving the Unipolar Moment: Realist Theories and U.S. Grand Strategy after the Cold War." *International Security* 21 (4): 49–88.

Mayda, Anna Maria. 2009. "International Migration: A Panel Data Analysis of the Determinants of Bilateral Flows." *Journal of Population Economics* 23 (4): 1249–1274.

Melander, Erik, Thérése Pettersson, and Lotta Themnér. 2016. "Organized Violence, 1989–2015." *Journal of Peace Research* 53 (5): 727–742.

"Migration in the Gulf—Open Doors but Different Laws." 2016. *Economist Magazine*. September 10, 39.

Morton, Matthew, Jeni Klugman, Lucia Hanmer, and Dorothe Singer. 2014. "Gender at Work : A Companion to the World Development Report on Jobs." Washington, D.C.: World Bank Group. http://documents.worldbank.org/curated/en/884131468332686103/Gender-at-work-a-companion-to-the-world-development-report-on-jobs.

Moses, Jonathon W. 2009. "The American Century? Migration and the Voluntary Social Contract." *Politics and Society* 37 (3): 454–476.

Myrskylä, Mikko, Joshua R Goldstein, and Yen-hsin Alice Cheng. 2013. "New Cohort Fertility Forecasts for the Developed World: Rises, Falls, and Reversals." *Population and Development Review* 39: 31–56.

Myrskylä, Mikko, Hans-Peter Kohler, and Francesco C. Billari. 2009. "Advances in Development Reverse Fertility Declines." *Nature* 460: 741–743.

National Intelligence Council. 2012. *Global Trends 2030: Alternative Worlds.* Washington, D.C.: CreateSpace Independent Publishing Platform.

Nguyen, Hong Thao, and Ton Nu Thanh Binh. 2019. "Maritime Militias in the South China Sea." June 13. National Bureau of Asian Research, Maritime Awareness Project. https://map.nbr.org/2019/06/maritime-militias-in-the-south-china-sea/#_ftn2.

Norris, Pippa, and Ronald Inglehart. 2009. *Cosmopolitan Communications: Cultural Diversity in a Globalized World.* Cambridge: Cambridge University Press.

———. 2016. "Trump, Brexit and the Rise of Populism: Economic Have-Nots and Cultural Backlash." American Political Science Association Annual Meeting. September 1–4. Philadelphia.

Nowrasteh, Alex. 2016. "Terrorism and Immigration: A Risk Analysis." September 13. Cato Institute Policy Analysis No. 798.

Oeppen, Jim, and James W Vaupel. 2002. "Demography. Broken Limits to Life Expectancy." *Science* 296: 1029–1031.

O'Neill, Jim, and Anna Stupnytska. 2009. *The Long-Term Outlook for the BRICS and N-11 Post Crisis.* Global Economics Paper No. 192. New York: Goldman Sachs.

Organization for Economic Cooperation and Development. 2013. "International Migration Outlook 2013." OECD Publishing. https://www.oecd.org.

Organski, A. F. Kenneth. 1958. *World Politics.* New York: Alfred A. Knopf.

Organski, A. F. Kenneth, and Jacek Kugler. 1980. *The War Ledger.* Chicago: University of Chicago Press.

Organski, A. F. Kenneth, Jacek Kugler, Timothy J Johnson, and Youssef Cohen. 1984. *Births, Deaths, and Taxes: The Demographic and Political Transitions.* Chicago: University of Chicago Press.

Østby, Gudrun. 2016. "Rural–Urban Migration, Inequality and Urban Social Disorder: Evidence from African and Asian cities." *Conflict Management and Peace Science* 33 (5): 491–515.

Palmer, Glenn, Vito D'Orazio, Michael Kenwick, and Matthew Lane. 2015. "The MID4 dataset, 2002–2010: Procedures, Coding Rules and Description." *Conflict Management and Peace Science* 32 (2): 222–242.

Paris, Roland, and Timothy D. Sisk. 2009. *The Dilemmas of Statebuilding: Confronting the Contradictions of Postwar Peace Operations.* New York: Routledge.

Petersen, William,. 1979. *Malthus.* Cambridge, Mass.: Harvard University Press.

Pew Research Center. 2013. *Second-Generation Americans A Portrait of the Adult Children of Immigrants.* Washington, D.C.: Pew Research Center.

Phillips, Tom. 2015. "China Ends One-Child Policy after 35 Years." *Guardian.* October 29. https://www.theguardian.com/world/2015/oct/29/china-abandons-one-child-policy.

Pinker, Steven. 2011. *The Better Angels of Our Nature: Why Violence Has Declined*. New York: Penguin Books.

Preston, Samuel H. 1984. "Children and the Elderly: Divergent Paths for America's Dependents." *Demography* 21 (4): 435–457.

———. 1986. "Changing Values and Falling Birth Rates." *Population and Development Review*. Supplement, Below-Replacement Fertility in Industrial Societies: Causes, Consequences, Policies 12: 176–195.

Pritchett, Lant H. 1994. "Desired Fertility and the Impact of Population Policies." *Population and Development Review* 20 (1): 1–55.

Ramsden, Edmund. 2009. "Confronting the Stigma of Eugenics: Genetics, Demography and the Problems of Population." *Social Studies of Science* 39 (6): 853–884.

Rodrik, Dani. 2013. "Unconditional Convergence in Manufacturing." *Quarterly Journal of Economics* 128 (1): 165–204.

———. 2014. "The Past, Present, and Future of Economic Growth." In *Towards a Better Global Economy: Policy Implications for Citizens Worldwide in the 21st Century*, by Franklin Allen, Jere R Behrman, Nancy Birdsall, Shahrokh Fardoust, Dani Rodrik, Andrew Steer and Arvind Subramanian. Oxford: Oxford University Press Online. https://doi.org/10.1093/acprof:oso/9780198723455.001.0001.

———. 2015. "Premature Deindustrialization." IAS School of Social Science Economics Working Paper No. 107: 1–51

Rosen, Christine. 2004. *Preaching Eugenics: Religious Leaders and the American Eugenics Movement*. Oxford: Oxford University Press.

Russo, Anthony, and Joe Russo, dirs. 2019. *Avengers: Endgame*. Los Angeles: Marvel Studios.

Rousseau, Jean-Jacques. 1984. *A Discourse on Inequality*. 1754 ed. Translated by Maurice Cranston. Internet Archive. *https://archive.org/*.

———. 1913. *The Social Contract or Principles of Political Right*. 1762 ed. London: J. M. Dent and Sons. Internet Archive. *https://archive.org/*.

Samuelson, Paul. 1958. "An Exact Consumption-Loan Model of Interest with or without the Social Contrivance of Money." *Journal of Political Economy* 66 (6): 467–482.

Satellite Sentinel Project . 2012. *Making the World a Witness: Report on the Pilot Phase*. Boston: Harvard Humanitarian Initiative.

Sauvy, Alfred. 1969. *General Theory of Population*. New York: Basic Books.

Schweller, Randall L., and Xiaoyu Pu. 2011. "After Unipolarity: China's Visions of International Order in an Era of U.S. Decline." *International Security* 36 (1): 41–72.

Sen, Amartya. 2003. "Missing Women—Revisited." *British Medical Journal* 327 (7427): 1297–1298.

Seybolt, Taylor B., Jay D. Aronson, and Baruch Fischhoff, eds. 2013. *Counting Civilian Casualties*. Oxford: Oxford University Press.

Solow, Robert M. 1956. "A Contribution to the Theory of Economic Growth." *Quarterly Journal of Economics* 70: 65–94.

Southern Poverty Law Center. 2022. "Whose Heritage 3rd Edition: Public Symbols of the Confederacy." Montgomery, Ala.: Southern Poverty Law Center.

Stowell, Nicholas. 2021. "Silver Tsunami: The Political Demography of Aging Populations." PhD diss., Claremont Graduate University.

Swift, Jonathan. 2005. *Gulliver's Travels*. Edited by Ian Higgins. Oxford: Oxford University Press.

Tammen, Ronald, Jacek Kugler, Douglas Lemke, Alan C. Stam III, Mark Abdollahian, Carole Alsharabati, Brian Efird, and A. F. K. Organski. 2000. *Power Transitions: Strategies for the 21st Century*. New York: Chatham House.

Teitelbaum, Michael S. 1975. "Relevance of Demographic Transition Theory for Developing Countries." *Science* 188 (4187): 420–425.

Teitelbaum, Michael S., and Jay Winter. 1998. *A Question of Numbers: High Migration, Low Fertility and the Politics of National Identity*. New York: Hill and Wang.

———. 2013. *The Global Spread of Fertility Decline: Population, Fear, and Uncertainty*. New Haven, Conn.: Yale University Press.

Thorp, Willard. 1941. "Postwar Depressions." *American Economic Review* 30 (5): 352–361.

Tilly, Charles, ed. 1978. *Fertility, Historical Studies of Changing*. Princeton, N.J.: Princeton University Press.

United Nations, Department of Economic and Social Affairs (UN DESA). 1955. *Methods of Appraisal of Quality of Basic Data for Population Estimates*. Population Studies 23. New York: United Nations Publication.

———. Population Division. 2015a. *Demographic Components of Future Population Growth: 2015 Revision*. New York: United Nations.

———. Population Division. 2015b. *World Population Prospects: The 2015 Revision*. DVD ed. New York: United Nations.

United Nations, Office of Drugs and Crime. 2019. *Global Study on Homicide 2019 Edition*. New York: United Nations. https://www.unodc.org/unodc/en/data-and-analysis/global-study-on-homicide.html.

Uppsala Conflict Data Program (UCDP). 2016. Overview of UCDP Data. http://www.pcr.uu.se/data/overview_ucdp_data/.

Urdal, Henrik. 2006. "A Clash of Generations? Youth Bulges and Political Violence." *International Studies Quarterly* 50 (3): 607–629.

Urlanis, Boris Tsezarevich. 1971. *Wars and Population*. Moscow: Progress Publishers.

U.S. Census Bureau. 2016a. "Historical Estimates of World Population." https://www.census.gov/en.html.

———. 2016b. "U.S. Trade in Goods and Services—Balance of Payments (BOP) Basis." Economic Indicator Division, Database. https://www.census.gov/foreign-trade/statistics/historical/gands.pdf.

U.S. Department of Justice, Federal Bureau of Investigation. 2014. "Crime in the United States 2013." November. https://ucr.fbi.gov/crime-in-the-u.s/2013/crime-in-the-u.s.-2013/violent-crime/murder-topic-page/murdermain_final.

Vanhuysse, Pieter, and Achim Goerres. 2012. *Aging Populations in Post-Industrial Democracies*. Abingdon: Routledge.

Vaughn, Matthew, dir. 2015. *Kingsman: The Secret Service*. London, England: Marv Films, Cloudy Productions, and TSG Entertainment.

Vollmer, Sebastian, Hajo Holzmann, Florian Ketterer, Stephan Klasen, and David Canning. 2013. "The Emergence of Three Human Development Clubs." *PLoS ONE* 8 (3): e57624. https://doi.org/10.1371/journal.pone.005762.

Walt, Stephen M. 2009. "Alliances in a Unipolar World." *World Politics* 61 (1): 86–120.

Waltz, Kenneth N. 1979. *Theory of International Politics*. Reading, Mass: Addison-Wesley.

———. 1997. "Evaluating Theories." *American Political Science Review* 91 (4): 915–916.

Wang, Gabe T. 1999. *China's Population: Problems, Thoughts and Policies*. Aldershot, UK: Ashgate.

Weidmann, Nils B. 2009. "Geography as Motivation and Opportunity." *Journal of Conflict Resolution* 53 (4): 526–543.

Weiner, Myron. 1971. "Political Demography: An Inquiry into the Consequences of Population Change." In *Rapid Population Growth: Consequences and Policy Implications*. Prepared by a Study Committee of the Office of the Foreign Secretary: National Academy of the Sciences. Baltimore: Johns Hopkins University Press.

Weiner, Myron, and Sharon Stanton Russell. 2001. *Demography and National Security*. New York: Berghahn Books.

Weiner, Myron, and Michael S Teitelbaum. 2001. *Political Demography, Demographic Engineering*. New York: Berghahn.

Wheeler, Hugh. 1975. "Effects of War on Industrial Growth." *Society* 12: 48–52.

White, Tyrene. 2006. *China's Longest Campaign: Birth Planning in the People's Republic, 1949–2005*. Ithaca, N.Y.: Cornell University Press.

Winckler, Onn. 2002. "The Demographic Dilemma of the Arab World: The Employment Aspect." *Journal of Contemporary History* 37 (4): 617–636.

Wohlforth, William C. 1999a. "The Stability of a Unipolar World." *International Security* 24 (1): 5–41.

———. 1999b. "Unipolarity, Status Competition, and Great Power War." *World Politics* 61 (1): 28–57.

Wong, Larry. 2007. "The Canadian Chinese Exclusion Act and the Veterans Who Overcame It." *Chinese America: History and Perspectives*, 219–221.

World Bank. 2016. *World Development Indicators 2016*. August 10. Washington, D.C.: World Bank. https://openknowledge.worldbank.org/handle/10986/23969.

World Economic Forum. 2015. *The Global Gender Gap Report 2015*. Geneva: World Economic Forum.

World Trade Organization. 2016. WTO: 2016 News Items Reports on Recent Trade Developments. July 22. https://www.wto.org/english/news_e/news16_e/trdev_22jul16_e.htm.

Wrigley, Edward A. 2004. *Poverty, Progress, and Population*. Cambridge: Cambridge University Press.

Xinhuanet. 2015. "China to Allow Two Children for All Couples." Edited by Huaxia. October 29. http://news.xinhuanet.com/english/2015-10/29/c_134763645.htm.

Yoshihara, Susan, and Douglas A Sylva. 2012. *Population Decline and the Remaking of Great Power Politics*. Washington, D.C.: Potomac Books.

Zhu, Wei Xing, Li Lu, and Therese Hesketh. 2009. "China's Excess Males, Sex Selective Abortion and One Child Policy: Analysis of Data from 2005 National Inter-census Survey." *British Medical Journal* 338: 1136–1141.

INDEX

technological advancements: developmental role, 151; family planning and, 106; life expectancy and, 57–58; violence's impacts on, 103–104
textile industry, migration flows and, 76–78. *See also* labor markets
trade relations and policies, 150–151, 153. *See also* economic conditions and policies
Trump, Donald, 86, 87
Two Treatises of Government (Locke), 68

Ukraine, 137–138, 182
United Arab Emirates (UAE), immigration policies, 94, 96
United Kingdom, Brexit and, 86, 146–147
United States: American Dream, 163–166; anti-immigration policies, 75, 160–166; China and power dynamics, 25, 169–174; COVID response, 12; global influence, 132–133; as immigrant destination, 73, 78–79; immigration and power potentials, 170, 171; immigration rates and trends, 165–169; Iraq invasion, 136–137; undocumented residents, 89; violence in, 89–90, 102
unity and national identity: cultural narratives, role of, 118–120; political polarization and, 37–38. *See also* international system and norms
urbanization, 36, 118. *See also* population growth
USMCA (United States-Mexico-Canada Agreement), 147. *See also* international system and norms

Vietnam, 114–115
violence: history of societal violence, 102–103; impacts on society, 103–104; overview of trends and impacts, 99–102; youth and risk of, 151, 178–179
visas and immigration policies, 90, 94–95

war: China-U.S. parity and risk of war, 172–174; colonization and, 133–135; consequences of, 104–109, 116, 135–141; COVID impacts versus, 11; decline in, 99–101, *100*; demographic impacts of, 15–16, 107–108, 181–182; loss measurement, 106–107; nuclear weapons and, 141–142; overview of research about, 105–106; population growth after, 106, 108, 109–113
women: changing roles of, 123–124; discrimination, effects of, 126–127, 158–159; education impacts for, 120–121, 124–125; fertility rates and rights of, 16–17, 22, 23, 38. *See also* discrimination; fertility rates
work force. *See* labor markets
World Trade Organization (WTO), 142, 144, 151. *See also* international system and norms
World War II, *110*, 111. *See also* modern age

xenophobia. *See* immigration; policies, government

youth bulge. *See* baby booms

www.ingramcontent.com/pod-product-compliance
Lightning Source LLC
Chambersburg PA
CBHW031129270326
41929CB00011B/1561

* 9 780820 364155 *